Reverberations

Also by Dietrich Fischer-Dieskau

WAGNER AND NIETZSCHE

THE FISCHER-DIESKAU BOOK OF LIEDER

SCHUBERT'S SONGS

Reverberations

THE MEMOIRS
OF
DIETRICH
FISCHER-DIESKAU

Translated by RUTH HEIN

Fromm International Publishing Corporation

NEW YORK

Translation Copyright © 1989
Fromm International Publishing Corporation

First Fromm Paperback Edition 1990

Originally published as *Nachklang*
Copyright © 1987 Deutsche Verlags-Anstalt GmbH

Designed by Jacques Chazaud

Printed in the United States of America

First U.S. Edition

Library of Congress Cataloging-in-Publication Data
Fischer-Dieskau, Dietrich, 1925–
[Nachklang. English]
Reverberations: the memoirs of Dietrich Fischer-Dieskau /
translated by Ruth Hein.
p.   cm.
Translation of: Nachklang.

1. Fischer-Dieskau, Dietrich, 1925–   2. Singers—Germany (West)—
-Biography. I. Title.
ML420.F51A3   1989
782.1′092′4—dc19
[B]   89-30749
                                                              CIP
                                                              MN

ISBN 0-88064-122-3 (pbk.)

For Julia

Reverberations

Prelude

Every writer of memoirs is condemned to record fragments. A lieder singer has little cause to object, since he
thrives on his love for small forms. And surely the reader
will indulge him if he chooses to preface each chapter
with lines from Schubert lieder he has frequently sung.
The best way of crossing the sea of detail in search of the
meaningful moment is to believe that whatever has been,
is. And whatever was, has become eternal, lifted out of
time, which we enter before birth and leave when we die.

The past seems to me so closely connected in so many
ways to the present because today and tomorrow always
live in memory. We call everything our own by recalling
it. This book was begun as an attempt to illuminate what

has become shadowy, to retrieve early encounters and experiences and bring them to the surface. But these memories have come to include later friendships—a garland of faces, sketches for a portrait. The collection cannot be complete, nor is it intended to be.

Berlin is the city of my birth. I grew up in Berlin, and it has my loyalty to this day: I'm a rare case. When a Berliner stops to look in the mirror, he will not immediately see what distinguishes him from the residents of other cities. In Berlin I have been in turn schoolboy, university student, soldier, opera singer, and professor at a professional school. In my sixty-two years as a Berliner I have seen the city by day and by night and in every season. I have walked around its lakes and driven along its rivers—and stood on every one of its podiums. My private memories whisper arrogantly in my ear: Over there in the Olympia-Stadion, on Berlin's last birthday measured in round numbers, you pretended to be a child in the crowd of people, directed by Niedecken-Gebhard, the "set designer of the Reich." Over there, in the glass showcase of the armory, you stared in amazement at the incredibly small uniform worn by Frederick the Great. And there is the room in the Admiralspalast where you sat across from Ernst Legal and tried to make him understand that you had more to gain from accepting the offer from the Städtische Oper than you did from the invitation to start in the studio of the Staatsoper. And though I still remember the air of the suburban train stations that we breathed on our way to school, it is no easier for me than it would be for a stranger to write about the fate of the city.

What Berlin always failed to accomplish in its glory days succeeded when the city was in ruins. Berlin became beloved for its courage and its helplessness. It is rooted in the hearts and minds of those who have left and is imbued with almost as much nostalgia as Old Vienna. The situation has changed over the years, and today many are beginning to look at Berlin's charms with quite different eyes (and not only for the tax breaks it provides). They whisper to each other the news that, after all, Berlin has once again come alive, the intellectual hub of the republic. After the turbulence of the student riots, it is true, the pace grew a little more circumspect and thoughtful, so that even the broad avenues with the thickly ranked greenery stood out more handsomely than in any other city of the same size. Though the air here occasionally seems to be in a bad mood, thanks to air pollution, when the wind blows and the sun shines, the city still smells as wonderfully of nothing at all as it used to, stimulating the brain cells, increasing energy.

Berlin's energy was destroyed in peacetime by waves of mischief, during the war by bombs. I had a close view of both. The frenzy of erecting monuments and statues in the period before the First World War encourages pangs of nostalgia, and there is increasing indignation at teenagers who smear graffiti over fountains and statues. I grew up in those western suburbs where in 1933 ugliness was fought against, and where a beginning was made to turn Berlin into an attractive, exciting city once again. But then Hitler and his architects crisscrossed the city, and we of the younger generation grew up among their arrogant monstrosities, which have not yet entirely disappeared, that presaged the massive bombings, and were

---

followed by a dry spell that left people to grope in the dark.

I have seen Unter den Linden when it was still in full bloom. The broad avenue held a strong attraction for me as the perfect expression of what may be called the Prussian style. The last great creation in this style was the monument to Frederick the Great by Christian Rauch, unveiled in 1851. I could never pass it without stopping and taking a look at my ancestor, General of the Artillery von Dieskau, his countenance one among various officers. It was only right for him to be part of the monument, since his ballistic inventions had helped his royal friend to win battles. The monarch showed his gratitude by following the coffin into the Old Garrison Church, his head bared.

The arrangement of the "Linden" was called into question after 1900. The police and the banks pushed to the forefront, and they spoiled the work of Kaiser Wilhelm II's architect by adding on to his buildings. Of course the phrase "Prussian style" is a makeshift, because the strollers from Castle Bridge to the Brandenburg Gate see a mixture of French, Italian, and German elements. The style was created not only by its artists but also by its builders. With the exception of Friedrich Wilhelm I, all the Hohenzollern were touched by the muses.

Right alongside the senselessly destroyed castle, the dictators of the left rebuilt the Royal Opera House in accordance with Frederick's style. The reconstruction of the building that punctuates the sightline demonstrated that the avenue was getting its second wind. And even those cultural, and especially literary, activities that are un-Prussian though native to Berlin, which we had sorely missed after the destruction by National Socialism, are gradually coming back. Even if one literary café does not a

---

4

literary city make, there are, especially in the area of literature, the healthily controversial Akademie der Künste and a series of institutions that communicate with it.

Berlin is the site of my first profound musical experiences, especially of opera and concerts, which resulted in my choice of career. Singing is a fundamental form of expression for Berliners. Oddly enough, their pleasure in song does not conflict with their irony and their delicate sense of the comic. Thus no one laughed when a hundred men suddenly rose to their feet to sing a sentimental song in close harmony. Thanks to Carl Friedrich Zelter and his "Liedertafel," a Berlin invention, the male choruses known as *Männerchöre* came into being. Besides the major amateur choruses and orchestras, there were countless musical societies that combined an ideology and a passion for music.

All these together furnished the soil for this city of music, this huge audience of concertgoers, who helped me as well when I was ready to give recitals. I was a member of the chorus in the old Singakademie (a building, by the way, designed not by Karl Friedrich Schinkel but by one of his pupils). A quite different architectural mood is represented by the Philharmonia, destroyed by wartime bombing, which was originally built as a roller-skating rink and was adapted to a concert hall during the late 1880s. I often sat below the large organ that stood against the back wall, behind the orchestra, acquiring a crucial familiarity with works, orchestration, or points of conducting. The listener is comfortable in Hans Scharoun's new Philharmonia building, and the acoustics are adequate in most seats. The soloist, however, with his vocal energy projected in only one direction, finds it difficult to reach all those who surround him. The Deutsche Oper, with its 1950s style that has not grown nostalgic, is stark, like all of my beloved Berlin. It has much else to offer, however: excellent performers in every section, a benevolent and cordial spirit of teamwork, and outstanding musical productions.

1

"Wo mich das Leben freundlich begrüsste"

My first memory is of terror. (If, that is, I forget the delicious sensation that followed my crying as a baby. That sensation is still present in my life, but now it comes from singing.) I was two years old, sitting on the lawn with my beloved calico beagle, who had a pacifier hanging around his neck. At that moment a roar of thunder tore through the air. I slitted my eyes and looked up: A metal monster darkened the sun in a frightening way. It was probably an early airplane, still rare in those days. Of course I screamed my head off. The maid, Else, came running and transplanted me to the blue stroller, a chair on four wheels, in order to distract me by a walk round the garden.

I loved this vehicle. Its movable wooden slats served to frame my line of vision and became armrests when they were let down. Else did more than look after us children; she was the maid-of-all-work. Bright as a button, good-looking, her face turning scarlet as she worked, the young Silesian woman of about twenty-five was beloved by the whole family. She looked after me and my two brothers, did the washing, ironed, cooked, and cleaned. On her day off she put on a cloche hat in the latest style and immediately looked worldly. A boyfriend named Bruno, who wore a peaked cap, turned up now and then. But Else wasn't really all that fond of him, and one day, when she refused to go with him, he pulled out a pistol and forced her to comply. That was the last time we saw the dangerous suitor. Fortunately Else returned safe and sound.

When I was four, my parents went away on a short vacation, leaving their three sons behind. I developed terrible stomach pains and screamed for three days. Finally Else got the clever idea of delivering me to a nearby hospital, where I was relieved of my appendix at the last minute. Back from the hospital, I basked in the pampering and the granting of otherwise ignored wishes, such as a complete zoo of wooden animals.

When I was ten, Else married. For a while she came to see us occasionally, but gradually the visits stopped. I was sad to see her go.

I was born into a well-to-do family, growing up as a member of what today would be called the upper middle class. My father's passionate devotion to music was unrequited. He was the first member of his family with musical ambitions, even going so far as to compose original works. My mother's father, a military architect for the imperial government, sang as a hobby; he was a tenor. My father's first wife, who had died young, had, according to my mother, been an accomplished pianist.

My father, Dr. Albert Fischer, had a knack for promoting the love of music, displaying great initiative and skill at organization. As principal of the academic high school in the Zehlendorf district of Berlin and as an advisor to the school board, he produced so-called war-bond concerts during the First World War. All this took place before he added his mother's maiden name—von Dieskau—to his own. The concerts were held in the auditorium of one of the three secondary schools he supervised. Time and again I was to rummage through the yellowing programs of these concerts, crammed with the names of famous artists: Pauline de Ahna, who was accompanied on the piano by her husband, Richard Strauss; Emmy Destinn, the star of the royal opera; Francesco d'Adrade; Claire Dux, the lyric soprano, who was also a permanent member of the royal opera; and Hugo Rüdel, director of sacred music.

But sponsoring concerts was not my father's only deviation from his regular profession—though, as he put it, without "coming up with more than six on one throw of the dice." He also functioned as a writer and theater manager. He had wanted to train as a professional musician, but Grandfather had put his foot down and forbidden such a career, since it was widely known to be "unprofitable."

My father's eight brothers and sisters were all musical, just as they were all addicted to practical jokes. Having been born late in my parents' lives, I never knew my grandparents. But I can still hear my father tell the story of the time he and his brothers fixed the church clock in the small town of Ziesar near Magdeburg so that it struck thirteen. They also used to wipe the inky nibs of their pens on the curtain while their soft-hearted, indulgent mother had just enough strength to chide gently: "You know how much you upset Daddy when you carry on like that. . . ."

In spite of all interdictions, my father would not stop composing. I can still see him bent over the score of his singspiel *Sesenheim*. Though the work was performed a number of times at Berlin's Theater des Westens in the late 1920s, he continued to revise and improve it to the end of his days. "Your works will survive you"—but not this one, because as early as 1927 Franz Lehar presented his operetta *Friederike*, using the same subject, Goethe's love for Friederike von Sesenheim; furthermore, the role of Goethe in Lehar's work was sung by the very popular Richard Tauber. The success of the operetta put an end once and for all to any hopes my father might still have harbored. The pages and pages covered with writing and musical notations during many a long night became a family treasure, cherished even as the sheets turned yellow and brittle.

Every Sunday morning my father's sensitive fingers would glide over the piano keys until they settled into the heavy chords of old Protestant chorales. It was then that we saw the side of my father that he had inherited from *his* father. A Lutheran minister, Grandfather published a book on church music around 1870. The huge tome has become a highly respected standard work; it is still in print.

Lying under the piano like a burrowing animal, listening intently to the loud sounds eerily nearby that my father coaxed out of the piano—that was my greatest delight. When I was four years old I heard some excerpts from *Lohengrin* on the radio (or so my father told me later) and fell completely under the spell of my first encounter with opera. For days I ran around feverishly.

After 1925 my father became a cosponsor of what was known as the Secondary-School Theater of Berlin. Unfortunately only the wealthier students could take advantage of this opportunity to attend classical plays, operas, and concerts for a nominal admission fee. I was eager to assimilate immediately whatever I had seen and heard. I recited with an excess of emotion, often without the slightest idea of what I was declaiming. I acted out my speeches and poems at the top of my lungs to the maid in the kitchen until she gave notice and fled the premises. My repertoire included the better-known poems of Schiller and Goethe. Years later, when I was a prisoner of war, I could still recite them to my fellow prisoners.

I was won over to poetry at an early age. I have been in its thrall all my life because I was made to read it, because it gave me pleasure, and because I eventually came to understand what I was reading. I also tried my hand at writing but could never get past the opening lines. Many of my blue school notebooks were filled with childish attempts at "novels" and verse dramas that never went beyond "I went into a garden . . ." or "The sun shone on the castle of Adlersfried . . ."

But by the time I was thirteen, I was thoroughly familiar with the more important musical works, mostly through recordings. By the mid-1930s superb performances were available on records; the same ones are being rerecorded even now. I made the turntable serve my need to communicate. If some friend of my mother's from out of town came to stay with us, I immediately accosted her brashly: "I've arranged a wonderful program just for you, you *have* to listen!"

During this time I was a student at the academic high school in Zehlendorf. The enormous pseudo-Renaissance building was more likely to frighten than reassure a child. The elementary school I had attended had not been much more confidence-inspiring, but I worshiped my first-grade teacher—not because I learned so much from him, but because he liked to hear me sing. He confided to my astonished mother that I had "the voice of an angel." Herr Tapper was my refuge whenever I, who had been sent to school a year early, was the butt of the other students' scorn and derision. And I never understood why. Why were they laughing at my hair (which my mother liked to curl)? Why did they use me to test their strength? Thin-skinned and exposed, I always stood stock still. But once I attacked the oldest and meanest of them when he came up to me menacingly in the schoolyard. Blind with rage, fists flailing, I lowered my head and charged him, without the slightest effect except that I was left bloody and flat on my back. Then Herr Tapper came up with a splendid idea: He assigned the ruffian to be my bodyguard and to keep me safe from all attacks by the others. From that moment on I enjoyed peace.

My father had recently retired, but in his Zehlendorf school I enjoyed all the "privileges of my birth." Scarcely any teacher there had not at one time or another benefited from my father's kindness and sense of fair play. The faculty repaid him by showing me great leniency.

Like any bourgeois of the turn of the century, my father never forgot his first evening at the theater; now he passed on to his children what playwrights through the centuries had taught him. When the curtain rose, I thought

I was in the presence of princes. Gold and crimson, lights and greasepaint, that indefinable odor that wafted from the stage to the audience's nostrils while the curtain rose—we were smitten at once. Filled with high-flown sentiments and artifice, we would return from the matinees like sleepwalkers. Even though these time-honored German classics were often performed by second-rate casts, we also had opportunities to see Berlin's theatrical luminaries. We were amazed, exhausted, and—though we did not know it—a little better prepared for our careers.

But of course I was also drawn to the movies. First I went with school friends; later, during the war, my mother and I attended. We felt our way, blindly and yet seeing, through our century without tradition, distinguished from earlier times by our bad manners—though in retrospect they seem genteel compared to the present. At the time popular art had just begun to rear its head, anticipating some of the barbarousness that surrounds us nowadays in TV soap operas and terror-filled videos made expressly for young people.

During the war the movies became more than an amusement for women and children. We loved them, my mother and I, but we did not take them seriously, though I knew the voices and features of all the performers. We rarely discussed the films we had seen; we paid no more attention to them than we did to food. By the time I finally understood the real meaning, the cultural significance of a particular movie—beyond the names and voices of the performers—television had already begun to supply me with the films to satisfy my craving.

If the film at the local movie palace was already unreeling when we arrived, as often happened, we would grope our way down the aisle behind the usherette. I felt like someone who did not yet belong. Above our heads a white beam of light cut through the hall, you could see the motes of dust dancing in the air; colored lightbulbs ran along the walls; and the penetrating smell of disinfectant made my throat constrict. My legs rubbed past other legs. On the screen it was always raining, even when the sun was shining, even in indoor settings. And if a flash of lightning shot through the auditorium, no one seemed surprised. When we relaxed at the end of the movie and the lights came back on, I felt as if I had suddenly been robbed of something wonderful, replaced by ugly folding seats, whitewashed walls, a floor covered with drying spittle and scraps of paper. When we passed the projection booth on our way to the street, I would beg for a snippet of discarded film. At home I patched it into the motley reel of earlier acquisitions. Thanks to a little hand-cranked projector, I could view the result shivering with pleasure.

I had a penchant for begging on the streetcar as well. I began by placing the correct change in the conductor's open palm, saying, "Fifteen pfennigs." The conductor pushed the ticket at me and repeated "Fifteen" with a rising intonation in his lifeless, mechanical voice. This was my chance to ask, "D'you have a used-up pad?" And the long-suffering man (after all, I was not his only tormentor) held out two or three pads from which the tickets had been torn, leaving only the stubs. They were perfect for stick-figure drawings that became moving-picture stories if you flicked the pages quickly along your thumb.

I should have mentioned earlier that the "Brown wave" of National Socialism broke over us when I was barely eight years old, and the curriculum in my father's schools no longer focused on the world it had viewed in the past. What is certain is that this "apprenticeship" slipped past me without making much of an impression on my music-crazy self.

On January 30, 1933, when triumphal marches blared from the radio and the reporters' voices crowed with ecstasy, when shouts of *Heil* thundered among the crowds, no one—except for a few far-sighted people, political sophisticates—could have suspected where the overwhelming enthusiasm would lead. Eight years old, I arranged my toy army band in front of the radio and made believe that the tin soldiers were producing all these wonderful marching rhythms.

Some years earlier, when my father had retired, he had been obliged to relinquish his lavishly appointed principal's quarters. Now we all shared an apartment on Holbeinstrasse in Lichterfelde, another Berlin district. At the other end of the city, Father earned a little money by teaching in a private school. Herr Jarow, an old bandleader, lived near us in the almost rural neighborhood of Dürerstrasse, where horse-drawn carriages lumbered over the bumpy cobblestones, past rain-drenched carts. On the way to my lesson I was more concerned with drumming on the picket fences and gates along my way than with the lesson ahead of me. Herr Jarow was my first piano teacher. My father had frequently consulted him in his never-ending effort to cast the score of *Sesenheim* in an increasingly professional form. Herr Jarow's interest in my unspeakable tinkling was nonexistent. He always greeted me with "Would you like a piece of cake?" or, "Would you like me to show you my coin collection?"

Sometimes I stopped to watch Adolf Drescher, a philosophizing shoemaker, whose Dürerstrasse shop was next door to the musician's home. Drescher would stare dolefully straight ahead whenever he stopped working for a minute; brooding on the craziness of the modern world made him morose. When he began to speak, he swallowed his words almost at once, since all he saw was a lout who would be unable to understand anyway. But I kept coming. Whenever I stepped through the door, my throat constricted from the odor of leather and tobacco. He coated threads with tar, he punched holes, he nailed soles onto the lasts, he shaped heels—and always there was the hum of the rotating brushes and finishers. Later, whenever I performed the stage business of Hans Sachs in the second act of *Die Meistersinger*, where I had to make a shoe, I thought of my early days and that shoemaker.

It took me a long time to get used to going to the grocery store, armed with a long shopping list, for I was excessively timid. The first few times Herden, the grocer who ran the old-fashioned store, encouraged me by slipping me a small bag of chocolates. I was not a spoiled child; I had to wash dishes and perform other household tasks; very frequently it was my job to carry coals up the three flights from the cellar. They ended up in the ornate tile stove, where in winter delicious-smelling apples sizzled.

I shut myself off from reality and lived in a make-believe world. Even if it was not as sumptuous as Mö-ricke's "Orplid," at least I had created it all by myself. I could count my friends on the fingers of one hand.

My second piano teacher was Joachim Seyer-Stephan. A former child prodigy and a protégé of Ferruccio Busoni, he was now eking out a meager existence by giving lessons to old ladies and children who had not a trace of talent. Although under his tutelage I managed to gain at least a vague idea of Walter Niemann's *Salonstückchen*, I was more interested in another activity practiced in the high-rise apartment on Fortstrasse in Zehlendorf, where my teacher's father, Friedrich Seyer, painted his pictures. When he was not absorbed in his own works, a stylistic blend of romanticism reminiscent of the Pre-Raphaelites and a hint of Buddhism, he would copy a painting by Botticelli, his particular favorite. For the first time something got through my shell—I became caught up in lines and colors. How was it possible to duplicate a painting so precisely? How did one get such bizarre ideas and capture them in watercolors? For hours I squatted next to the painter at his work, and now and then I too picked up a colored pencil to draw a picture. Once, when I had made a pencil portrait of Seyer-Stephan (I was all of eleven years old), my patient host said, "You could easily become a painter."

I forgot his encouragement for a time, in part because of the extremely dull art instruction we were given in school; drawing the head of the Horseman of Bamberg over and over for two whole years was sheer torture. It was only much later that I recalled his words.

My daily walk to and from school led me past the train station at the Botanical Gardens. I always dawdled on the overpass to breathe in the sweet steam from the locomotives chugging by below. One morning in 1938 a friend and I were innocently walking up the hill to the bridge when the sight of glaring white letters, ugly drawings, arrows pointing to stores, words of abuse, obscenities, all scrawled on the pavement, brought to a stop first our feet and then our hearts. The door to Friedländer's men's tailoring shop gaped wide open, the furniture store next door was half-empty, the plate-glass windows all around were smeared over. People passed by with frozen expressions. For the second time in my life I found myself face to face with crime and violence.

The first time had been during an "excursion" of our Hitler Youth troop, when suddenly all the ten- and twelve-year-olds were egged on by the older boys to attack an "enemy" troop. The bloody brawl that developed put me in a state of shock for quite a while. It was not unlike the state I was in now, at the sight of this filth. The incident left us mute; without a word we began the long walk back to Zehlendorf.

The time had already come when we had to deal with mendacious, secretive behavior, which probably seemed shady to us even then and later certainly appeared rather ridiculous. This was the form our survival took: No one had control of his own life, and everyone was made to pay for something he had not started, in the no-man's-land between school and home according to rules and customs.

Sometimes I was amazed that human beings were so easily capable of such things. And yet: If we wanted to get out of Latin, we had only to urge Schmidt, the top student, to interrupt the lesson as quickly as possible. He would ask the confirmed Nazi behind the teacher's desk, "What is your opinion sir, on the lies the Minister of Propaganda uttered this morning in the *Völkischer Beobachter?*"

The teacher's dull features would change to red-faced outrage. "Now, listen here . . ." This would be followed by a time-consuming discussion during which, strangely enough, it was never acknowledged that the entire class disagreed with him. So it is not surprising that I picked up precious little Latin in school, not to mention pleasure in the stylistic wonders to be found in Tacitus and Cicero. Perhaps my greatest regret is that I am unable to read

Vergil in the original, for as soon as I began to sing, I gave precedence to careful study of French, English, and Italian.

Besides teachers who were dyed-in-the-wool Nazis, there was also Dr. Meyer, who managed to evade the prescribed "German greeting"—the *Heil Hitler* spoken while raising the right arm—by slightly raising his left hand, in which he held his briefcase, and muttering, "Heitler."

And who exactly were the enemies of the solid citizens at that time? The Socialists, the Communists, for many the Jews—but very definitely not in our family. It is true that not even the most sagacious person could act in such a way as to prevent the decline of a segment of the West, along with a large part of European Jewry. To a ten-year-old, participating, wearing a uniform, developing his talents meant everything. But disenchantment with the new form of daily life set in almost at once. My temperament rejected the "outings"; the brawls that ended in bloody noses and worse; the exertions intended to make us "fit"; the banal "home nights"; the routine orders during excursions that said when we could, and could not, urinate, determined by the platoon leader personally; singing the wretched songs that were the standard tunes of National Socialist youth groups, for which I, as senior member and flank man, had to give the pitch. As a sign of our blood-thirstiness we wore on our belts a knife engraved with the phrase "Blood and Honor," symbolic of a national paroxysm that had set out to turn the whole world into a blood bath.

No one can know what he may be capable of. A man could find out that he was a Nazi, get the fright of a lifetime but recover quickly from the shock, and just as quickly think himself a man again. On one occasion, when I was

19

eight years old, I returned from one of our overnight excursions, when we slept in tents, with a high fever that put me in bed for several days, during which time I was a particularly attentive eavesdropper on Uncle Werner Ludwig and my father as they engaged in another one of their verbal sparring matches. They referred to the Party bigwigs as "jumping jacks."

Twice I saw the bigwigs for myself. The first time was when we gathered early in the morning to take part in a Youth rally that night in the Olympia-Stadion. After interminable waiting, for which I had not fortified myself by bringing along anything to eat, we were given a watery soup. Tarry torches were pressed into our hands before we started on our march, all the way through Berlin. Finally we were standing semiconscious in the stadium's center oval. Numbed by the acrid odor of the torches, we stood, column after column, and listened to the words of the screaming Minister for Propaganda, Josef Goebbels: "When there is an argument between young and old, youth is always in the right." He thus managed to combine both a revolutionary point of view and the seduction of his audience. But at the time I did not understand what was happening.

The other occasion was during a motorcade of the "Führer" through the center of the city, past the Labor Ministry; my half-brother Achim had reserved places at a window for us, so that for once we might be at the center of the action. After we had been waiting for about an hour, the shouts of the crowd on the sidewalks began to swell to a roar: "Führer, command us; we will follow." And then we saw him, standing in the open car; that is, from our high window we saw the light-brown top of his cap and the right arm robotically raised in the "German salute," his outstretched fingers repeatedly straying toward his left shoulder and balling into a fist as if to squash the same people he had only just acknowledged with his salute. I arrived at this observation only in retrospect, but even at the time I had an oddly clear understanding that an absurd form of playacting was being forced on us even if the dictator's face was hidden from us.

My father had made great progress with his plans to reform the secondary schools. He had already established three of them in Zehlendorf and with colleagues had developed the prototype of German secondary schools. His program brought him to the favorable attention of the ruling powers; by a hair, Hitler would have put him in charge of German education. Age and illness protected my father from his own basically naive ideas, and when the crucial time came, he was no longer being considered.

Werner, my uncle on my mother's side, enjoyed mingling the smoke from his pipe with my father's cigarette mist. And sometimes the argument for and against the Nazis would grow heated; thus I acquired a basis for comparison at an early age. The clearer discernment, however, as I noticed quite frequently in the early years, rarely seemed to include public opposition. My older half-brother, Achim, never visited us in our Lichterfelde apartment without at once covering the telephone with a pillow. But having done that, he spoke mainly about petty quarrels and annoyances in his job in the Ministry of Labor, and only rarely about more serious issues.

The movie newsreels brought us the first terrifying hints of concentration camps. It became impossible to claim that we knew nothing about them. But people buried their heads in the sand, preferring what they believed to be the security of the moment. Did that make those who

21

remained passive equally guilty? Were we boys guilty when, walking to school, we silently passed by the filth scrawled in the road? Everyone knew what was going on, but we were not brave enough to bring up this particular topic in school. Of course anyone could see and understand if only he took the trouble to think. But people were not informed enough. The broad stratum of the middle class was perhaps even more ignorant than were the workers, who had been schooled by the German Socialist Party and by their trade unions. Nevertheless, the daily object lessons played out in the streets really should have made many more people suspicious.

Rosenfeld, who had a tailoring business right next to the train station, suddenly disappeared. The apartment below ours housed a family from Upper Silesia with a wonderful grandmother who could tell stories like no one else. One day a truck drove up, and the entire family was herded into it. They took only a few personal belongings, among them the oldest son's wooden train set, which I loved dearly. Many of the neighbors watched with stony faces as the grandmother leaned on her grandchildren because of her swollen feet. No one moved; by this time such scenes must have become commonplace. Probably the passersby spoke to each other with a little more urgency, smoked a cigarette, and went on their way.

An elderly woman moved into the vacated apartment. She was outraged by every musical sound from upstairs— and in our family there were four people who made at least a little music every day. Whenever my mother said, "Shush," almost inevitably the answer was, "Oh yes, Frau Hermanns is wringing her hands again."

In school they began to teach us to spy. "Boys, if you want to do the right thing, you'll keep your eyes and ears

22

wide open ... Werner Nelke, are you listening? The enemies of our nation are everywhere."

And sure enough, a few days later the news was whispered from ear to ear: Werner's father had been arrested. The newspapers contained hints that the Jews were being "dealt with." Could it have been that we did not believe such indications? Of course we did. Generally people escaped into cynicism. Neighbors complained to neighbors about the vaguely perceived but steadily growing danger of crime and war. My bearded uncle, the retired president of the senate, with his smooth forehead and his long pipe, always said what was on his mind; his bitter condemnations did not spare the Nazis. My father was not among those who slaughtered Jews and burned books; but I have a feeling that they could have persuaded me, for example, to follow their ideology. If today someone has some private objection to the "system," he has no reason to feel smug, since he is free to express his feelings. Hitler imitated Stalin and had us brainwashed until we truly believed that "Without Hitler, we'd drop dead on the spot."

Once a year, when it was beginning to feel like Christmas, my mother and I got off the streetcar at Leipziger Platz and entered the temple of the Wertheim department store. This dream castle was my idea of absolute perfection, and in fact no other department store in the world approached its splendor. Later on the Kaufhaus des Westens entered the competition, but while it may have been flashier, it was more like department stores all over the world. In my memory Wertheim's streamers of glowing lights still glitter above the lobby, my glance still slides along the fountain court, the rug department, and the walls of semiprecious stones. But compared to the pleasures of the Christmas decorations, these everyday glories were merely frosting on the cake.

Because of my father's age and retirement, our family, with three children, had very little disposable income at this time. How good to be able to fall back on a widowed uncle, such as Uncle Werner! Of course the ill-tempered old man showed no signs of a love for children. His own two offspring had put him through too much misery. He liked visiting with my father, whose social life was greatly reduced after he retired. I was much too young and silly for most of what was spoken between the two men, but the puffs of smoke coming from the cigar and the long curved pipe appealed to me. Once again there was a chance of turning something into music in my mind: quick or slow puffs setting the pace for an imaginary train engine. . . .

Every Easter candy eggs and chocolate eggs spilled out from Uncle Werner's cornucopia. At Christmas our wishes for military gear, such as helmets, swords, air guns, and toy soldiers, were the first to be granted. But I'm told that when I was eight I said, "Being a soldier is too hard. I think I'd rather be a poet."

On our birthdays a different kind of treasure mysteriously appeared on the table where the presents were laid out. When I was only five, I found two genuine toy theaters, their curtains open and scenery in place. Everything—even the puppets—was made of cardboard covered with hand-painted prints, rich nourishment to a child's imagination. What was it that persuaded the good prophet to set me up with, of all things, the second act of *Tannhäuser*, the battle of the singers in the Wartburg? From that moment on, playing with this bewitching toy took up much of my free time. I read out loud from paperback editions of plays at the same time that I pushed the figures on and off the stage. How pleasant compared to reading novels: The casts of characters, with names and degrees of relationship, made them marvelously easy to follow. Hardly any of the classics were immune to my joy in delineating different characters in different voices, without understanding anything of what I was declaiming. My repertoire ranged all the way from Schiller to Wildenbruch. True, when I tried to tackle *Wallenstein*, I found that the huge cast of characters defeated all my efforts at rhetoric and stage effects. My audience was made up of other children on birthdays, school friends, or my poor afflicted brother, who had been born physically and mentally handicapped. All those years I shared a room with Martin, I came to feel his suffering. His nature—which, because of his inadequate body, was expressed over and over in a glance, a sigh—and his immobility affected me as well.

I was just as influenced by the message my uncle conveyed with the gift of the toy theater. But it was almost impossible to discern his pleasure in my new games in his expression. If only he had taken some notice of my enthusiasm! From then on, all sorts of places became the arena for my theatrics; as I sat in the bay window of the dining room, on one of the benches designed by my father himself in the late-romantic style, while my older brother, Klaus, was practicing the piano right beside me, I would pull on the cord that opened the thin curtains, and at once a stage was revealed: horse-drawn wagons clattered past, at the center of the embankment a small boy stood singing, the ragman shouted, and pedestrians hurried past. Even dust motes dancing in the sunlight could become actors. And when the piano piece by Chopin or Brahms came to an end, I would pull the curtain closed with slow solemnity. I always remembered to count the number of passersby I saw in about ten minutes; they represented the latecomers. By the time I was nine, I already had gone so far (without any real justification) as to use these counts to work out the future audiences for "my" public appearances, even though I did not exactly know what talents I might have to offer. Eighty auditors in ten minutes was the record. Later I was amazed that in the short period of about six minutes so many more people could crowd into a concert hall.

A recording of *Der Freischütz* came with the toy theater. This was a good deed on my uncle's part. And whenever we were invited to visit him in his home on the top floor of an apartment house, situated opposite the Zehlendorf-West train station, he would drag me off to the conservatory adjacent to his bedroom, wind up a small music box, lay a pile of little metal records alongside that I could play, and leave me to my own devices. The idea was to prevent me from being bored, so that I would not interrupt or disturb the grown-ups as they chatted. The only time I felt uneasy was at supper, when my uncle would press a loaf of bread to his chest, just below his full beard, so as to cut slices personally for his guests. Before we sat down, I would finger the carvings on the massive sideboard, shiny from long use. I found the varieties of shell ornaments irresistible—they were so wonderfully labyrinthine. The life-size photographs of my late Aunt Gertrude sometimes made me fearful; they were displayed on every chair she had ever sat on. My uncle, a passionate photographer, also spent hours recording the likenesses of the rest of the family. It was quite possible that after a long wait the longed-for "first shot" would be blank, since

Uncle had forgotten to put a plate into the camera. Later I often made the pilgrimage to Zehlendorf-West, because my mother considered it desirable for me to have the benefits of my uncle's tutoring in Latin. As soon as I sat down next to him at the desk, he would take one pipe after another from the wall rack and begin to clean them. My sense of smell, already oversensitive, made it hard for me to concentrate on the passage I was supposed to translate, and my discomfort would throw the old man into fits of silent giggles.

After he and his housekeeper had survived all the rigors of the war, he became a late victim of despotism. When the eighty-year-old, disregarding the strain, carried the garbage can down four flights to the yard, he was stopped by a Russian soldier. "You weapons?" My uncle, who loved to whittle and tinker, carried a pocket knife. The discovery of this cost him his life; the Russian shot him in the head.

How far have I traveled from those who are no longer with us? The dead have a great deal to say, and yet they say very little. They cannot be contained in the brief sketches that are all memory leaves us. They should not be seen from a single point of view. They hold our interest, and a book could be devoted to each one of them. But that activity is opposed by a secret prohibition, almost a curse. What else is a human life but a series of shocks, the penultimate one of which is old age and the final one death?

In the labyrinth of my imagination I also take my bearings from their voices. They have lost nothing of their resonance—that has to do with my professionally trained ear. Nor is there any need for faded photographs and album pages at Christmas or All Souls' Day. In the course of a long life the dead do not have to be trotted out as images, perhaps lit by votive candles. We should find other ways of paying homage to their existence, which now lives only in memory and in shadow. I have become convinced that we advance through the strength that comes to us from the dead.

My future began to take shape in the imaginary theater behind the curtains and between the cardboard scenery cut from broadsheets—also among volumes of Goethe and Schiller shelved above those of Wieland, Heine, and Lenau. Because there was not enough space, some of my father's books were kept on a simple shelf that ran along the wall in the corridor; but the greater part were kept in a very tall case decorated in bad taste. At the center stood Meyer's twenty-four-volume encyclopedia, from which I derived a certain amount of precocious knowledge. The classics, heavy old volumes in thickly gilded bindings, were lavishly encrusted with figures and portraits; you could feel them with your fingertips. The texts were embellished with the usual illustrations in bad late-nineteenth-century taste. Beside them stood the good Cotta editions of German poets, more modestly illustrated. All of them were destroyed in the fire bombings.

As long as my father was alive, my access to the books, with their infinite number of penciled marginal notes, was limited or secret. I made up for it by browsing through Woermann's history of art so often that I could recite all the picture captions by heart, without looking at them— a feat that astonished my father the one time he tested me.

I am sure it would have been good for me if my father or mother, or one of my many aunts, had enjoyed reading out loud. But I was hardly ever the recipient of such a boon—most likely because I myself was too preoccupied with reading out loud. I had a great yearning to exercise my own voice. And yet I cannot imagine anything more beneficial to a child than to hear good literature read aloud. When I was in the sixth grade, Dr. Mayer, our enterprising German teacher, made us read (unfortunately without acting) classic plays aloud, assigning us roles. It did not take very long for him to discover that I stood out among my fellow students who, stuttering mightily, robbed the reading of any illusion. Because I could read with expression, I was allowed to read the lead part in whatever play we were studying.

But for the time being there was a lack of good books or even of any recommendations along that line. My father died just when I was beginning to be interested in serious books, and my mother was loath to make suggestions. I was enthralled by the feeling of loss and self-forgetting in *Buddenbrooks*, after I had already devoured Felix Dahn, Gustav Freytag, and Henryk Sienkiewicz without any lasting effects. When I laid aside Gottfried Keller's *Leute von Seldwyla*, I followed up with shallow novels that did not exactly advance my intellectual growth. I cannot recall the names of these successful authors, who must have made a lot of money.

Now, as I am jotting down these lines, I imagine, without much joy, my impending old age and infirmity. I think of the deaths of those I have loved and still love. But I am unable to imagine my own death, since from the beginning I adjusted to the idea of a dubious reincarnation. It is, for example, possible to acquire a kind of immortality by impressing songs on records, an act that makes use of voice, eyes, and the breathing mechanism. Once such work is finished, these organs collapse, only to flutter away like swallows in the form of discs, coming to roost in many collections. A couple of hundred records, twice as many sides, the interpreter's picture on the sleeve—so I become an icon both practical and terrifying. That is how I imagined fame to be when I was very young. But I ignored death, which goes hand in hand with fame. I worked out a form of immortality for myself that unfortunately did not take into account that every title vanishes from the catalogues as quickly as it appears. But this insight—along with abandoning pretentious gestures—came only when I was actually recording.

The first conductor I met, in whom I immediately inspired terror, was named Walther Schartner. I was all of eleven years old, and had gone with my parents to a spa in the Iser Mountains of Czechoslovakia, where my father was taking the cure. (It turned out to be in vain; he died the following year.) Every afternoon and evening the musicians in the obligatory bandstand in the park played to satisfy even the most demanding tastes. The players were a slightly condensed version of the municipal orchestra of Görlitz, the Silesian county town that in its own way was aspiring to culture. I in my short pants had often stood behind Herr Schartner and—uncharacteristically without my usual shyness—vigorously beat time right along with him. One night posters announced a conducting contest for the patrons. Avid as I was to take center stage, I would not rest; I assaulted the nerves of my venerable father, the privy councilor. (He was seventy-two. Schubert was still alive when my grandfather was born.) Finally he took me to the spa office, somewhat skeptical and certain that I would be turned away. Schartner raised his bushy eyebrows slightly; but then he could not have been more enthusiastic. He was shocked only when, asked for a suitable piece, I replied, "The overture to *Freischütz.*"

The conductor's dismay was understandable; he could not know that the curly-haired boy was intimately familiar with this work from his toy theater. What did we finally agree on? First, the Badenweiler March, very popular at the time and holding no dangers for the conductor; then, with somewhat greater daring, the Blue Danube Waltz. With my usual recklessness, I refused a score and conducted "by heart"—which is to say, as I happened to feel like doing. I did not realize that there is a tricky pause near the end of the piece. As the hurdle approached, the friendly first horn player, even while he played, sent me desperate signals with his left eyebrow, but ignorant as I was, I couldn't figure out what he meant. Promptly and vigorously I flourished my baton into the silence. The embarrassment seemed to me monumental. But it is unlikely that many in the audience were aware of what had happened, and the applause for the "charming little boy" was spectacular. I myself wasted a great deal of energy on embarrassment over my sailor suit with the bow on the chest, not exactly appropriate attire for a conductor but forced on me by my mother. My parents and friends spent days trying to console me for the grief of my "disgrace." The only one to succeed completely, however, was Susanne, my second girlfriend, whom I had met at the spa.

I no longer remember my father's reaction. Nor has much else concerning him stayed in my memory. Each of the rare occasions when he took me for a walk resulted in a grave decision. If we headed for the steamboat landing on the Wannsee, past the chicken that laid tin eggs, I was

determined to be a sea captain when I grew up. But the
first sight of smoking train monsters caused me to exclaim, "I'm going to be an engineer."

Once—about two years before Hitler seized power—
we were standing facing President Hindenburg's official
residence. The handsome mansion, guarded by helmeted
soldiers, the beautifully wrought iron gate—all led to my
decision to become president. My memory is no longer
very clear, but I am told that in a school composition I
delivered myself of the bon mot, "Hindenburg is a Field
Marshal whose hair stands on end."

I do have a vague memory of roughhousing with my
seventy-year-old father, smelling the smoke of his cigar,
and hearing the soft rasp of his breathing. From time to
time I interrupted him as he played solitaire in bed and
begged him to draw a new figure for my theater. "Daddy,
make me a prince!" became the catch phrase in our family
for an unwelcome distraction.

Once my father returned to the arena of his life's work
as an honored guest, when he was invited to address the
graduating class. I can still see him deliberately bypassing
the speaker's lectern to his left, standing beside it for an
informal speech, only occasionally leaning on the edge.
He also took his key ring out of his pocket, running it
soundlessly through his fingers while he was thinking.
The fact that he also spoke very softly, so as to emphasize
the absence of emotion in his remarks, made me squirm,
since his words were almost unintelligible from beyond
the sixth row. It was quite a contrast when his successor
in office, Herr Wicht, spoke in a booming voice for the
formal conclusion before dismissing the students from the
auditorium with a typical two-fingered gesture closely resembling the "German greeting."

I fully intended to distinguish myself by standing out brilliantly, in my father's manner. This was an especially strong desire because I was convinced that everyone was repelled by me. At nine and ten I still had a baby's snub nose and eyes that lay deep in their sockets. Though I enjoyed the cries of enchantment uttered by certain aunts whenever they saw me, I did not believe them.

During my vacations in Ottobeuren I played with Irma, the brewer's daughter, who was a year younger than me; as soon as I was with her, I became even more obsessed with the conviction of my own ugliness. She was nine years old, with silky blond hair and green eyes. She sang the Queen of the Night's coloratura arias without any difficulty and danced prettily on her toes. I was shy and dared not tell her that I admired her. But she had no need of such assurances; she teased and taunted me, and my confusion grew.

My next infatuation was with a boy, a classmate who not only shone academically but also brought along his German shepherd dog every day, leaving him in the care of a neighbor during school. He was just beginning to do chemical experiments in the basement of his house, and one day I was shocked, first by his absence, then by the news that his house had exploded and he had lost his life.

Two years later I fell in love just as passionately with Susanne, whom I have already mentioned. My love lasted through the summer at the spa and ended only when I saw Carola at the skating rink in Berlin and fell in love with her. The rink was a place of horror. My mother, who believed in physical exercise, literally had to drag me there. I grew sick and tired of falling; at the best of times I could not trust my overly long legs. It took an eternity for me to get to the point where I could even move from the spot with short pushes on twisted ankles. This earned me a scathing look from my beloved, who refused to stay by my side even for a little while. I told my father about my misfortune as soon as I got back home. It was one of the very few instances when we had a "conversation"; he was more inclined to jokes and grandfatherly feelings than to talking seriously with me.

After a severe bout of pneumonia, which he caught after explaining the stars to my mother on a cold night, he required careful nursing, which with great pride I took on, as far as going up and down the stairs and his brief stay in the garden were concerned. I stationed a chair on the landing, for a rest midway, and was happy to be allowed to support him in the upward climb by placing his arm across my shoulders. Then they took him to the hospital, and to make my mother's life easier, I was sent to stay with my half-brother Achim and his family in the Zehlendorfer Fischtal.

Achim, a son of my father's first marriage, was twenty years older than I. He has walked with me, often from afar but always lovingly, during the longest stretch of my life. Among the numerous figures of near and distant relatives, he was the closest of all to me because he so much resembled the father I lost so early. Achim, too, always remembered our father with special warmth and admiration; he was to take my father's place. I could confide in him, confess, complain—never without his loving concern. Achim made his life into a work of art of sympathetic understanding, which those who knew him less well dared to call "smothering." But that precisely was his sensitivity; he was not a revolutionary, an iconoclast, or a lofty artist. He had an unobtrusive authority with which he helped the whole scattered family. My wife Julia mourns the person who had immediately and unconditionally taken her to his heart.

Achim was the first person of our acquaintance to drive a car, a rickety DKW, and he did so very cautiously. I'll never forget the snail-like drive to a family reunion in Ziesar, where I saw with delight the first cows and pigs of my life. Amid the converging burghers Achim, gentlemanly in a double-breasted suit, his elegant wife at his side, stood out like a stranger. He represented something that the larger group had striven for but had never attained, and his appearance was observed not without envious displeasure. On the drive back to Berlin—it was around the time of the 1936 Olympics—we found ourselves on the rising stretch of road just outside Potsdam stuck in an endless line of cars, which made us three hours late getting home.

Achim and Annie's love story remained a romance to the very end; they complemented each other in an almost ideal way. Somewhat cautious and judicious in judgment, Achim caught fire from Annie's liveliness and spontaneity, and surely she also helped to develop his taste. It was from him that I learned how exciting an enthusiasm for antique furniture can be, how it can enhance one's knowledge. "I've just bought another wonderful old bureau, I don't even know where to put it." I often heard him make such statements, even while I was billeted in the Fischtal during my father's last illness, so as to set my mother free to devote all her time to caring for the patient.

A few weeks after we buried my father, I was dashing excitedly about, helping to set the supper table for some guests, pestering my grief-stricken mother about whether what I was doing was right or not, where to place a particular thing or where to find another. Suddenly Achim, who had arrived early, slapped me soundly. The blow destroyed all my pride at helping and being competent. It took a while before I understood the feeling that had motivated the concerned stepson.

In the Fischtal soft, sloping meadows invited us to play, and I immediately adapted them to theatrical purposes. When a certain Peter Steiger in my class was chosen for some minor role in a Nazi movie, I suddenly found the boy terrifically interesting. I took him to the Fischtal, and in a state of ecstasy we played at "falling" and "dying" by letting ourselves roll down the steep slopes. In general I preferred death scenes whenever possible. So my friend Hansi Wunschel would happily take the part of a stern judge, and my feelings were deeply hurt if, after suspenseful deliberation, he decided not to condemn me to death. We probably chose this boy to be our spokesman because his speech was untinged by the local dialect. He often rang our doorbell, and my mother was thoroughly charmed by the six-year-old's carefully chosen words: "Madam, would you be so kind as to see if Dieter is at home? We wish to play with him."

I would have liked to have known my father's feelings about this friend and his equally well-spoken younger brother. We were playmates during the time when my father became seriously ill, and then cruel death walked through our door. When the family assembled in the living room, I gradually came to understand what the women's weeping meant.

Learning of my father's death filled me with grief and fear. Outside the cemetery chapel, seeing the endless lines of students from "his" schools that filed past us to shake hands, my grief—the emotion of a twelve-year-old—became mingled both with the feeling that I was inappropriately dressed in my Hitler Youth uniform and with pride because all of them felt sorry for me, the fatherless boy. Since I had not witnessed my father's death, I secretly hoped to see him again. For a long time I thought I spied him at any moment among the passersby in the street. Whenever I saw a stocky man with a florid face, taking little steps, my heart grew warm. I loved my father, but until he died I never knew the depth of my love.

School subjects interested me less and less; my curiosity was increasingly aroused by music. Our "singing" teacher, Wilhelm Forck, who had a pleasant tenor voice, conducted the school chorus. One day he placed a chair in front of the singers and called on me: "Dieter, get up there and conduct."

The music happened to be the Sanctus from Schubert's Mass in G Major. Because I was no more hesitant than I was competent at the job, I was allowed to conduct another selection as well, Schumann's "Der deutsche Rhein."

Not long after my father's death the parents of my school friend Hansi Wunschel invited me to spend the summer with them. This was the first time I had traveled on my own. Hansi's father had moved from Berlin to Traunstein, where he had been promoted to head of the local tax office. Somehow the stern man who enjoyed correcting me in a harsh voice must have found something in me to like, and the short summer weeks were filled with adventures. Once the four Wunschels and I got on bicycles to glide smoothly down the streets from Traunstein to Salzburg, there to venture a glimpse behind the scenes of the hustle and bustle of the Festspiele. They were just setting up the scenery for *Fidelio* in the Schauspielhaus; the stage doors were wide open, and my hungry eyes were able to stare into the mysterious dusk.

At home in the official residence in Traunstein, I found out that I had never learned good table manners. Sitting next to Frau Wunschel, I helped myself without first offering the bowl to her. "Such manners! The lady has to be served first," Herr Wunschel scolded. Ilse Wunschel's attempt to exonerate me died at birth and turned into respectful silence.

We also went mountain climbing. I did not cover myself with glory when, only a few steps before we had reached the summit of the Dirnbachhorn, I wilted and remained sitting alone. Later we came to a ski hut by a path that was hard to negotiate. Even though it was summer, my city shoes could hardly stand up to the rigors of such a hike. It had been raining, and inside my too thin shoes my socks were wet through and through. I held them out to the fire we had lit with all possible speed. At our back the bunk beds were waiting, and as happened to me later, when I was a prisoner of war, I, a clumsy climber, was assigned a top bunk—a source of still more embarrassment.

I cannot remember whether by the end of this vacation I had managed to overcome my shyness enough to produce an even halfway sensible word of thanks.

Whenever I see Hansi nowadays, it always seems to me that no time at all has passed since our last meeting.

Instead of concentrating on math, history, and geography, I searched my conscience, with a rigor strange in a twelve-year-old. I meditated on my nature, human destiny, the decay of matter, the immortality of the soul. Max, one of my school friends, was often forced to listen to me. He was the first person with whom I could make something like chamber music, since he played the clarinet. We stood together, begging signs around our necks, outside the Philharmonie or the Staatsoper, earning the money for tickets. Often we got stage seats, so that we could watch the expressions on Willem Mengelberg's and Oswald Kabasta's faces while they conducted. Delighted and thrilled, we would talk about the "gooseflesh men" who made us shudder with trumpets, horns, and drums at the climaxes.

We probably had only a dim idea that we were being offered merely excerpts from the full panoply of musical pleasures. It was better not to acknowledge such composers as Felix Mendelssohn and Gustav Mahler, Tchaikovsky and Debussy. And such names as Schönberg, Berg, and Webern did not ring in our ears. Today it seems incredible that young people were not taught about Sigmund Freud. I too had never heard of the man who unlocked new continents of the soul that remain to be explored to this day.

When we had raved our fill about the "gooseflesh men," our conversation turned to the mighty of the earth, and we agreed on the unreasonableness of their advice. Drunk with the spiritual wines of the afternoon at the Delphi, we sat in the midst of silent table telephones listening to Jean Omer, himself already close to being banned. As the Belgian musician played, Max took his turn at talking. The jazz tunes lifted his spirits and strengthened his patience with things to come.

For him these things came all too quickly and cruelly. We were able to sit in some café or other on Kantstrasse only a few times more, watching the girls and talking about marriage in our usual supercilious, ridiculous manner.

In my infatuation with music I increasingly neglected my studies. I also skimmed light novels by such writers as Rudolf Herzog and Friedrich Gerstäcker and ate gingerbread until I was sick. It may be that my constant self-analysis developed my intelligence, but it was a strain on my nerves. No sooner did I ask myself something like, "What am I thinking about?" than a flood of other questions and answers overwhelmed me. The philosophical discoveries I thought Max and I were making flattered our self-love enormously. Often I pretended to be a person of significance who was about to reveal new truths for the welfare of humankind. I looked on other mortals with the proud awareness of my own great achievement. But when I bumped into one of these mortals, I lost my composure in front of the least of them, and the more important I believed myself to be, the less I was able to show my feeling of superiority; I even felt ashamed of my most harmless remarks. Wrapped in such doubts, I dreamed of worldly success, encouraged by Max.

We both found dancing class stimulating, and I would not have wanted to miss a minute of it. Nevertheless, as soon as I found myself in the group, I was paralyzed by a morbid shyness. The sounds of current sentimental hits filled the room. Dazed by the loud records and dazzled by the glances of young girls, aroused by a thousand delicate scents emanating from the "ladies' " dresses, I lost all self-assurance, barely dared to open my mouth, and could only ask a very plain girl to dance with me. I'm sure I was labeled "boring." And to my horror, the loudspeaker blared out the suggestion that Herr Fischer-Dieskau not always ask the same Fräulein So-and-So to dance!

In our long conversations I agreed with the gentle Max that people were predestined to strive for moral perfection. Each one in his own modest sphere was obligated to discourage sin by the example of his own virtue. Occasionally we came down from such heights to discuss our future: military service, art, marriage, the best way to raise children.

Soon I was sent to confirmation class. I considered it a ridiculous business, since I was descended from a long line of clergymen and knew more than others about the matters under discussion. The contentious Pastor Petersen reminded us that we were living in peculiar times. Each Sunday he thundered from the pulpit against the Brown madness, and then there would be weeks and months during which he disappeared. But time and again—probably because he was well beyond the critical age—he came back and waggled his goatee and bellowed through Lichterfelde's Paulus-Kirche. Pastor Martin Niemöller acted no differently, except that he was absent from my brother Klaus' confirmation classes for even longer periods.

But then I sat in the Jesus-Christus-Kirche in Dahlem and devoured the ceremony with my eyes, never suspecting that this church would one day become an essential place for me, part of my artistic home. In the 1930s it stood at the center of the "Confessional Church," which boldly attacked the "German Christians" as an opportunistic, state-sanctioned organization. After the war the Berlin radio stations and record companies set up shop there, and the congregation benefited from the proceeds from records. I cannot number the works, the conductors, the other singers I encountered here. (The situation has not changed to this day.) I soon began to feel at home in the bright space, where unfortunately the loud hum of air-planes tended to drown out every other sound.

In the Jesus-Christus-Kirche I also heard sermons by Hellmut Gollwitzer, whose speech was rumored to be so erudite that no one could follow him. But I remember that though I was only a teenager, I had no trouble under-standing him when he exhorted us to practice freedom and independence of thought. Since those days Sigmund Freud has gained ascendancy over my religion. Of all that I have read, nothing has impressed me as profoundly as his insights. But the memory of those Confessional cler-gymen remains alive; they belonged to the only organized illegal group that existed at the time.

In Petersen's classes the beautiful Eva sat a few rows behind me. I turned my head to look at her so often that I made a bad impression on the instructor. Soon I was chasing after her, sniffing the air around her house, not daring to speak to her for the longest time. Then I walked her to class a few times, though she seemed embarrassed by my attention. And when I finally pressed a shy kiss on her lips, she boasted of the smart lieutenants who had taken her sailing on the Wannsee; there was no way, she made it clear, that I could even enter the competition. From then on I avoided her like the plague.

2

"Er wünscht sich mächtige Schwingen"

By the time I was sixteen, I had no hesitation about tackling Brahms' *Vier ernste Gesänge (Four Serious Songs)*. I sensed that my voice was acquiring a nice quality. I had heard these songs over and over as sung by Emmi Leisner, an alto. She interpreted them with verve and sensitivity, with energy and expression, with sonority and nobility, and with an instinctive sense of what was appropriate. The somewhat corpulent singer on the stage of the Beethoven-Saal acknowledged the impassioned boy sitting next to his mother in the first row with a welcoming smile. After one such evening of lieder—the program was made up entirely of Max Reger—my mother talked me out of my reluctance and took me backstage.

"There he is, my young admirer," the artist exclaimed.

To the question of whether she would be willing to give me singing lessons, she replied, "No. I think a man would be more effective. Go to see Georg A. Walter, the wonderful Bach interpreter. He'll keep me informed about your progress."

Georg A. Walter lived in the last house on Berlepsch-strasse in Zehlendorf. I auditioned for him, and he turned aside, catching his breath. His reply to my question whether I might study with him, was instant and whole-hearted: "Of course, my dear boy. Of course."

Walter belonged to the school of new Bach interpreters that formed in the 1920s. He began by assigning me vocalization exercises from Manuel Garcia's school of singing.

Soon, however, we abandoned these and a few introductory remarks on anatomy—which frequently referred, somewhat embarrassingly, to the *os pubis*—in order to concentrate on Bach cantatas, which Walter played very fluently and proudly at sight. A well-known evangelist and oratorio tenor, he of course felt deeply about these works. Secretly he yearned for the opera, and not infrequently he performed parts of Wagner's *Lohengrin* for me.

For a while I greatly enjoyed the change from technical work to actual music-making, but at the end of a year it was not enough for me. I still knew nothing about how to overcome the break in the vocal range and other technical details. So, with Walter's blessing, touchingly given, I ended my pilgrimages to Zehlendorf. Before that, there had been a student recital in the Meistersaal, where at the age of seventeen I dared, as the last item on the program, to bellow Hans Sachs' curtain speech ("Verach-

---

tet mir die Meister nicht") from Wagner's *Die Meistersinger.*

But now the conservatory lay ahead of me, as did lessons with Hermann Weissenborn (not to be confused with Günther Weissenborn, who for years was my accompanist whenever I toured Germany). As a recital singer, Hermann Weissenborn was much less successful than his colleague Walter. Berlin educators thought of him as a leader of the chorus. After long and obstinate application, I was accepted into his class. He already had too many students to whom he gave individual instruction.

I saw Walter again before starting in Weissenborn's class. My school was preparing a concert in which I was to sing the *Winterreise,* in response to my fervent desire (and my mother's) to perform the song cycle before a larger audience; Professor Walter was in the audience. In my zeal I miscalculated: Two songs (I don't remember which ones) were not properly memorized—so I simply left them out. When the concert was roughly at the halfway mark, the air raid sirens began to sound. It was January 30, 1943, the tenth anniversary of the Nazi seizure of power, and the British were commemorating it with heavy bombardment. My audience of two hundred or so in the Zehlendorf town hall joined me in fleeing to the basement. After about two hours, during which all hell broke loose outside, though fortunately not in Zehlendorf itself, we all went upstairs again for the second installment of the song cycle. It was a debut out of the ordinary, but it showed me that I could confront difficult circumstances and work through them to the end.

When the time came for my final secondary-school

examination, proudly called "music examination," few of my fellow students were left. Not only they but all the younger teachers as well had been snatched up into the armed forces. What remained were lovable old men like our music teacher, Seelmann, who was actually responsible for the German curriculum but who had an astonishing knack for improvising free piano versions of Wagner operas. He introduced us—with the help of a great deal of mimicry—to the Ring cycle of Bayreuth's patron saint. I cannot pretend that I didn't enjoy these one-man performances.

When I went to the "flophouse"—in those days the place best suited for catching up on sleep after the wakeful nights—terror of the nighttime bombings and the paramilitary polish in the Hitler Youth we had been forced to join dominated all our thoughts and feelings. Compared to such burdens, ordinary school life paled. Nevertheless, even school provided us with certain amusements. I no longer remember all the ways we thought up to frighten a certain, no longer young music teacher; we tormented her with sudden blackouts, with cupboard doors springing wide open, with deafening noise. . . . She would either flee or call me to the grand piano, hoping for some solidarity-based silence from the class. Time after time I showed off my limited repertoire of piano works, and silence would descend on the classroom.

It seemed to Max and me that everything was covered by a veil of unreality. We saw boundless sadness in people's eyes. Around this time I began to understand that our world had become too complicated for human beings, that the principal theme of our time would be flight, blind running from madness, from violence, from decay. Max was one of the first to fall, shortly after he was drafted.

The biology professor remained behind to give the music exam. He asked me to speak on parallels to Bach's *Phoebus and Pan*. It took me a while to remember, but I recalled just in time that it was one of Bach's "parodies," with numerous note-for-note references to the *Bauern-kantate*. In the eighteenth century one of my ancestors had used the latter at the ceremony to mark the acquisition of his estate. (It is true that soon after, the impoverished von Dieskau family was forced to sell the little Renaissance castle near Halle that was part of the estate.) Given such a topic, which I had studied beforehand, I did very well. The other subjects could not be taken too seriously; since there were only three students left in the graduating class, the school authorities were unwilling to let anyone fail. Except for me, a Dutch boy, and a polio victim, everyone else had been drafted. A feeling of guilt still haunts me for our crime: We pooled our money so that the Dutch boy could bribe the janitor—in those days still called "the porter"—to let us have the questions for the oral exam.

Immediately after this masterly achievement I presented myself for an audition at the conservatory. I waited for hours in a huge crowd of women before I was given the chance to offer up my rendition of "Wegweiser" from the *Winterreise* so the committee could judge my abilities. I was so hungry and exhausted that I could not immediately think of the words to the third stanza; Professor Weissenborn, a member of the group, was kind enough to prompt me.

When finally I settled down to the first hard work of my life (though it lasted for only six months), I realized

---

how much I still had to understand and master. Once again I was made to vocalize, and some of the exercises were the same ones I had already been assigned by Georg A. Walter—Garcia vocalizations. I was not unaware of the chain of connections. Julius Stockhausen, the Brahms enthusiast (he had been the first to sing the *Magelonen-Romanzen)*; Raimund von Zur Mühlen; and Johannes Messchaert—these great figures in the history of the art song had all emerged from Garcia's school; and Hermann Weissenborn had Messchaert to thank for the fact that he was a part of the Berliner Akademie. It was also Weissenborn who, when I sang more professionally, gave me a precious old edition of Garcia's *Art of Singing*. I believe that he enjoyed our lessons so much because I made him work hard. His face bright red, the old gentleman breathed heavily—I drained him dry. And he tried with all his might to save me from the draft, which threatened me after my first semester, by giving me inflated grades. But all his attempts were to no avail.

When the conscription notice came in the mail, the curtain that had concealed the things of this life was torn apart. How was I, an unworldly dreamer, to endure in the world thus revealed? Human experience taught us that there was no return from this state of mind to more easy-going spheres. Often I confided my misery to my cousin Edith, who suffered from a hip ailment and was confined to a wheelchair. She wrote to me when I was stationed in the Perleberger Kaserne, shortly before I was sent to the front: "If now, in spite of everything, the miracle of vanquishing war—that is, peace—were to happen, and everything were to flow back into the ordinary stream of life, your awareness that all beauty continues to give pain, that all joy is merely melancholy, cannot be erased. You stand apart from your unsuspecting contemporaries."

On the other hand, at twenty, life can be hard to bear at the best of times. Why should it have been different in those days?

I had turned my antennae in the right direction. Edith Schmidt was the daughter of my beloved uncle, Dr. Martin Fischer, a physician, who not long before had been run over by a truck when he was bicycling, as was his usual practice, while paying house calls on his patients in Zehlendorf. Edith looked like her father; her disability, however, increasingly limited her movements and deformed her. The mother of three beautiful daughters, she helped support the family with translations from the French and English. With her we could do parodies and imitations to work off our feelings of hatred and mockery for the brawlers and shouters in the Sportspalast and Olympia-Stadion. The man of the house, himself slightly tinged with Brown, tended to flee the premises, fearful and annoyed, during such performances.

While I was stationed in Italy, even in the apocalyptic conditions of the time, I could still detect something of the waning beauty of the country, and I found the Italians wiser in their way than our problematic people. In the meantime Edith looked after my mother, calling her a "silent heroine, worthy of the utmost admiration and love." At the front, when we were engaged in a struggle to the death, I often took refuge in the memory of our conversations about the Greeks and about the consolation that could be found in their history and wisdom. Time and again people struggle with their destiny, are severely tested and strengthened by the experience, mature and wane; then new generations rush in, not a whit wiser, entering on the same ordeal all the way to the painful yet sweet resolution.

Edith also kept me informed about home: "Went to visit your mother today—marvelous. Irmel played—Haydn, Telemann, Martini, and Brahms. She has a soul for the cello, and I love her already. It was wonderful, over coffee at the festively set table, sun streaming into the room, flaming-red grape leaves, and your letter at the center. Everything around your mother is so alive!!"

Irmgard Poppen had sensed the "elective affinity" and attached herself to Edith. I had met her at the conservatory just before I was drafted. A girl with a handsome profile sat a few rows in front of me in Professor Mahling's class on music history. My heart, which was beating wildly, made me speak to her. She came from Freiburg im Breisgau and proudly called herself a "Bobbele"—the local word for a native of that enchanted region. In the three or four days left to me before I had to report (with my few possessions in a cardboard box) I asked her to go to the theater with me. We saw a performance of *Johannisfeuer* by Hermann Sudermann (with Hannsgeorg Laubenthal, Maria Koppenhöfer, and Paul Wegener), Jürgen Fehling's last directing job in Berlin before the end of the Thousand Year Reich, and not long before the bombing of the Staatsschauspiel, which has since come back to life as the Schauspielhaus in East Berlin. Recently I saw the spot again at the foot of the great staircase where we had agreed to meet that night in 1943. The occasion was an evening of lieder I performed with Hartmut Höll in the theater converted into a recital hall.

Before I entered the service, Irmel and I even found an opportunity to make music together, though there was no piano in her lodgings. But accompanying her on a harmonium, I realized with great pleasure what a highly talented cellist she was. That night the bombing was severe, but I was only marginally aware of the flaming inferno and the acrid smoke as I made my way back home.

Edith could not stop raving about Irmel: "She is one of those people who genuinely live by their own inner law—with the greatest naturalness and freedom, undeluded by external norms, and since she has a very modest mind and a warm heart, every one of her actions, every glance, every word is true, pure, natural, and a joy. To this is added a gentle cheerfulness, that glows from within, as it were, not loudly but steadily."

Edith's thought-provoking letters helped me through many of the realities of wartime in Berlin that we heard about. Conditions were the same as those I had experienced before I left, with the night bombings continuing. If I wanted to describe life at the front, I usually employed a number of code words and referred to myself as Otto. Each of Edith's letters asked, "What does Otto think?"

During this period my mother was forced to hand Martin over to an institution outside Berlin, and soon the Nazis did to him what they always did with cases like his: They starved him to death as quickly as possible. My mother, who had organized her whole life around taking care of him, suffered infinitely more from his death than she had from his torments while he lived. Edith wrote: "I have felt so sorry for her so many times, and I admire the way she copes! Now the poor child will be a melancholy memory for all of you."

For Edith her house in Zehlendorf became another

melancholy memory; during the last months of the war the Schmidts fled to the vicinity of Stade, where both later died. But before that time Edith, at the age of fifty, went back to school under that "formidable headmistress, life," after the end of the war. None of the friends who had to live through the hell that Berlin became were their old selves. It seemed that the inner bonds had been broken, that they could not recover from the horrors of the war and its end. A further torment was the hunt to satisfy the most primitive needs, the daily guerrilla warfare that had a poisonous effect on everyone, and in which it was precisely the best who failed. Edith ached finally to hear the Badenweiler March played without fear that the neighbors would deplore its jazziness. But her piano had not made the trek to the country. There was only a radio, acquired by trading in her wristwatch, which she loved because it held so many memories. "Let me tell you about the crazy homesickness we carry around with us here. All you need is a quick shot of the Grunewald in a movie or you have a vivid memory of a street corner—and right away there's a stab to your heart and you're sick for hours."

These sketches of a lost time, which can never return, bring it back to living memory.

3

"Dessen Ohren Mordgebrüll umhallte"

Today I see the diary pages excerpted here as my attempt at preserving an inner life in chaotic surroundings, not unlike the will people exerted after the war to construct a new culture. Even the horrible aspects of the years 1943–1947 remain part of my emotional baggage. I am not willing to relinquish any of it; it gives me the strength on which I live to this day.

How productive were the times in Berlin? I may have lived too much only for music; now the total readjustment is especially hard. My job here in Fürstenwalde is cleaning the horses, the rest of the time I act as coachman. . . .

King-sized Russia. Endless mud. Poems by Morgen-

---

stern. It is a good idea to learn them by heart, to have something to fall back on. . . .

If at least we were properly outfitted! Summer clothing in the Russian winter. I worry a lot about how they came through the last heavy attack at home. This Ahrimanian time is terrible, a time that does not live up to its definition. The avenging catastrophe is upon us. . . .

We meet a lot of old soldiers from the East whose tales make us feel very insignificant. One officer just told us all about the extensive destruction in Berlin—the conservatory also received a direct hit. . . .

Lots of cold, lots of slush, and even more storms. Every day horses die for lack of food. The animals look awful. By now soldiers returning from leave in Berlin have told me details of the night bombings. If only half of what they say is true, the people must have endured terrible things. Everyone here is totally discouraged. . . .

Irmel is studying the Pfitzner duet (probably the wonderfully strange one, with orchestra) with Max Strub, the Pfitzner enthusiast and expert. . . .

Our dear, beautiful Lichterfelde apartment is completely bombed out. Of course I went there at once, since I did not know how Mother had come through the heavy attack. She was well, and the loss of all our furniture faded into the background. Only a few things could be saved. Most of the scores burned, as did both instruments. I saw the grand piano, without its legs, shoved down all the flights of stairs, lying in the cellar. Record collection and record player saved. With her customary energy, Mother did not lose her head; she had already made all necessary arrangements. All I had to do was take care of the move—by handcart—to Achim's Dahlem apartment, where some space was available. We set up at least one room almost normally, so that the second day of my leave was no longer an extreme-emergency leave. Theater, concerts, a lot of other music—defying the irrational world. Actually we are very proficient at this. . . .

Time spent with Irmel . . .

Until the parting, this leave was as complete and perfect as one could wish. Time and military life were forgotten. Now, back in the old, cold surroundings, I can hardly believe the enormous new happiness I was granted at home. Instead of my earlier constant restlessness, a self-contained feeling of happiness. . . .

Then I stood at my father's grave, that quiet, familiar place. I had stopped being his son, I was him. . . .

It is astonishingly easy to go into this great uncertainty. Fortified. If I should not return, my life will have had meaning simply through meeting Irmel. . . .

Huge massing of the army, units from every German region. Entrainment. Departure for the front. . . .

Now we are surrounded by mountains. Mightier and more awesome than any I have ever seen. Glow and gleam alter as day comes and goes. The valleys envelop us, and their splendor silences every thought. Whenever someone begins to point a timid finger, it drops again at once, only to move to yet another beautiful sight. A small railroad station at the Brenner Pass; we stop briefly, a clear and starry sky over the steep slopes in every direction. Standing watch in the night. The mountains have changed. They have become demonic. Countless peaks, each pushing the next one aside. Houses emerge in the half-dark, they look as if they belong somewhere else. Their pale slimness does not seem to fit in the foreground of the huge rugged mountains. In the bright morning a yellow sun lights up gray Verona. Narrow towers scrape the air. Everything is

---

new and different. The train has stopped in the middle of nowhere; for the first time our eyes rest on the Italian landscape. A couple of squatting figures might have just climbed down from the opera stage in their bright clothing. . . .

At our next stop we are harshly welcomed by low-flying aircraft. Though the train is able to proceed, some men and horses are dead or wounded. Twice the wave rolls over us while I am huddled in my dugout at the edge of the road. Noise and dust and screams stick in my memory. . . .

I will, I must bring to the surface what exists in me but is not yet conscious, I must express what it is that inspires me. . . .

I get along very well with the evacuated Italians who populate these mountains in great masses. I have also sung now and then, with great success and received the verdict, *"Un gran cantante!"* It is amazing how much even the poorest farmhand here knows about opera. Whenever we march and I must set one foot in front of the other while the night is dark as pitch, how often my eyes are kept open by thinking of home, of a faraway, wonderful future. Yesterday something strange happened to me. In the ancient cathedral of Vicopisano, a town hard hit by English bombs, I found an organ that still had some working parts, and I played it to my heart's content. Of course I soon had an audience of monks, and they asked me to sing as well. About fifty more people came into the church from the street, all of them pale, emaciated, careworn. Transfigured expressions, and the assurance that for a moment or two they had forgotten all about the war. Then (it was a long time since I had eaten) they shared with me the little food they had, and were happy as kings to see me enjoy it. Only when we are completely separated can we understand that we belong together. . . .

Alone in an ancient shepherd's hut. No one far and wide, 1500 m. altitude. . . .

This afternoon pretended, as so often, that I was supervising the Italian workmen, with a splendid view of the wide, softly curving heights of the Appenines. . . .

Cloud formations in fascinating colors, mountain rain with a purple overture, bright sunlight in front of eerie dark cloud masses that move with amazing rapidity over the disheveled crests. Epilogue: interplaying of all the colors to happy effect, glittering lights on all the slopes, impassable roads. . . .

Reading *Lebendiges Theater* [Living Theater] by the stage designer Ludwig Sievert. . . .

Once more we are back to living in mud and holes in the ground. . . .

With every new army report fear of the future increases. Will all hope, all waiting have been in vain? From somewhere or other distant Sunday bells make a ghostly sound as they summon the faithful to Mass. . . .

The rough types sitting in the cellar down below symbolize modern humanity for me, as it burdened itself with this war. Perhaps many of them became frightened as they examined the state of their souls, outraged by the wilderness that has taken root there. . . .

Brahms' Third Symphony. You could write volumes about it. Thank God I know it by heart. What is so moving, with all the formal terseness and rigor, is the unconscious content, which can be expressed only in music. . . .

A strange thing has happened to all hopes for the future. When you are stuck in the everyday life of the front and bury your head, common sense absolutely forbids thinking about a happy outcome. So many are dying. Over the graves, forgetfulness. It is almost taken for granted that we think of ourselves as part of that group, and yet there is something stubborn that keeps saying, *you* are going to live. . . .

As soon as I receive my "daily ration" of nine cartridges, which I am ordered to use, I shoot them into the night sky. . . .

Unreal living conditions. To the left, earth; to the right, earth; above us a tent flap offering hardly any shelter at all. In my dugout there is someone from western Prussia who rubs himself with rancid butter twice a day to compensate for the lack of washing facilities. . . .

A few days ago I read the army report: how horrifying. Freiburg bombarded. Not enough that everything here threatens to overwhelm us past the point where we can cope. Without a company commander who writes poetry, sings, composes music, plays the cello, and talks about philosophy I would surely have a worse time of it. He is a comfort in this gray Advent period with few thoughts of Christmas, and unfortunately I am also kept from writing home often enough. . . .

In despair about my failed life, about people who think only of material things, about the political future, which is entirely black. . . .

Suddenly I am in paradise. Four days of rest and relaxation in the frontline convalescent hospital. We have learned to ask for very little. Things that until recently we took for granted have acquired the stature of the seven wonders of the world. Lying in a bed. Being able to sleep, to eat at a table with a cloth and real dishes, served by waitresses; living in heated rooms. To play the piano— and there is a radio. Time to think and write. . . .

The division has a musician, Bruno Penzien, who is in charge of everything connected with music. Yesterday he and four others came to regale us with a noisy night of music. I asked him whether I might be allowed to sing tonight, when there is to be a social gathering. He immediately questioned me at length, but this morning he arrived carrying a thick packet of scores, and we began to make music together uninterruptedly. First old songs, then Brahms symphonies arranged for four hands; finally he played to perfection everything I wanted to hear: Bach, Beethoven, Mozart, Reger, endlessly. Perspiring with excitement, I parted from him, but I kept thinking about the evening for a long time. He promised to come back. How was I to bear the change to the inferno afterward? Nevertheless, my gratitude for the present is great. . . .

Actually did sing two things last night. Did some drawing too, to the amusement of many. But the best: Bruno Penzien came back, had bought all sorts of things in Bologna, and we made music, almost the entire *Dichterliebe* and *Schöne Müllerin*, and some Bach arias. Bruno found the parting equally hard. . . .

Ordered to report. During nightly rounds through sheaves of flares I enjoy the romanticism of the landscape. . . .

Even in this bunker world the incomprehensible magic of Christmas Eve. The damp mud walls covered with white canvas. The green of fir trees, tinsel, candles. In the "official" celebration sang some three-part settings; afterward the whole battalion provided with music and song transmitted by telephone. . . .

Even the roughest men try to be agreeable. Around midnight, out into the moonlit snow landscape, singing "Im Stall bei Esel, Ochs und Rind" for three voices. . . .

Sang to the wounded, whose rapture moved me considerably. . . .

Now there is nothing but cold, wet clothes that grow stiff and icy. Never been so cold before in my life. The cover at the front of my dugout too stiff to move. . . .

No more meditations on the future. Considering only the life we still have. Thinking of nothing but saving ourselves. We are prepared for our destiny. The front seems frozen, and every night we must either dig foxholes or move on, under indescribably difficult conditions. Berlin threatened at close range. . . .

A voice comes from loudspeakers across the mountain slopes, crying, "Desert! Join our side!" [Later on I found confirmation in his book *Der Wendepunkt* that the voice was Klaus Mann's.] Given the completely changed living conditions that will prevail after the war, all of us will have great trouble in turning the strange into the familiar. The relation of person to person will take on a different coloration because of the sickness. . . .

Confused, frightening news from home. Tomorrow, Good Friday, I shall stuff my head once more with the *St. Matthew Passion*. "We sit down with tears." . . .

My nerves get the best of me a lot lately. Uncertainty, hunger, trench warfare probably account for it. . . .

While we are getting our food, a grenade explodes not two meters away. No splinters hit me, but the tendons on my right foot refuse to work. Hematoma. Back with the medic to the "field hospital" set up in a small farmhouse. After two weeks we are discharged. They hand us five rounds of ammunition: "Try to find your unit." I limp along among all the fleeing vehicles retreating along the road in the direction of the Po River. A supply truck gives me a lift, and when all traffic comes to a stop, it turns off into

---

a neighboring village. Sleep on straw in a barn, not without night watches because of the partisans, who take no prisoners. Then we spread white sheets on the roofs. Success, the airplanes spare us. And then the tank fire comes closer and closer. Finally black Amis stand before us and in mime recount a major battle. Patting us down and taking our watches. They let me keep Irmel's picture and my little diary. . . .

Taken prisoner. . . .

Driving endlessly. Far too many of us—more than fifty—stand on the back of the open truck, always in danger of falling off, thanks to the wild driving of the black man at the wheel. Italians along the side of the road spit and throw stones. The way the Americans coming toward us look and behave makes me sure that they were and are far superior to our soldiers. After nine weeks of famine, five of us in a tent for two, finally, in a camp near Livorno. . . .

One evening a GI came to the camp and told us he had heard something on the radio about a new kind of bomb that had been dropped somewhere over Japan. Soon we learned details. . . .

It is hard to send letters into an uncertain distance. No sign of life from home yet. Regular cautious attempts at information remain unanswered. Very lonely in the midst of many people. . . .

My current work in the orderly room allows me to type up from memory all kinds of poems, to make an anthology that can be copied and passed around. That puts some kind of lid on complete stupidity. Now and then, like the beats of a kettledrum, dreadful news reaches us, as for example the huge surge of rapes by the Russians in Berlin. . . .

After almost a year now, finally the first mail delivery, an enormous joy . . . Irmel is well and waiting for me. . . .

In the meantime I am named one of the few cultural officers in the Pisa-Livorno sector. Travel from camp to camp with evenings of lieder, recitations, and piano performances. One of those Steinway uprights available in every Ami unit on my truck, Werner Burgert, the accompanist, and I in front next to the driver—thus we rush along the dusty country roads. Often, admittedly, the "art barracks" are almost empty. At the windows, grimacing faces, making fun of me because of the "heavy music." We hardly care at all, since what is important is music. Pisa, with its military hospital something of a center of culture, has its own small orchestra under Herbert Trantow, a former ballet conductor at the Berlin Royal Opera. Recently he accompanied me in the *Winterreise*, which I sang to an audience of German nurses and patients. Eugen Andergassen is performing in plays he has written himself and in Max Mell's *Apostelspiel*. But sooner or later everything runs out of steam, since initiative is lacking. Resolutions once made are cast aside. It's not possible to go on working with no one but oneself. . . .

We performed the Christmas Oratorio by Schütz with a small chorus and a couple of instrumentalists. I sang all the solo parts. We read *Don Carlos* with scenery and lighting, typically German infantile efforts. . . .

Back again in Pisa. The young composer Werner Hübschmann, one of Hermann Grabner's students, and I tackle harmony and counterpoint. Founded a men's chorus. How can leanings toward acting, singing, conducting, and painting be reconciled? No one would believe how much each of these possibilities attracts me! . . .

Thanks to Wilhelm Reiniger's wonderful service, felt something like an Easter spirit. I sang Bach. My twenty-first birthday in the camp, with nothing but thoughts of Irmel. . . .

Some of my friends, who used to study literature and languages, and I are dying to go along on one of the trucks that drive into the city. After all, we want to have seen the Leaning Tower and the cathedral at least once. Women sit on the steps of the cathedral and shout to our backs, *"Che belli giovani!"*—What handsome young men! But no sooner have we entered the baptistry than American military policemen appear in the doorway, whistling and shouting orders. The people outside have earned a little cash or a cigarette by tattling on us. Taken off to an interrogation prison for a couple of days, sharing a cell with two black Americans who keep busy day and night dramatically shaking the iron bars and shouting. Back in our camp, after a while there is suddenly a legal hearing. And the commandant grins as he says, "In future please satisfy your artistic interests inside the barbed-wire fence!" . . .

Sudden transfer to Foggia. At a time when we had come to believe that we would finally be allowed to go home. . . .

I am rather proud of the fact that I was the first person in this southern solitude to have organized a serious entertainment: a one-man performance in a church hall containing a harmonium, on which I accompanied myself. Compromises are unavoidable. . . .

"Scraps" from the construction of the great airport are the seeds from which a theater barracks with about five hundred seats is growing. The play is *Der Vetter aus Dingsda*. Director and principal actor: guess who? A veritable waterfall burbled on the stage, and Fritz Kauber painted the scenery of fantastic rooms. Nothing special results from all our talents here—after all, the women's parts are played by men—but it distracts us from the oppressive thoughts of life's emptiness. . . .

I feel as if on the outside a few chosen ones were trying desperately to preserve the validity of the past for our age. So many are feverishly waiting for something new that we can greet with wonder. How can we creatively continue to keep up the tradition of what has gone before on our own? . . . No one to teach us, far and wide. . . . Not free to take lessons from Italian civilians. . . .

Back in Pisa . . . Every night a female captain leaves me a collection of 2000 records in the handsome room with the fireplace. Gustav Adolf Trumpff, the musicologist, returned with me from Foggia. He enjoys listening as well. Also found Detlev Jürges there, still organist for the field-hospital chaplain. There is another lieder recital. Found the scores for it more or less accidentally. Attendance and success quite considerable. They say I have gained in depth, have become more assured overall. Probably due to the "provincial" days in Foggia . . .

And once again in the priest's small study, over papal cigars with cherubs on the band and a scent like perfume, blissfully warm at the stove. The people I'm with, all, like me, unfulfilled. Always the same faces. . . .

Concert with Detlev: Brahms and Ravel for four hands. Charming nitpickers in the audience, offensive and lacking all objectivity. An instructive and amusing experience . . .

Bliss to re-create art, bliss also the ability not to close oneself off to works. Actually, sheer ingratitude, the artist's longing to be understood by everyone. Ingratitude, to mock at things while our senses are closed against them.

A commandment that those who understand remain steadfast and draw in those whose feelings and mind fail. A small circle consciously or unconsciously continues to develop the artistic taste of even the common man, ignoring a delay of decades. I share the opinion Axel von Ambesser expressed in *Das Abgründige in Herrn Gerstenberg*, that we may never nourish ourselves exclusively with what was thought and created before us . . .

April 1947: The American commandant, smiling complacently, says, "Those two (Detlev and me) make such great music, they can wait a while." How cordial of him! I sing in an American soldiers' club, hit songs with a German band. On orders, of course. So I arm myself with indifference, and for the rest, and especially now, I can let the real music get to me. . . .

With Detlev, studying songs by Debussy. Enchanting—like everything of his I know. Lately much occupied with impressionists, in part performing, in part listening to the radio and records. . . .

Furtwängler permitted to conduct again. On the radio I hear his first appearance in Florence with the orchestra of the Accademia Santa Cecilia. Things have not advanced to this point in Berlin, it seems . . .

Sent home, shortly after Detlev, in June 1947, with the last American hospital train. Destination, Göppingen. All they left me is the "patient" uniform—that is, pajamas—and a wooden footlocker that a buddy made for me some time ago. Am embarrassed because of the way I look to Irmel, who came to get me and take me to Freiburg by train.

4

"Vorüber die stöhnende Klage"

Soon after arriving in Freiburg, the returning soldier had a chance to show what he could do. Before a scheduled performance of Brahms' *German Requiem* in Müllheim in Baden, the baritone soloist fell ill. I was asked to step in for him, and even without rehearsal I managed to hold my own with the well-known soprano Tilla Brien. Theodor Egel, the conductor, promised me additional engagements, and in the years to come he kept his promise to the letter.

His chorale also sang in the Freiburg church where Irmel and I were married in 1949. She had been associated with the conductor for a long time as the continuo player in Bach's Passions, often with Karl Erb in the part of the

Evangelist. When Egel said farewell to his chorale in 1982 with a deeply moving performance of the *St. Matthew Passion* in Freiburg Cathedral, I was privileged to be one of the soloists.

Hermann Meinhard Poppen, my father-in-law's brother, conducted the Bach Society of Heidelberg, a praiseworthy choral society that rescued many new oratorios from obscurity, including Max Reger's "Hundredth Psalm," at a time when Poppen was still a student of the composer as well as his general assistant. Hermann was a typical old-fashioned conductor: an outstanding organist and pianist, paternally looking after everyone and everything connected with his concerts, even such details as ticket sales and setting up chairs and music stands. He was a swearing, nervous automobile driver.

Hermann and his kind-hearted wife, Emmy, were persuaded to put me up in their home for a few nights in 1947, during my first trip through the Neckar area. Anyone who recalls the considerable material burden such an invitation imposed at that time will appreciate my host's reluctance to welcome the young stranger to his table. Of course we came to know each other through music, and Hermann did not hesitate to invite me to participate in a performance of Max Reger's *Einsiedler* in the Heidelberg castle. He thus became the first conductor to engage me professionally.

Many other performances followed, the Bach Passions as well as the Brahms Requiem, the last involving a test of courage in the Ludwigshafen church. The soprano did not show up for the only soloists' rehearsal. When the orchestra nevertheless struck up the accompaniment to her solo section, I began—first humming, then singing outright one octave lower—to sing the soprano part. I was given an ovation by the chorus and the orchestra.

Once I traveled to Heidelberg to take over the part of the peasant in Schönberg's *Gurrelieder* in one of the first postwar performances of the work in Germany. When I arrived at the gloomy brownstone town hall, I could feel the tension in the air. Though Poppen was able to complete the orchestra rehearsals, the music for the soloists and the orchestral scores for these sections did not arrive until the last moment. As is so often the case, the publisher allowed only a very few copies of the vocal and orchestral scores to circulate. These were so studded with insertions in bright colors that had been added from generation to generation that they were almost illegible, looking more like abstract art. When the orchestra began to play, the musicians frequently found themselves divining rather than reading the subdivided string sections and complicated entrances of the wind instruments. After a while only an occasional ragged shred of sound could be heard from one corner of the stage. Finally a single violin played a few isolated notes, and the conductor dropped his hands, discouraged. "What can we do now, Dieter?"

"Maybe, at least for the interludes, we could make some small cuts when the orchestra is playing alone."

"Yes, but how? Help me."

"Here is a D major, and another one three pages further on, so—"

Beggars can't be choosers. And no one in the audience noticed anything amiss. More than once I have mentally begged Schönberg's forgiveness for this performance, cut

---

69

by a few minutes. Perhaps he has forgiven me, if only because his songs appear so often on my programs.

At that time, in 1947, Irmel went on a short tour along Lake Constance with the Nauber Quartet, playing second cello in the Schubert quintet. I was allowed to carry music stands and place the scores on them—until, that is, the first violinist discovered that his assistant was exercising his voice in the corner of a tavern and "forced" me to sing for the whole quartet.

Whenever I mentioned to anyone my intention of returning to Berlin, to my mother and my teacher, I was met by pitying looks. The reports of extreme conditions there could only add to our gloomy ideas of life in Berlin. But I went home all the same.

The railroad journey was unbelievably uncomfortable. I was jammed and squeezed in among all the other people and luggage, with endless stops and a night spent sitting on my cardboard suitcase in the Hanover central railroad station, which was like a gloomy inferno. I thought with longing of my wooden suitcase from my prisoner-of-war period, which would have done better service as a seat. Everywhere were starved, ragged figures, disconcerting overcrowding, dirt, and muttered curses. And then the first shocking sight of the incredibly disfigured silhouette of Potsdam.

Nevertheless, in Berlin I was soon considerably busier than I had been in Freiburg. The Berlin climate is stimulating—as I continue to insist, no matter how polluted the air may have become. At that time I was eager to take care of my mother, who was under tremendous strain; after all she had endured during the war, her nerves were worn to a frazzle. Her life had been endangered first by the night bombings and then by Russian soldiers, who were determined to shoot her along with a group of other women. She saved twenty lives with her quick wit; she was able to make the Russian with the submachine gun understand that it was not the women of Dahlem but Russian forces that had exploded a grenade right next to the Russian soldiers. The women breathed a sigh of relief at having been left alive and unmolested.

During the three months that followed, my mother had to stand by as the Russians filled the two floors of our row house with stinking excrement, turning it into a giant toilet. She and a neighbor worked for months trying to make it livable again. How many other horrors had I missed by my absence? People did not speak much about what they had endured. Did life turn out so well for us so soon because we did not make use of all our opportunities for inner renewal? Did we fail at so much because life turned out so well for us so soon?

When I returned, the Cold War was already in the making. East and West had drifted apart in the city—no wall was needed to separate them. "The daily struggles, the daily cares" that Ernst Reuter spoke of openly when talking to the West were still a fact of life—for both parts of the city. But everything that was to become important in postwar culture was in place. The Russians had been the first to order that theater and concert performances employ Germans. The process expressed both the desire to entertain and the humanist conscience—conflicting motives. Though Germans were to be reeducated from "murderers" into civilized beings, the occupiers placed the primary emphasis on the welfare of their own troops. The Russian example was effective, as was the Russian victors' patronage of the arts in the form of licenses and funds. The Americans, the British, and the French promptly copied them. But their purposes had begun to take fundamentally different directions.

Konstantin Simonov's play *The Russian Question* and the other works that became part of the repertory persuaded many artists active in the Eastern sector to come over to the West, since they were not willing to participate in anti-American propaganda. In both parts of the city performances sold out at once; tickets were even bartered for coal briquets and boxes of nails, of which the theaters were so much in need. Boleslav Barlog, who had just taken the future of the Schlosspark-Theater into his hands, was fond of saying that whenever the medical head of the Steglitz hospital required most of the available electricity for surgery, the theater would lose its power in the middle of a performance. Barlog turned a shabby movie house—or, more accurately, a pile of rubble—into a widely respected showcase for young talent and a gathering place for older, more experienced theater people.

But hunger still plagued the city. Many singers and actors were too weak to last through a whole performance. The most persistent ritual of Berliners still was standing in line for bread. Not a day went by without some drama or other. And right next to some temporary stage where *The Countess Maritza* was being performed, the "rubble women" (the women who cleared the bomb sites) handed each other their pails full of debris in a sort of bucket brigade. Every shed, every garage could serve as a temple to the muses. The demand kept pace with the lavish supply. Every night long queues led to the box offices (where, after everything, it was still necessary to stand in line).

* * *

So we had the house back, the one we had moved to with our few bits and pieces when we could no longer stay in Lichterfelde. The old woman my mother had become welcomed me at the door of the apartment on Schützallee; she was shrunken, her face was wrinkled, her eyes filled with tears of joy. She ran to me and hugged her Dieter, her baby. I felt as if I were bringing her the gift of my youth and my first successes. I scolded her for always writing to me that she was too lonely and wanted to die. I denied that she had any right to complain, because after all, here I was, bursting with optimism and good health. My regal egotism charmed a wan smile to her lips.

But Berlin looked awful: the Tiergarten razed to the ground, the landscape of ruins extending for miles and disfiguring the city, the people exhausted and starved. Firewood was a rare commodity; I too was sent to the woods to dig stumps out of the ground. Everything that was at all edible was still rationed. My mother made spreads for bread from yeast; we fried potatoes without fat, tossing them quickly from one side of the pan to the other.

Now suddenly the citizens, unaccustomed to such goings on, were confronted with public assemblies where they had a vote. There was required labor, intended to satisfy the democracy that had been newly "decreed." In the Western sectors denazification—a farce in any case— had already entered its final phase by the time I returned. In almost every family there were "these and those," there were embarrassing secrets or secrets finally revealed. A few years later matters had already progressed so far that the American occupying forces admitted with a sigh of relief, "It's time to put an end to it."

The Americans tolerated wholesale amnesia more readily than the other occupation forces did. But we should remain keenly aware today of the miracle that democracy was for Germany in those days, in spite of the criticism leveled even then at the "special interests" that were clearly being pursued by American policies. In both the East and the West the responsible parties fanned the flames of the Cold War, in their rivalry speeding up the process of reconstruction—including the defense systems. Without the conflict with Moscow, we could not have imagined Germany as the heart of American foreign policy.

Even in the years before 1949—that is, even before the so-called economic miracle—there was an intellectual upsurge in art, literature, theater, and music. That we should also live in some comfort and make a profit—these were less important aims, secondary to the expression of the creative urge and the satisfaction of our artistic needs—as were traveling and getting to know the "world" outside. Where would my mother have been able to lay her hands on the money for travel? Though I was earning some pocket money by giving English lessons, it was sufficient at most to buy a few books printed on cheap paper, or to invite someone now and again to go to the movies or the theater, or to accompany me to a café.

What was most important to me in 1947 was to gain ground for artistic work as soon as possible—which meant studying. I therefore threw myself into my classes with Hermann Weissenborn, who embraced me warmly on my return. And once again the stocky gentleman with the bushy eyebrows and the pink cheeks found himself breathing hard at certain moments of intense pedagogic effort. During every lesson I was given more encouragement and guidance than I would have believed possible in the past few years. What I was lacking—melodic facility—was our primary subject. The feeling of finally being able to take my voice in for repairs in a safe harbor, as it were, was priceless. In spite of all the work that soon began to overwhelm me, I continued my classes with Weissenborn, with only brief interruptions, until his death in 1959. He unfailingly corrected me and showed me new paths, even if he almost never praised me. At most, after a successful premiere of a lieder recital, I might hear the sarcastic remark, "Long live improvisation!"

In my opinion meager praise is what makes a good teacher. Of course the bearer of the vox humana, which is deeply connected to the psyche, wants to be treated with the utmost care and concern. But no ambitious student should be satisfied to be showered with rose water. Those who want to say something instructive must make a judgment call each time between praise and criticism, for which there is no set formula. I shall have more to say on this subject when I come to talk about Karl Böhm.

Strictly speaking, I had only one teacher, Hermann Weissenborn. I never learned much from the others. During most of my life I have been more of a teacher than a student—probably not a great distinction nowadays. By this I also mean that fellow singers, conductors, and pianists always took it well when I made suggestions about their work. The more clearly the "soloist" is able to communicate his interpretation, the more help he is to others who share in the performance. The great singers I have encountered surely did not acquire their greatness from those we customarily call teachers.

75

My teacher never got any engagements for me, as teachers sometimes do nowadays. I considered this an entirely positive approach. Only by example (and not by shortcuts based on career decisions) can critical understanding and its relationship to interpretation be learned. Only rarely does a teacher's rational and instinctive understanding of the music spark originality in the student's point of view. With Weissenborn, technique and interpretation always went hand in hand, and his unerring ear was more sensitive to my weaknesses than any microphone could ever be. An outsider, hearing what he shouted feverishly to me in the heat of battle, would have thought it madness: "Don't draw breath here. What about your phrasing? Place the note at the back. Raise the palate. The elevator is going up. Relax your jaw. . . ."

There was no "method," merely improvised exercises adapted to the lesson at hand. And these led me straight to the only smooth path.

Shortly before Christmas 1947 the American radio station finally opened its doors to me; I was promised an audition. At that time Professor Elsa Schiller was in charge of music at RIAS, the new network in the American sector. She had been a professional pianist and, as a Jew, had lived through terrible times under the Nazis.

Those of us who had not been driven out only gradually began to understand and empathize with the sufferings of the emigrants and the victims of persecution. In the prisoner-of-war camps there had been only silence on these questions. I was eventually to meet many survivors, and each time I could not rid myself of a sense of infinite shame and guilt, although actually I had not been a participant. None of those who had been expelled or tortured had had an easy time making a place and a home for themselves in the countries in which they took refuge in the 1930s. This was especially true because at that time the world had not yet shrunk in language and customs to the extent it has today, when it is scarcely a hardship for anyone to have to live in another country for a couple of years. In those days it was not every emigrant, every migrant who could turn himself into an immigrant, and not every refugee could become a citizen. And the wall, the endless wall of the dead? I can only say that it was no easy task for me to visit Holland or England or Scandinavia for the first time.

But music has a stronger power to forge connections among people than is dreamed of by politicians, and I am grateful for having had this intimacy to fall back on. Recently in Holland I was given a small silver laurel wreath engraved with the words, "To the beloved enemy."

At that time, in 1947, there was an atmosphere of departure. Those of us who lived in the American sector felt clearly privileged. The army helped us when they could—all the propaganda from yesterday, the Brown time, had been wrong. CARE packages arrived, bringing us well-chosen goods. An officer who had noticed that I was not cleanly shaven anonymously sent me a razor to be used with water. The Americans gave parties for the children. They opened libraries, satisfying some of the enormous thirst for the literature we had been deprived of. Everyone read an unbelievable amount. I too threw myself into works by Thomas Wolfe, Theodore Dreiser, John Steinbeck, Thornton Wilder, and Eugene O'Neill. In Berlin we looked on General Lucius D. Clay as a piece of great good luck, no matter how much he was attacked by his compatriots at home. On the firing line, as it were, he practiced pragmatism, and in full view of the East he initiated the process of economic recovery. In the shadow of this occupation force German young people received not "reeducation" but real education. The first stipends for trips to the United States were handed out. And we caught up on Hollywood movies. Those that were trashily sentimental inclined us to nausea; others fascinated us with their outstanding actors: Greta Garbo, Humphrey Bogart, Ingrid Bergman, Bette Davis, and a long roster of other stars. Charlie Chaplin, Buster Keaton, and Harold Lloyd conveyed a breath of the freedom of the absurd. I felt closer to them than to any of the others.

A concert in the Dorotheen-Gymnasium in the Dahlem section of Berlin led to my first invitation to participate in a panel discussion. Annelies Schmidt, a cellist, was the moderator that night, which was part of the series "The Artist Presents." Hanns Heinz Stuckenschmidt, at that time the chief critic of the *Neue Zeitung*, bestowed measured praise on me, allowing that I had a good chance of advancing in my profession. Later he was to mention me countless times in the *Frankfurter Allgemeine Zeitung*, and always I was left with a sense of sympathetic goodwill. It was a heady moment for me when he, the sovereign critic, who had taste and standards, who was never handicapped by an inappropriate bias, suggested to me "from afar"— having known me for thirty years—that we address each other by the familiar "Du."

After waiting for the audition at the radio station in a long line of applicants from every possible field, I passed with distinction with a Bach aria. The RIAS chamber orchestra, under its conductor Karl Ristenpart, was at that time performing most of the Bach cantatas, and I was allowed to take the bass part in almost all of them. I often sang with the highly musical and intelligent tenor, Helmut Krebs. He was my partner in many oratorios, from Bartók's *Die Zauberhirsche* (under Fricsay) to Bach's *Passion of St. John*, as well as in operatic assignments.

Elsa Schiller showed no reluctance to let me record the complete *Winterreise* on tape, an unusual venture at that time. Unfortunately she was not especially taken with the pianist, a friend of mine I had brought to the recording sessions. She therefore cut the second session short and ordered the taping to begin from scratch, this time with the "house pianist," Klaus Billing. But this session too suffered delays, because at the time, December 1947, the recorders and tapes were not as reliable as we take for granted today. After eleven hours of taping, the technical staff, directed by the head of production, Ernst Rittel, announced that a technical defect had unfortunately shown up that made the first eight songs unfit for broadcasting. Billing and I, weary to the bone, did that part of the cycle over, which took us until one o'clock in the morning. This required considerable stamina, especially as in those days there was nothing like a commissary or even a sip of coffee while we worked.

Elsa Schiller was taking quite a risk using a barely known twenty-two-year-old singer for this recording, but its success justified her daring. Today it is not easy for me to judge my work on that taping. It seems to me homogeneous, though burdened with errors of tempo. In general a certain mournfulness prevails that I would not tolerate today. However, the experiment was successful enough to be broadcast again and again, until finally a pirate recording was put on the market by an Italian company.

79

No sooner had the tape been aired for the first time than my telephone rang. Peter Anders, the premier tenor of the 1930s—more recently "promoted" to heldentenor—spoke enthusiastically about my voice. He did not forget to tell me that his interpretation of Schubert's *Die schöne Müllerin* would be heard the following week. Once again I was charmed by Anders' rich timbre and—as so often in later years—distressed by the infrequency of his lieder recitals. Shortly before his premature death, which he met while rushing, as usual, from one theater to another along the autobahn, we met one last time. In Humperdinck's *Königskinder*, that mixture of originality and imitation of Wagner, Anders sang the King's Son and I the Spielmann. My feelings about this opera are the same as Joseph Keilberth's: "In this work no one gets to the end scot-free. The floods of tears fall on the bridges of the violins as well as the vocal cords to such an extent that it is unthinkable to continue."

The Bach cantatas were also broadcast by many radio stations, and soon they were heard in France and Italy as well. Frau Schiller followed my subsequent activities with affectionate interest, introduced me to various pianists (once to Michael Raucheisen, who had been so famous in the 1930s), and was delighted when years later we paid her a visit in her retirement cottage in the Salzkammergut. The plump lady with the compelling dark eyes worked in Berlin for about ten years, after which she put in roughly the same amount of time as the head of the most important record firm in Hamburg. She was the embodiment of the type of artistic director, now so sorely missed, who was in sole charge of such a company. She always spoke to the point. In fact, her candor could be cutting. She could not, would not, put up with sanctimoniousness and fawning.

To a young conductor who had apologized once too often for his presence in front of the orchestra she said, "Please, not so much modesty. You're not good enough for that."

After Irmel and I, both still very young, had married, it was time to say good-bye to the Schützallee and hurt Mother by putting a little distance between us. There was a house in the Charlottenburg district that belonged to an aunt, Eva Bruhn, who for a time during the 1920s had been a quite well-known soprano. This was to be our new home, although we only had one bedroom at one corner of the long bungalow, with the baby grand standing right next to the beds.

As the years passed we gradually worked our way through the connecting room and little by little took over the house. Two Jewish women had survived the war here, thanks to the dauntless compassion of Frau Berger, the caretaker. One of them remained—until her death, never paying rent—in the basement apartment, and was happy to iron and sew for us. But the other woman, Frau Kantorowicz, lived in our midst, as it were, and always felt "jumped" like a checkers piece when we wanted to get from the back rooms to the apartment entrance. Soon she had had enough and found herself a less frequented terrain. The Kilians, a family of four, lived in the room where I now keep my papers. They had piled up briquets along the walls; we had to find them a new place to live. What today is the music room was subdivided by cardboard walls through which every whisper could be heard. Frau Beckmann and Herr Ey-Steineck, who was in the process of shedding his impossible military uniform and turn himself back into a civilian, soon moved out of the corner they shared, which could be reached only by way of the kitchen.

In 1951, after an anxious four days of labor, our son Mathias was born in the Paulinenhaus hospital just around the corner. He was followed in 1954 by Martin. Both were splendid boys; I'm sure that as a father I made the usual foolish mistakes. In any case, with hindsight I see myself in those days as far too young for the role of someone "vested with the rights of upbringing."

Until he accepted an engagement in Frankfurt am Main, Hansgeorg Laubenthal and his family lived on the top floor. The sturdy concrete roof had protected their apartment during the war, since the countless fire bombs had burned themselves out on the flat terrace without causing any permanent damage. A few years after we moved in, Laubenthal, a youthful matinee idol—who must have been fifty if he was a day, but who was still performing Romeo and Ferdinand at the Deutsches Theater— decided to take singing lessons from me. I did not have the time to accommodate him, but he auditioned for me, and it was fascinating to observe a performer who had had years of practice in speaking with great suppleness and pliability growing stiff as soon as the tones he uttered were sung. *Pagliacci* and *Traviata* were torture to the human ear. . . . After a number of stage rehearsals, Laubenthal abandoned the role of Alfredo in *La Traviata*, since he was quite incapable of ridding himself of this tension.

When the Laubenthals left, Erik Ode and his wife, Hilde Volk, moved in above us. I very much enjoyed their stay. Many actors came to visit, and we met many new and interesting people at their parties. I especially recall Gustav Knuth's pleasure in storytelling, Walter Gross' dry wit, and the charm of Herr and Frau Meisel-Lingen. Ernst Stankowski came down to our apartment to sing, accom-

panying himself on the guitar. Karl Skraup told stories of
Vienna twenty years ago and how, despite the lavish productions, all the actors had been in dire financial straits.
The Odes' apartment offered us a glimpse through the
fence of our youthful isolation. Otherwise, however, being
alone together satisfied us so completely during those
early years that we had only a few close friends. But we
both came from large families, and on both sides relatives
clung to us, sometimes weighing us down, and kept us
busy during such leisure time as we had.

In 1950 Irmel and I both happened to be giving concerts
in Italy, and we treated ourselves to a side trip into the
past. We went to Pisa, the place where I had stayed longest
as a prisoner of war. The sun was hot, as always in July.
A walk through the city showed how much it had suffered.
Quite nearby too was the site of that front where I had
spent almost a year in a foxhole. Later, as a prisoner of
war of the Americans, I stayed in a military hospital for
almost the entire second year. Not as a patient, but as
"cultural officer." I was generously assigned a bed with
springs, though where it stood was not far from those
places in the ceiling that gave a direct view of the sky.
Outside the city gates we rediscovered the spot where I
had presented my very first *Dichterliebe* and many other
selections in the semidestroyed assembly room before an
audience of fellow prisoners. The building still stood,
badly delapidated, ringed by the same barbed wire that
by then, of course, presented no obstacle to nightly excursions. In the distance I recognized the castle, as if
Schinkel had conjured it into the landscape that I had tried
to immortalize with colored pencils. It was hard to believe

that this desert had served as an oasis for so many inmates of various camps in the surrounding area, who arrived in buses for our readings, plays, and concerts.

We looked for and found the villa, like a little rural castle, where the family of the painter Tealdi lived. I was especially drawn to it because I had fallen in love with the Tealdi's beautiful daughter Orietta when the family paid a friendly call on the hospital commander and I was asked to sing as a "divertimento." Soon after—and without the guards' permission—my pal Detlev and I stole over the moonlit fields to the Tealdis, for a serenade. As befits a romantic-platonic love story, I was also permitted to give Orietta a few piano lessons. Now she was far away in Rome and married, but the dreamlike atmosphere of the family home was unchanged. A plump servant opened the huge gate; she stood there helplessly until she finally remembered: *"L'artista!"*

And once again, as he had done that other time, the tall father came striding from the sun-drenched garden, where he had been painting. Pleased to see us, he led us into the hall, called his wife, asked about our life. The various things in the room—the metal sculptures, the beautiful old pitchers, the luxurious leafy plants—still stood in the same places. Among Tealdi's many oil paintings lay an old violin, which he occasionally tortured. Then Orietta's youngest sister, with her husband and baby, came into the room, dazzlingly beautiful and cordial. My singing had not been forgotten. When we left, Padrone Tealdi handed me a small, prettily framed picture he had painted, and for Irmel he plucked a lemon from its tree, handing it to her with a gallant bow.

* * *

84

How I would have liked to have become better acquainted with the many interesting people I met through the years! Most of the time traveling, recitals, and operatic performances made it impossible. But I had the rare good fortune to make some genuine new friendships in later years, and I am still close to several people from the past whose steadfast devotion is a continuing joy. In 1951 Gerda Riebensahm attended a performance of the *German Requiem* in a Berlin church with me as one of the soloists; she immediately tried to get her husband, Hans Erich Riebensahm, who had studied with Artur Schnabel, to take an interest in my voice. This interest soon grew into a bond that has run through my life like an unbreakable thread ever since, although Hans Erich served as my accompanist at only one concert. In good times and bad the two of them are affectionate listeners, and I can always count on them for fruitful exchanges of opinion on the most diverse subjects, from housekeeping to philosophy. My greatest enjoyment comes when we listen to music together and venture onto totally new and unknown musical ground. Listening, reading, and discussions have opened up new vistas beyond our original more purely aesthetic pleasures. Not least, at many of Hans Erich's concerts, as well as within my own four walls, his pianistic skills provided my ear with standards of clarity and awareness that have withstood the test of time. Bach's *Well-Tempered Clavier*, Beethoven's sonatas, Schubert's late piano works, and Schumann's major cycles—the focal points of his piano recitals—are particularly close to his heart. His art has little that is accommodating or virtuosic, but for all that it is more precise and concentrated on the work.

Hans Erich is friend, admirer, and critic all in one. He

opens himself to the other. A headstrong East Prussian, he can also be aggressive and unsparing, which, after the first mild shock, is good for me every time. It hurts me whenever he describes his own life as "botched," perhaps because he has no talent for the empty gesture and shallow adroitness on the stage. Gerda, sophisticated and lively, takes his side whenever he feels that we have done the wrong thing or need support. Her cheerfulness conceals an ability to commit herself steadfastly to a cause. Unfortunately it has been some time since Gerda, who studied with Leonid Kreutzer, has played the piano; I regret this all the more when I recall how wonderfully she and Irmel performed Schubert's Arpeggione Sonata. When she talks about something she has read, psychology dominates. She describes characters vividly and with insight. She is enthusiastic about psychoanalysis and psychotherapy.

In the early 1950s Gerda and Hans Erich Riebensahm introduced me to Dr. Harald Schulz-Hencke, one of the early champions of psychotherapy. He suggested that the next time we were in London, we look up his colleague Dr. Walter Schindler. This psychiatrist, odd both inside and out, questioning his teacher Sigmund Freud, had heard me sing the *Winterreise* a few years earlier at the Royal Festival Hall and had been impressed. A spectacularly ugly man—freckled, half-bald, with thick lips, jug-handle ears, and a paunch—from the great emigrant enclave in London, who strangely took a keen interest in military drill, he invited us to his small apartment.

I had the sense that he understood me thoroughly. He urged me to put more space between my exhausting engagements—but not, as every other adviser never tired of suggesting, to "take better care" of myself. Schindler's idea was that I needed time to continue educating myself, to broaden my horizons. Such study and reflection would enable me to renew my understanding of each composer's originality, and to express it. To strengthen my performances, I should study other countries and people, attend university lectures, take part in excursions, and, especially, read. I doubt that anyone, especially in those early days when I was blocked by all the new material I had to assimilate, could have told me anything that could have been more helpful and prepared me better for the future. I still live my life largely according to Schindler's prescriptions.

I adored my profession, my career. I was entirely in thrall to opera and recitals. I felt bittersweet echoes of my childhood faith, which had sustained me so richly, especially as a prisoner of war. But singing gave me a different kind of strength, perhaps a more genuine one. Schindler was aware of my feelings, writing to me many times on the subject. Once he remembered that more than ten years earlier he had improvised a meal of sausages and raspberry juice for Irmel, "your unforgettable wife," and me. On that day, he wrote, I had seemed very youthful, a quality that was even now (1970) expressed in my voice. "Youthfulness is the declaration of all that is living. Life should surely always be young and endure. I mean life in the metaphysical sense, of course. You share in it to the utmost extent possible by putting humanity into your art."

Though I choke a little when I reread this letter, I cherish my memory of the humanist. On another occasion he wrote, "The way you used your voice, as usual, did not remain outside us listeners; it led in a tremendous way deep into my feelings, which put me in touch with the spirit of music. What happiness for you, to be the communicator of such experiences."

The first time I heard the name and voice of Hertha Klust was when I was five years old and my great-uncle gave me the puppet theater. At that time little magnesium flares and flashlights were used to produce stage effects to the music of "condensed operas" on wax recordings. More than once I staged *Der Freischütz* for my friends. In 1948 Hertha told me, beaming, that at the time of the recording—1919—she had been asked at the last minute to replace the singer scheduled in the role of First Bridesmaid who had fallen ill. And in fact the voice on the old record did not sound professional.

The idea of condensed operas came from a veteran of the old Lindenoper, the director Hermann Weigert, who was shortly to emigrate to the United States, where he married Astrid Varnay. Ignominiously shortened, but not spliced into a medley, these versions included a running commentary and even parts of the spoken dialogue. By the way, it was in 1955, with Weigert as my "coach," that I came to understand the special subtlety of the part of the Herald in *Lohengrin*—an otherwise fairly undifferentiated role—at the Bayreuth Festival; I had learned the intricacies so well that the press generally discussed at greatest length my performance in the shortest part. The critic from the *Rhein- und Ruhr Zeitung* of Essen wrote, "Most impressive: DFD in the role of Heerrufer, who made this character the key for understanding the work, not least through the power of the effortless flow of his voice."

Hertha and I appeared together for the first time in

1949, on the stage of the Titania-Palast in the Steglitz section of Berlin, to perform Schubert's *Schöne Müllerin*. Since there had been scarcely any advertising for the concert on the notice boards or in the subway, I was both pleased and startled to find myself facing a sold-out auditorium (about two thousand seats). Sometimes, it seems, it takes an enthusiastic whispering campaign to fill a hall as huge as this 1920s movie palace, where West Berlin's concert scene was centered after the war. (The Titania-Palast, with its outstanding acoustics, has long since died an ugly death amid department and chain stores.)

Our successful concert was followed by a strange review (which was surpassed in brevity probably only by Alfred Kerr's "*Ugh, Gliese!*" in the 1920s). Hans-Joachim Moser, a former singer and one of the most important musicologists of the day, could bring himself to write only a one-sentence review of the evening: "The most one can object to in the rendition of 'Die Schöne Müllerin' by D.F.D. and H.K. is that the baritone did not pause long enough between songs."

God bless Moser for his criticism—forever after I was careful to cleanse myself of this sin. Moser, a frequent guest at my house in later years, was always fond of quoting himself, a quirk that may excuse the numerousness of his books. "Once I wrote . . ." or "On another page I say . . ." But he sprinkled knowledge and minor errors of fact into the conversation in such a virtuosic manner that he fascinated all listeners. Drawing on his wide experience, he gave me long lists of little-known songs for voice and piano, most of which I later performed.

But back to Hertha. In 1949 Heinz Tietjen engaged her to coach at the Städtische Oper; working with her provided me, still unschooled in sight-reading and speed-memorization, with a source of practical experience. The lady with the elegant head of gray hair, though hard of hearing, trained me in the role of Jochanaan in *Salome* after we had developed two programs of lieder. Not only were the scores basically unnecessary, since Hertha knew every note by heart, she also sang all the other parts and cued me. Her performances might sometimes be improvised, but not always. In some concerts she seemed to me too dry; but she needed this clarity to help her bad hearing, which she admirably compensated for with feeling.

One evening when we performed selections from Hugo Wolf's *Spanisches Liederbuch* and *Italienisches Liederbuch*, something dreadful happened. Immediately after the opening chords the piano pedal jammed, producing a cacophany of sounds and echo effects. In despair we stopped, left the stage, and waited for the piano to be repaired. Ever since that night I have urged my accompanists to try out the piano, preferably the day before the concert. . . .

In her casual morning working style, Hertha liked to sit at the piano with her legs crossed and a cigarette dangling from her lips. (Those were the days when people still smoked. After the blockade was lifted and the admirable airlift had ended, the trade in cigarettes had been reestablished more or less efficiently again.) Puffing away, she drilled the difficult *Doktor Faust* by Busoni into my brain, as well as the role of Mandryka in *Arabella*. In this latter work she simulated the part of Graf Waldner with a marvelous bass.

I no longer remember how I happened to be admitted to a soloists' rehearsal for *Tristan und Isolde*, which Hertha accompanied and Furtwängler was conducting before his only postwar appearance at the Städtische Oper. When he realized that his pianist was paying little attention to the score before her but was playing many more, and at times more important, notes than were written in the piano reduction, Furtwängler raised his eyebrows and could not resist saying, "Bravo, I've never heard *Tristan* coached this way!"

When Hertha lost her sister, with whom she had been living for a long time, she shed many a tear at my grand piano. The loneliness of her last years and her approaching death cast a shadow over her life. But when we played Schubert's "Divertissement à l'hongroise" for four hands without my making too much of a fool of myself, her face would gradually clear, and she would return to the wonderful old stories she so loved to tell. Such as the tale of one pitiful Tosca, who found that a jealous colleague had placed a trampoline instead of the soft pillows behind the Castel Sant'Angelo. After Tosca jumped to her death from the platform, the supposed corpse bounced back several times into the sightlines of the astonished audience. "One more round trip," someone in the audience shouted.

The list of exceptional singers Hertha accompanied is long. There is a recording of Schumann songs set to Heine poems on which she is the accompanist, though the label mistakenly credits Gerald Moore. Despite persistent efforts, I have not yet succeeded in providing the pianist with her right to exist on the record sleeve. On the other hand, her name is clearly legible on an early collection of Beethoven lieder. During this recording we had the time and inclination to go beyond the prepared program, and we added a number of songs that we sight-read.

* * *

After a short period of "denazification," Heinz Tietjen resumed the management of Berlin's theaters. The powerful head of all the government stages in Berlin during the Nazi period was a controversial character. His way of behaving like an éminence grise behind the scenes and out of sight, showing himself in public as little as possible, gave rise to the witticism "There has never been any such person as Tietjen."

When I began to work at the opera, I was admonished by an assistant director never to make untoward remarks onstage—Tietjen, he claimed, had installed a microphone in his office. (Today such a practice would no longer be considered unusual. As it is, all sounds onstage are broadcast to the entire house.)

Tietjen was in need of a lyric baritone for his first premiere, Verdi's *Don Carlo*, which was scheduled to open soon. He had heard of me and asked me to audition. I agreed reluctantly. I had come to doubt the wisdom of singing opera from the many grave warnings I had received: "After a year, tops, your voice will be shot"; "Your voice is much too delicate." As a result, my confidence was badly undermined. But now, after I had bellowed Renato's aria from *A Masked Ball*, Tietjen led me to an adjoining room, excluding the public, and there he had me sing a few lieder as well.

Then, quite casually, the corners of his mouth twitching, Tietjen spoke. "You'll sing the part of Posa with me in four weeks."

My knees were knocking. I dared to remind him that my stage experience was absolutely nil, and that I had never taken any acting lessons. Tietjen's reply did little to allay my fears. "There are going to be childhood diseases.

But the extra arms and legs usually disappear. By the way, recitals should remain your first activity."

It was due to Tietjen's understanding and care, and the fact that he released me from excessive obligations that I was able to meet my extensive recital schedule, which was so important to me. And for the sake of concerts I refused a number of invitations to work in opera that I began to receive, especially after my appearances as Wolfram in 1950 (1954 in Bayreuth) and Amfortas. Tietjen can be charged with much that was bad, with intrigues and underhandedness, but I wish more managers were as considerate as he of young beginners.

It matters a great deal what role one chooses for one's debut on the stage, which in music means the whole world. Verdi's virility and purity, represented so clearly in Posa, left an indelible trace on my future, not only creatively but as a man. I was privileged to begin my life on the stage with Verdi. When at the age of twenty-four I studied *La Forza del Destino*, I realized shortly before opening night that the baritone role of Carlo would still be overtaxing my abilities. In a confidential conversation with Tietjen, I told him, trembling, that I would have to give up the part. His understandable initial anger soon gave way to acquiescence and empathy.

Just recently I discovered, hidden under ivy leaves in the Waldfriedhof in Berlin's Westend, a tiny plaque reading "Ludwig Suthaus." The heldentenor was one of the heroes of Tietjen's tenure at the royal opera and a special favorite of Furtwängler in the roles of Siegmund, Loge, and Tristan. He was valued not only for his absolutely dependable musicianship but also for the ability of his voice, tinged with a baritone quality, to express a broad

93

range of emotions. Suthaus sang Tannhäuser at my debut as Wolfram, and during rehearsal Tietjen never tired of pointing out to me the singer's economy of means—a tip I was unable to appreciate at the time, since I then had the crazy idea that it was important to be original at every stage of rehearsals. Suthaus did not always make it easy for me: Almost every time the hunting party came onstage in the second scene, he, with his back to the audience, made a different distorted face at us, so that we had a hard time suppressing our laughter; especially I, who was wholly unprepared. So it could happen that the text of my first aria, "Als du in kühnem Sange," might escape me to such an extent that once, mindful of the conductor's desperate gestures and the sinister silence of the prompter, I sang two whole lines to the syllables "la, la."

During the long second-act ensemble, which was performed uncut, Suthaus initiated those of us who had not yet tried it into the joys of using the wrong words without anyone in the audience noticing. For example, the line "Elisabeth, die keusche Jungfrau—und der Sünder" (Elisabeth, the chaste virgin—and sinner) became "Elisabeth, die keusche Jungfrau—und sechs Kinder" (Elisabeth, the chaste virgin—and six children). The pleasure was reminiscent of school pranks and teacher-baiting. After we had practiced for hours with the conductor the line "Dich wird dies Schwert dennoch erreichen" (This sword will touch you all the same), which was to be sung very quickly, it was a pleasure for the tormented Minnesinger to sing instead, "Das ist zu schwer, das muss man streichen" (It is too hard, we'll have to cut it).

By 1948 many of the voices from the 1930s had fallen silent. I was thoroughly familiar with all their names, since as a schoolboy I had found it impossible to pass any notice board without stopping to study the repertories and casts. And at home I filled the columns of old ledgers with imaginary seasons and the ideal group of performers. After the war I met some of those legendary figures who had meant so much to me, and was privileged to act and sing with them. Thus in Hamburg I was surprised to meet Rudolf Bockelmann, a heavyset hero of Wagnerian opera, whom I had idolized since childhood. At first I did not recognize him—the postwar famine had emaciated him. He had also stopped performing, like so many other famous people who never managed to climb out of the abyss of the immediate postwar period. Bockelmann's Sachs, Amfortas, and Wotan helped determine my conception of these roles. Because he also often sang lieder, his hearty approbation meant all the more to me.

Remaining true to one's audience guarantees knowledgeable listeners. When the audience is familiar with a singer's style of presentation, it will have a pretty good idea of the hurdles and dangers of the role he is performing. It was therefore a very special pleasure to observe the admirers of the sixty-year-old Helge Roswaenge from the proscenium box. During especially high notes their faces reflected concern for their idol. Now and then his followers even protected the tenor with premature bravos before the impending perils of head tones. Twenty-six years old, playing the part of Marcello in Puccini's *La Bohème*, I stood on the stage beside the older man and fully appreciated his collegial, dramatically sovereign presence.

I did not respond to some friendly approaches from colleagues because when I was young and people still occasionally told me the truth, I was called either eccentric or conceited. Today I can only agree with them. It is

95

an unfortunate fact that, aside from a few pleasant exceptions that I intend to mention, I did not fit in very well with the kind of people I had to work with most of the time. If your colleagues leave you alone, you may feel lonely; but at least you don't feel harassed. In any case, I can't complain. All of them were decent to me until age and fame automatically put some distance between us.

Max Lorenz, the heldentenor whom Tietjen was able to protect from the Nazis in spite of his homosexual tendencies, was still performing. He appeared in several of the early *Tannhäuser* performances in which I sang Wolfram. Since it did not seem necessary to hold special rehearsals, he saw me for the first time when he was lying collapsed in front of the picture of the Madonna. At my words "Er ist es!" he jumped up, stared at me, and shouted fairly loudly, "Ist der noch jung!" (Is he ever young!) Later, when we were taking our curtain calls, he muttered, "Just like me when I was starting out. . . ."

As with some of his other favorite singers from the Staatsoper, Tietjen had happily put Lorenz under contract for his new company, as well as Margarete Klose (my first Venus). A short time later Lorenz sang one more Siegmund in *Die Walküre*, and on that occasion I heard him make the most glorious Freudian slip when he changed Wagner's text from "Es zog mich zu Männern und— [drawn out and soft!] Frauen!" (I was drawn to men and— women) to "Es zog mich zu Frauen und—Männern!" (I was drawn to women and—men).

Lorenz's wife, by the way, several years older than he and so strikingly ugly that she could be called beautiful, was wonderful at bearing the brunt of her husband's instability; even with his great wit, he could be extremely depressed. Her Berlin idiom was more cutting and coarse than any taxi driver's. When I appeared for the first time at the Munich Festival in 1951, singing Wolfram, Lorenz was the Tannhäuser. A few colleagues, headed by Helena Braun and Karl Schmitt-Walter, met me at the stage door of the Prinzregententheater to wish me luck. The oppressive summer heat, still heavy after a violent thunderstorm, lay over the theater, which had not been aired out (and which even then had a small hole in the ceiling through which rain fell). After the tale of Rome in the third act, not long before the end of the opera, Lorenz, who had grown tired, let himself fall and did not get up again. "You go on singing by yourself, boy, I've had it," I heard him say softly. And so I stammered out my few remaining lines solo to the bitter end, without any help from Tannhäuser.

It was not so much Maria Müller herself as her blond wig that was responsible for Hitler's being infatuated with her. But I was more smitten with this woman's artistry than I can describe. Already seriously ill, she twice sang Elisabeth with me (the names of the other sopranos in the role with whom I have sung would fill pages). During all her scenes I stood in the wings weeping copiously. Her slightly bent, frail figure radiated the purest essence of the role. Suffering and strain resonated in her no longer fresh voice with a power that unlocked all emotion.

Among the younger singers true friendships seldom came about. By chance you become part of an ensemble; you have to learn to work cooperatively with the other members. If you are teamed with someone of the opposite sex, you may even fall in love. That condition usually lasts only as long as you are working together and ends when you move on. The rare fortunate chance does sometimes occur when a friendship can grow, but seldom as it would if you had chosen the circumstances and wanted to establish something permanent, not because of the occasion but because you really believed that the relationship would deepen in time.

Ljuba Welitsch was Tietjen's Salome in a new production of the Strauss opera. Shortly afterward I was to sing in a new recording with Inge Borkh. Unfortunately the promised rehearsals with the manager did not take place. Tietjen had telephoned to Vienna to promise his help. But he only sent two letters with a few "instructions." I was referred to Herr S., a remnant from the Brown days, whom Tietjen allowed to earn a pittance at the Städtische Oper. So I was facing Herr S. even while I was already anxiously scanning the narrow, dark staircase (without a handrail, of course) that led down to the cistern. At the best of times nonathletic people are anxious at the prospect of feeling their way down stairs, and with my long legs I always associated the role of Jochanaan with stair phobias. Herr S. took a broad stance in front of me— though at some distance, since he was short and stocky. He unbuttoned his jacket, stuck out his paunch, smiled delicately, and in his best Berlin dialect said, "You're a conscientious singer! And you know what goes on around here. There's a hole, you climb up, and when you get to the top, you act sort of holy, and then you go back down." That was my only rehearsal. I had to work out the rest for myself by personal creative initiative.

The only private lecture on acting I received from Tietjen—though there was an audience—was during a reception with others from the opera, which made it especially embarrassing. At intervals he convulsively stretched his hands out to me and made horrendous faces. I was to show the appropriate expression in reply as quickly as possible when he called out, "Be— anxious! Be— angry! Be— friendly! . . . Okay, that's not bad at all!"

A number of Salomes have slunk around me in the course of my career. The action always presents Jochanaan, who is more or less rooted to the spot, with problems that have little to do with the work itself. When Salome circles around Jochanaan on the cistern, I did not always avoid the danger of standing in the star's light. My reaction to such whispered instructions as "More to the left, further to the front" was the utmost contortion of the upper part of my body so as not to cast a shadow. And yet the women had so much more freedom to move! Fortunately Tietjen announced in a letter that "standing stiffly on the rim of the fountain" was out of the question. "Richard Strauss was thinking of the very young John the Baptist, and he intends the character to undergo John's three temptations in his big scene with Salome."

And even without direct instructions this is what I tried to "carve out" very distinctly. Wieland Wagner's "cleared" stage *ante portas* was already prefigured in the totally abstract stage design by Josef Fenneker, which consisted entirely of a highly polished wooden floor with hangings to mark out spaces. I must also mention the mixed blessing of loudspeakers "supporting" the singers behind the scenes. In earlier days, Jochanaan in his off-stage scenes was allowed to sing directly, but invisibly, to the public through a scrim at the rim of the fountain. Technology bypassed that, and whenever I sang Jochanaan, a microphone and the assistant conductor that went with it were forced on me. Once the loudspeaker roared so loudly that panic almost broke out in the audience.

Another time my voice sank inaudibly into the orchestra flute section.

One day we took our *Salome* production to Wiesbaden and its festival, where we appeared in the pretty Wilhelminian theater building. Ernst Reuter, the Social Democratic mayor of Berlin, traveled with us. A heavyset man who walked with a cane and wore a beret, he and I had first met outdoors at a private concert in a house on the Kurfürstendamm. Now he went with us after the performance to a wine tasting in a Hessian vineyard. Our buses did not arrive until after midnight, after all of us, Reuter included, had begun to grow impatient. Our speech somewhat slurred in spite of the bite of cheese that followed every tasting, we got up to leave around two o'clock in the morning. I made motions of getting into my coat. Reuter reached over to help me, and when I respectfully declined, he said, "Surely I will be allowed to help our Wolfram put on his coat." Every Berliner who survived the blockade with him, and with the help of Lucius D. Clay, will remember Reuter with gratitude.

In 1949 Fricsay prepared a new staging of *Fidelio* with the unforgettable Christel Goltz. He inserted the "Leonore Overture" No. 3 after the somewhat flat so-called *Hüpf-Finale* with great effectiveness. I was playing the part of the Minister, Fernando. During the rehearsal with the orchestra I suddenly felt a violent blow on my back, administered by someone's knee, so that I stumbled forward a couple of feet. It was Tietjen, using this ungentle way to propel me to the spot where he wanted me.

After leaving Berlin, Tietjen headed the Hamburg Staatsoper for two years. He invited me to appear there in *A Masked Ball*. When, boyishly and in high spirits, he swung himself up to sit on my makeup table and talk to me, I sensed that the expectation of imminent liberation from the slavery of management, which was to occur in 1955, made him extremely happy. Unfortunately I saw him conducting only as a member of the audience, where I was impressed by his impulsive interpretations of *Götterdämmerung* and *Ariadne auf Naxos*.

5

"Harmonien hör' ich klingen"

My first appearance as Posa in Verdi's *Don Carlo* was conducted by Ferenc Fricsay. The young Hungarian had just earned his spurs abroad by substituting for Otto Klemperer at the world premiere of Gottfried von Einem's *Dantons Tod.* Tietjen, with his finely honed instincts, rightly expected an electrifying success with this novelty. What is now the site of the Deutsche Oper of Berlin was then the gaping ruin of the old Goebbels house. But the manager's section right next to it had been spared in all its ugliness. And if during the Soviet blockade Berlin's housewives had only two hours of electricity a day, here neither the elevator nor the heat was working. Many voice coaches wore two suits in the icy rooms.

Shivering all over, I climbed the stairs to the little rehearsal room, where I found Fricsay wearing a fake-leather coat. He seemed grumpy and looked me up and down as I stood before him in a suit that was much too small for me. I resembled a shy graduate more than I did a Marchese. But then he could hardly believe his ears: "An Italian baritone here in Berlin?"

And from then on he was kind and considerate as he prepared my stage debut with me; he also drilled me thoroughly in stage business and movement. Although he limped slightly, he introduced me to all the ins and outs of Spanish grandeedom, tossing his cape, doffing his hat, and twirling his sword. He used his pretty tenor voice to masterfully demonstrate the opening tones.

Unfortunately Tietjen did not live up to his promise of keeping an eye on my stage rehearsals. He left me entirely in the hands of Julius Kapp, who was a competent chief dramaturge but a weak director; his instructions were usually confined to "You enter left and exit stage right." My partner as King Philip, Josef Reindl, had just been called back to Berlin from the Rhineland by Tietjen. This excellent colleague insisted on holding private stage rehearsals with me at our house. "After all, I mustn't steal the whole show from you," he said with a grin.

Although I had an extraordinary opera debut, I knew only too well that I owed my success to my singing rather than my acting. As I repeated the part in subsequent performances, I physically grew out of the Watteau image that seemed essential to Josef Fenneker, the stage designer. My costume had been padded in the shoulders, chest, and thighs, since I looked so slight. Soon the extra thickness would prove unnecessary—after about ninety performances I was able to give the role greater three-dimensionality.

I learned, and not for the last time, that a performer does not really begin to learn his part until after the premiere, since an audience is required for him really to come to terms with a role. Only gradually does he rise to the demands of the task and the full expression of his talent, as well as uninhibited, passionate absorption in the character he plays. Usually the press is gone long before this fusion can be achieved.

In order to "sensualize [my] world theater," as one critic put it, I also sang seemingly insignificant minor roles, and learned from them. Even *Freischütz*, with which I had grown so familiar as a child, came my way, and I received confirmation that thanks to my intensity, the role of Ottokar had suddenly come to life. One day, during the dialogue passage, Agathe spoke her line "Schiess nicht, Max, ich bin die Taube!" (Max, don't shoot, I am the dove!) much too soon. I therefore had no idea what to do with my challenge to Max that he venture "noch einen Schuss, wie heute früh deine drei ersten" (one more shot, like your three earlier ones this morning). Nonplussed, I continued stammering out the text.

After Fricsay's departure for Munich to head its opera, he asked me to sing Pizarro in Beethoven's *Fidelio*, to be performed in the Herkules-Saal. I felt it was significant that this was the first time I sang a villain. The occasion is equally memorable for me as the time I got into a unique argument over the recording technique. As so often, the volume gauge gave only very tentative indications during the vigorous forte passages and during the piano passages did not move at all. The technician tried to help by adjusting toward forte in the wrong place, and I blew up. For days the whole cast, Fricsay most of all, was grateful to me for flying off the handle. From then on the sensitive microphone took its bearings from the piano passages, and in the end everything sounded as it should, even during the strongest fortissimo.

As was his custom, Fricsay kept the orchestra sound very lean and transparent. His unflagging attentiveness fascinated me. During recording sessions he would adjust the number of strings, at times with every measure, in order to achieve the desired subtleties. Perspiring but elated, I returned home after the wonderful recording sessions with Fricsay of French and Italian arias, which I began by fearing and came to love all the more. Unusually sparing in his instructions, he let us feel his respect and flexibility, which mean so much—perhaps everything—to a soloist. And the members of Berlin's RIAS symphony orchestra, known and familiar to me from its beginnings, enjoyed the occasion.

This was also the time to concentrate on foreign languages; no one should sing words he does not understand. A knowledge of languages instills self-confidence, freeing one from provincialism. Three is a good number; in my case they were Italian, French, and English—the languages that would be most useful in my work. At forty I began to learn Russian for a recording of *Eugene Onegin* that never materialized. But all my later attempts to add to my knowledge only confirmed the old German proverb that the grown man will never learn what the boy missed learning.

Fricsay relished improvising on many occasions. When at the last minute the scheduled alto in Handel's *Judas Maccabaeus* could not perform, he agreed to my suggestion that I sing the alto arias as well. Fricsay rehearsed with extreme intensity. During the performances he usually limited himself to a minimum of signals, since he felt confident in relying on everything we had rehearsed.

I consider the recording sessions as rehearsals, because during them Fricsay could take the concepts and intuitions of the preliminary rehearsal and translate them immediately into results, a process he especially enjoyed.

He was particularly interested in recording technology. In this his vocation and his avocation overlapped, just as he had a passion for playing with all gadgets. Even then Fricsay was enjoying multimedia productions of the kind we take for granted nowadays. I am not entirely certain, however, whether his artistic "orthodoxy" would have approved of every modern instance of such mixtures. He was never swayed by commercial considerations to make artistic compromises. Fricsay had acquired a reputation as a champion of modernism, stemming from the time he had taken over the production of von Einem's *Dantons Tod* in Salzburg. But like so many conductors who complain of the labors of rehearsing and mastering modern works and wish for a more enthusiastic response to their efforts, Fricsay too was eager to shed the role of champion and tried to conduct only such works as were pleasing to his listeners. Nevertheless, what he sowed in the way of receptiveness to the music of his countrymen Bartók and Kodály is still bearing fruit.

Ernst von Siemens unobtrusively acted as Fricsay's Maecenas. The fate of Deutsche Grammophon Gesellschaft was close to von Siemens's heart. Even during my early visits to his impressive villa at the Starnberger See I could sense his feeling for all forms of art. It was difficult to tear my eyes away from the priceless paintings that lined the walls, even as Herr von Siemens was urging us to join him in the record room to hear some of his treasures on shellac. As long as he headed the family firm, his democratic and liberal attitude set the tone for the company. The benevolent employer extended his unassuming helpfulness to his "annex," Deutsche Grammophon, as well, at times through his "right-hand man," Siegfried Janzen. As one of his protégés, my success may gratify von Siemens, a devoted concertgoer, to this day.

It was during the first recording rehearsal for scenes from Hans Werner Henze's *Elegy for Young Lovers*, conducted by the composer, that the conductor Otto Gerdes burst in to say that Ferenc Fricsay had died. This news put an end to a period of my life as well as the orchestra's— for all of us who had been his allies in the new beginning in Berlin. On hearing the news many of us ran outside, so as to be able to grieve unobserved. I mourned the loss of the conductor and friend who thought most highly of me; I especially missed the way he quietly kept an eye on my work, never wavering in his belief in my talent.

He had undergone surgery nine times, and the unremitting pain that plagued him as he worked occasionally caused outbursts of temper; but sunshine could follow immediately after such thunderstorms when, as if liberated and unmindful of his listeners' impatience, he began to tell endless amusing stories. All of us had the same selfish reaction to the news of his death: Pity us, who are left behind. But our first thought should have been: Finally he is released from his torments.

He left his orchestra to Berlin, and in the decades that followed, that orchestra would prove its mettle hundreds of times. I remember with emotion the countless occasions when I worked with the Radio-Sinfonie-Orchester, as it was now called. This collaboration had begun even before the Fricsay era, when I was the soloist in the *Weih-nachtskantate*, by my friend and fellow prisoner-of-war Herbert Trantow, and in the radio opera *Hirotas und Gerline* by Siegfried Borris. The applause for Fricsay's conducting of Orff's revised *Carmina Burana* in the Titania-Palast in 1950 is unforgettable.

The orchestra accompanied my first more significant recorded operatic roles (Bizet's *Pearl Fishers* and Gluck's *Iphigenia in Aulis*, conducted by Artur Rother; Donizetti's *Lucia di Lammermoor*, conducted by Fricsay). The first performance by a baritone of Gluck's *Orfeo*, a success shared by the orchestra, was a high point for me.

Many of the old familiar faces (Rudolf Schulz, Helga Schon, Edmund Metzeltin, Hans Mahlke, Heinrich Geuser, Walter Lutz, Hans Schrader, and many others) have made way for new ones, who have become no less familiar. Under Lorin Maazel and Riccardo Chailly, the RSO has continued to develop handsomely, continually raising its own high standards. And even when it was a matter of deciphering forgotten, complex scores, such as Spontini's *Olimpia* and Spohr's *Faust*, it turned out that these musicians invariably leaped the hurdles with virtuosity and drive. It is true that in these instances, as well as in rehearsals of Reimann's opera *Lear*, we had help from Gerd Albrecht, the scrupulous specialist for complications.

I went to London for the first time in 1951. Emmi Tillett lured me there with a performance of Frederick Delius' *Mass of Life* sung in the original German. That grand old lady of concert management reminded me of my mother

109

in many ways (and the two of them got along splendidly), except that Emmi's sharp-tongued English wit and her Jaguar, which she dashingly raced through the countryside and the streets of London, put her one up on my mother. No visit to London was complete without seeing her, no concert there turned out well without her encouragement.

It was at her home that I got to know the pianist Solomon (Solomon Cuttner) a little better. Until then I had spoken to him only once, briefly, in a hotel lobby in Montreal. Since that time he had often sat in the front row at my recitals in the Royal Festival Hall. And now, when I might have talked with him at leisure, I found him felled by a stroke, his senses and mind alert but his tongue paralyzed, his hands paralyzed, no longer able to perform and teach. Nevertheless his eyes shone with curiosity and interest, and I admired his courage. We were in the charming, cluttered rooms of Emmi's apartment, where she proudly showed us many of her treasures, including a watercolor painted by Churchill.

I have always refused to hand my life over to agents. That is why even in the early days I permitted myself a private secretary, who represented my interests and executed my wishes.

During the 1950s pleasure in performing drove me to arrange musical evenings in Berlin's Westend at which an average of fifty visitors met informally—musicians, actors, friends, relatives. (What I had to offer then is available today through a variety of "features" on television and radio.) I recorded a little lecture on tape, interspersing it with numerous examples on records and cassettes; at the same time I projected on a screen pictures from my constantly growing collection of "snippets." Diether Warneck and his wife, Traudel, attended some of these performances, of which there were about a hundred altogether. I had just been forced to part with my previous secretary, Franz Offermann, and Irmel thought she saw a possible successor in the young man, who was making his way as best he could since his university graduation. Her good instinct has proved true to this day, inaugurating a relationship that began informally and developed into a genuine alliance. Of course we have not always liked each other. I am surely not an easy person to work for, since nature has not blessed me with abundant patience, nor do I always carry through my intentions. Accompanying me and taking care of my business correspondence and telephone calls, acting as travel agent, driving me (who cannot drive) over long distances—all these have helped Diether Warneck to realize himself. He learned, and so did I.

The famous exceptions to the unfortunately reliable rule that agents promote only their own clients have scarcity value. In this connection I want to remember Rudolf Wylach, who began to develop his concert society in Wuppertal in 1934 and after the war expanded his activities throughout West Germany in an exemplary manner. Many of the younger concert managers let him teach them and help them when they had to arrange concert tours. Perhaps the many recital tours with me, along with the trips he arranged with the Bamberger Sinfoniker and the Vienna Philharmonic, contributed to his success.

Our collaboration began with a recital that had foolishly been scheduled for the Hamburg Musikhalle. Günther Weissenborn was to accompany me in Schumann's *Dichterliebe*. When we hurried to the stage, I was taken aback by the sight of yawning empty rows of seats. Only about a third of them were occupied. The situation was soon to change, however, after extravagant reviews, and since that night I am especially pleased at the young, enthusiastic audiences that attend my Hamburg performances.

The next time I saw Wylach—a serious, good-natured man, with small, cheerful eyes—he complained of the impending recession in the concert world (which he correctly connected with the spread of television). I always objected to the increase in ticket prices that was a result of the recession; it was excessive, and it was implemented much too swiftly. Of course I could not counter the general tendency in every case.

On occasion Wylach thanked me for all our joint undertakings and for the fact that I "trusted" him so much. He was one of the very few in his profession who developed an inner connection with what "his" artists performed. He never missed any concert, not even when, already fatally ill, he could walk only with tiny steps. When in enthusiasm he came back to the dressing room, he usually had tears in his eyes. Over the years a kind of friendship developed between us, though the age difference and the troublesome business relationship prevented it from developing into an easy closeness. Furthermore, Rudolf Wylach came from a generation that did not address others with the familiar "Du" as is the custom today. He was a wine connoisseur, and each Christmas he sent me a case of some exquisite vintage. If any year the gift had not arrived, I would have had cause for worry. Today I am happy that his daughter Karin, conscientiously continuing his work, has not broken with this pleasant custom.

Rudolf Wylach also insisted on appearing in person at almost all my concerts to check that my requests concerning lighting in the hall and piano tuning had been carried out. On one occasion one of the lighting technicians, arriving after we had been waiting a long time, grumbled, "But we only have orange, red, and blue."

"Why is that?"

And the poor man answered, "Recently we had a recital by Anneliese Rothenberger. She was very happy with our reds and blues and oranges. . . ."

Since I always try to appear as natural as possible to the audience, I much prefer a dull white. . . . How much Wylach contributed in practical terms to the success of my recitals is also shown in the following episode.

We were in the car for the short trip from Düsseldorf to a concert in Wuppertal. About halfway there we were overtaken by a fog so thick that it seemed the only way to proceed was at a snail's pace. When we thought we were close to our destination, the Wuppertal town hall, whose towers can be seen from a distance in clear weather, the head of a large dog rose from the fog and stared at us through the windshield. A huge St. Bernard. . . . Irritated at the delay and startled by the apparition, Irmel giggled, "Uncle Bruno!" I must admit that there was a certain resemblance to an uncle of ours, an industrialist. I discovered to my relief that the comical head of the dog concealed the figure of Wylach, who waved a huge sheet in the air—not the most practical thing, given the white brew around us—and slowly piloted us to the parking lot for the hall, which had been filled with an expectant audience for the last twenty minutes.

One of his wishes I was never able to satisfy except on records: to recite so-called melodramas, which he loved and remembered well from Ludwig Wüllner. Sometimes he muttered selections from Max von Schilling's "Hexenlied," one of Wüllner's showpieces. Once I told Wylach about the time when I was about four years old, walking at my father's side through Zehlendorf, not understanding why he was constantly raising his hat in every direction to greet acquaintances. One of them, a man wearing a black soft hat and cape, stopped and had a cordial conversation with my father. "That was Ludwig Wüllner," I was told without further explanation, and innocent as I was, I remembered for a long time the impression he made on me. Later I came to see Wüllner as an interesting object of study. The son of a famous conductor of the Brahms period, he was a versatile artist who casually, with few stage rehearsals, was sometimes "invited" to play such major dramatic roles as Lear and Faust for Max Reinhardt. But he also appeared as a heldentenor (Lohengrin!) on the opera stage, and held song recitals interlarded with recitations. (I have taken the liberty of appending to various recordings of lieder some of the melodramas from Wüllner's repertoire, from Schumann to Liszt.) It was said of the man with the piercing glance that his voice had not been outstanding, but that rumor may be an expression of envy. He was unwilling to give up performing and continued almost to his death in 1938.

Wylach listened with interest to my stories about Wüllner, as if he had never heard any of them before. I think back sadly to this gentleman, an entrepreneur of the utmost decency, who felt oppressed by the way things were shaping up in the music business.

Can anything change the current musical situation? Anyone who tries to disturb the deadly surface of uniformity with a new idea is immediately branded a utopian. In 1986 Justus Frantz did succeed in establishing the Schleswig-Holstein Festival, intended at long last to bring into the world of music some regions of northern Germany heretofore cut off from it. The design of a utopia always arises out of despair over the existing situation. When I consider the role of our current "supportive" competitions and music organizations, which sprout like weeds—according to the prevailing view flourishing as never before—I cannot decide whether their overwhelming vitality and the pressure they exert on young people is one of the causes of the death of mature musical sensibility or whether cause and effect are reversed. Can young talent be measured in quantitative terms? Is the fastest possible performance of technically difficult passages always the best? Is there an optimal rate of increase in the musical "proletariat"? Is more of the same better? And while we're on the subject: Must everything grow bigger? The myth of progress ends in a philosophy of power that greedily awaits the opportunity to rear its head. People who believe in progress see time and death as the enemy. But anyone who will not confront time will always be arming, unable to live without victory yet equally unable to escape death.

My first concert in London was to be conducted by Furtwängler's friend, the preeminent English conductor Sir Thomas Beecham. Any beginner had to feel that to appear with him was the be-all and end-all. Even during rehearsals I was aware of the care with which the old gentleman again and again perused the score whenever something did not emerge clearly enough. I did not know then that Beecham had been a close friend of Delius and an enthusiastic advocate of his music. In 1935 he delivered Delius' eulogy and since that time had repeatedly promoted the composer's work. But for this exception, Beecham was not overly fond of the moderns. There is a story that on one occasion, when he was rehearsing a new piece with the Royal Philharmonic Orchestra, he suddenly realized that all instruments had fallen silent.

"Gentlemen, what is the matter?" Beecham inquired.

The concertmaster replied, "Sir Thomas, we've come to the end of the work."

"Thank God!" the conductor shouted.

Beecham loved making jokes, and this alone endeared him to orchestras. But what impressed the musicians most was his astonishing capacity to improvise new shadings at the moment of performance.

Anyone entering the Albert Hall in London for the first time can only be awed at the huge oval, which nevertheless has quite good acoustics for most of its four thousand seats. Delius' somewhat florid sound, which we were intending to produce, fit well into the Victorian surroundings. When, in response to Beecham's evocative gestures, the sound was about to swell to a particularly powerful crescendo, he suddenly rapped his baton to bring us to a stop. Into the anxious silence all around he said, "A pretty piece, isn't it?"

On the night of the concert I had just calmly taken my place on my stool when a vigorous rising drumroll introduced "Rule Britannia." Startled, I realized that it was the custom here to begin not with the program but with the anthem, for which everyone had to stand. So I promptly jumped to my feet again. After that came the long, re-sounding piece to texts from Nietzsche's *Thus Spake Zar-athustra*, in which I easily hit my stride and at the end of which I had a good feeling about the performance. (It was confirmed for me the following day in excellent reviews.) But Irmel had tears in her eyes when she came backstage. "You looked like a fish, mouth open, mouth closed, and I couldn't hear a note from my box."

I tried to remain cheerful.

The following day I was asked to join Sir Thomas at tea at the Ritz, where he and Lady Beecham were most gracious hosts. In the middle of the conversation, which on my part was conducted in somewhat halting English, causing him to laugh more than once, he asked me, "Would you be willing to sing Hans Sachs next winter in a new production I'm conducting at Covent Garden?"

"Sir Thomas, your invitation is an honor, and it would give me great pleasure to accept. But at my age—you know that I'm all of twenty-seven—I don't think I'm ready for the part."

My attitude saddened him to such an extent that, rather than remain any longer, he went off to his room. It was difficult even then to find a good Sachs. And perhaps my refusal struck him as somewhat impertinent. It took about twenty-five years before I dared to take on the role of Wagner's shoemaker-poet.

Since 1952 I have been linked with Edinburgh and with some good friends there. I loved the city from the first moment I laid eyes on it. On sunny days a gentle breeze borne on an east wind from the sea is refreshing. The roofs of the old part of town climb on each other's shoulders, not always cozily. The evening light lends a glow to Princes Street, the main thoroughfare. One can wander over the terraces, trying to guess the dimensions of the old seventeenth-century town. I admired the beamed ceilings with their embellishments from a Scandinavian past. In Robert Louis Stevenson's house I was astonished at the life-size dolls on the staircase. While staying in the home of his descendants, I could not get enough of the golden evening panorama seen through the top-floor window. The melancholy sounds of the bagpipe are heard again and again and carry far. In the National Gallery I stood before Henry Raeburn's amazingly witty portraits. Over and over I felt that in this city we are intimately face-to-face with the past, and not only when we look at the pictures of the pavement artists. In the very first photo studio, of Hill and Adamson, I saw silver chloride plates from the 1840s.

And then there is the new town, designed in an architecturally attractive checkerboard pattern around 1750. In the squares and terraces of the historically preserved area stand the most handsome and most expensive houses in the city. At one time or another I stayed in several of them. And finally there are the Botanical Gardens: What better place for a traveler to stretch his limbs and loll about in comfort, under the weirdest, most unusual trees?

The 1952 Edinburgh Festival introduced me to Sir John Barbirolli and the Hallé Orchestra, which he had made his own. When I heard the name Barbirolli as a child, I imagined a master well along in years; now his youthfulness took me by surprise. Then again, a few years later I was startled by the rapidity with which he was aging, a process that could probably be ascribed to the little bottle he always carried concealed in his vest pocket. Barbirolli was not high-handed like Sir Thomas Beecham, nor a snob like Sir Malcolm Sargent, but a completely likable, cordial, unaffected person. His signals were precise, though not as razor-sharp as those of some of the other "moderns" of the period. He instinctively elicited the grandeur and the appropriate emotion from the works, calmly letting them ring out in the performance.

During the rehearsal for Brahms' *Four Serious Songs*, which was unfortunately being done in the somewhat "dusty," rather impressionistic orchestration by Sir Malcolm Sargent, the orchestra was not up to much. But Barbirolli did not interrupt, perhaps so as not to irritate the singer. There was little conversation, and no repetition after a single reading. Dissatisfied and worried, I trotted off to the George Hotel. But that evening, during the concert, the performance could not have been more integrated. Barbirolli had noticed the most subtle impulses of his soloist and in performance followed them sensitively. He was a genuine romantic among the postwar conductors.

Who was sitting alone in the auditorium of Usher Hall while we rehearsed? Kathleen Ferrier. This warmhearted interpreter, whose career would soon be cut short by her death from cancer, looked up at us unassumingly and with interest; after we had shaken hands, she expressed her most cordial approval of my work.

I saw Barbarolli again when we recorded Verdi's *Otello*, in which I sang Iago. It was one of the last times he conducted. Repeatedly the maestro broke off the session—for which each of us had had to sacrifice an hour to get there and back—and disappeared. After a lengthy search he would be found, reinvigorated for new deeds and jokes by his pocket flask. At that time his sight and hearing were no longer in top condition, and he gratefully accepted an offer of help that was surely seldom made. I suggested that when it came to the aria "Era la notte," which is sung softly, he beat time rather delicately, to make it easier for us to remain together in spite of the distance. The orchestra had its back to me, so they noticed nothing. Barbirolli, beaming, accepted my suggestion and was happy with the result. He liked to tell us that his father, a cellist, had taken part in the world premiere of *Otello* at La Scala in Milan and that he himself, a small child at the time, had been in the audience. He therefore maintained that the slow tempi he preferred were absolutely authentic; secretly, I had my doubts. The small, gentle Anglo-Italian died in 1970, at the age of seventy-one.

Along about the third year of my membership in the Städtische Oper—that is, in 1951—Leo Blech returned from exile in Stockholm. I came to know the old man, full of life and clear of mind, in connection with Franz Liszt's oratorio *Die heilige Elisabeth*, a work the composer had explicitly forbidden to be given as a staged performance. Blech, however, after his return from exile, insisted on repeating an old success with this, his favorite work. He immediately encountered resistance from the conceited young man I then was. At eleven o'clock at night I telephoned him to voice my conviction that the work lacked sufficient stage action. We did not hang up until two o'clock in the morning. He talked about the way things used to be, about the splendor of the music, how I was the only one who could realize his idea of the figure of the Landgrave—and on and on. I stood my ground for two hours, my heart pounding. Finally I capitulated and agreed.

Having won the debate, Blech worked especially hard with his opponent, and he did not rest during a rehearsal for both orchestra and stage performers until I had learned to keep my eyes simultaneously on him and on Elisabeth entering from the rear right. Thus he at least taught me a facility for opera, that hybrid of theater and music. Of the almost eighty performances, at each of which I was annoyed that my part was over before the intermission, owing to the Landgrave's death on the crusade, I almost slept through one. Shortly before the curtain was due to go up—when I had to be onstage—I got a telephone call at home from a desperate stage manager. I had thought the performance was set for the following day. My taxi slowly staggered to the opera house, and the curtain went up twenty minutes late.

This *Saint Elisabeth* cost me a lot of hair. There was still very little money for new wigs, and the first night my makeup man worked me over so roughly with the curling iron that the following morning I found almost my entire crowning glory in my hairbrush.

Blech was one of those rare conductors who are drawn to the arena at least an hour before the beginning of the performance. He would sit in his little room, pleased when now and then a member of the company paid him a visit. Then he would relate witty and lively stories of bygone days. He told me about the rousing battles in the days before the First World War when the Berlin Staatsoper was trying to wrest from Cosima Wagner the exclusive rights to produce *Parsifal* in Bayreuth. It was Blech who conducted the first production outside Bayreuth after Cosima, gritting her teeth, finally gave in.

I also sang Mozart under Blech's baton, at a concert in the Titania-Palast, which brought me together with an idol of the 1930s, the soprano Tiana Lemnitz, in duets from *Le Nozze di Figaro* and *Don Giovanni*. I preceded these with Agamemnon's major aria from Gluck's *Iphigenia in Aulis*. Blech implored me to use Wagner's arrangement, since its ending was so much more powerful. I insisted on the original version, but Blech was once again brilliantly persuasive, and I gave in.

An impression of Blech's conducting can be gleaned from listening to the recording of the 1927 performance of *Die Meistersinger* in Berlin. The orchestral sound is particularly well preserved: transparent, light, nothing drawn out. Of his colleague Robert Heger, Blech could say behind his back, "My *Carmen* is an hour shorter than his."

It is Irmel I have to thank for my meeting Wilhelm Furt-wängler. It was the summer of 1949, shortly before our wedding. Irmel was enrolled in a cello course at the Mozarteum in Salzburg, taught by Enrico Mainardi, the idol of all the young women. Since I still did not have valid identification papers after my return from the prisoner-of-war camp, the then director, Eberhard Preussner, furnished me with a document declaring that I was a student at the Mozarteum. Soon Irmel managed to get me involved in one of the popular "symposia," held in the Mozarteum's large auditorium. Mainardi was so taken with the Brahms *Four Serious Songs* that the very next day he informed his friend Furtwängler, "You've got to hear him."

Preussner allowed me to use his music room over the Salzach so that I might audition for "Jupiter" himself. Furtwängler kept me waiting a while, and I was glad to be able to prepare myself in solitude for the important moment. Suddenly the maestro walked briskly into the room, shook my hand, and muttered quite unnecessarily, "Furtwängler."

I'd set up the score of *Four Serious Songs* on the piano music rack. Glancing briefly at the pages, he sat down and at once began to play. Without interruption we made music with growing enthusiasm; I appreciated the unusual sonority of his playing.

"Thank you" was Furtwängler's only comment. He could not stay, he was already late for a private concert somewhere else. He therefore got up quickly, took me by the hand, and dragged me out to the Volkswagen that was known all over the city; Frau Elisabeth Furtwängler sat waiting in the car. During the preceding half hour I had noticed a certain fragility in him, but it was a touching vulnerability born of experiences, relationships, altered feelings between people. Its precondition is sensitivity; most people will see it as weakness. I consider a weakness on this level of consciousness an advantage, even a virtue.

I suspect that Furtwängler asked me to come along as a buffer; he did not look forward to still another occasion when he had to perform for a "world" that was more interested in other things. A well-known clarinetist was standing on the doorstep when we arrived at the house; he showed justified indignation at the prospect that some other soloist was intending to claim the audience's attention. But Furtwängler did not dignify him with so much as a glance and nonchalantly introduced me to the group, then started at once on the *Serious Songs*.

123

As early as the following summer I stood before the Vienna Philharmonic in the Salzburg Festival Hall to sing the *Songs of a Wayfarer* by Gustav Mahler. I had suggested the work unthinkingly, although it was new to me; I was quite unaware of the fact that Furtwängler did not care much for Mahler. But during the rehearsal he recalled a performance of it he had conducted a long time ago with Heinrich Rehkemper, and as if he were relieved, he decided that the songs were "worth hearing."

In November 1951, two days before the world premiere of Winfried Zillig's *Troilus und Cressida* in Berlin in which I was scheduled to sing Troilus, Furtwängler asked me to come to his new house in Dahlem. Because it was raining and the opening was close at hand, but especially because I had no real intention of accepting Furtwängler's invitation to sing Almaviva with him the following summer in Salzburg, I was about to send my regrets. But his chauffeur-driven car rolled up at my front door, so that I could tell him of my decision in person. Furtwängler was cordial and understanding; he soon shifted the conversation to his lifelong concern with his health, telling me how, after experimenting with various diets and pills, he had finally become convinced that there was only one thing that helped him prevent illness: to run by himself for an hour or two a day. Just finding the time to do this in itself required energy. Yeast and yoghurt—in addition to an otherwise normal diet without much meat— that, he explained, was the secret of his endurance. (Knowing how shaky his health was even then, a look at his appointment book of that time seems to confirm that his regimen had indeed been helpful.) But Furtwängler spoke at greatest length about his dream: to stop conducting once and for all the very next year in order to devote himself entirely to composing.

He was not able to realize his dream in the short time left to him. And it was evident that each time he returned to the conductor's podium he was partly in flight from the other challenge. His published letters contain countless heartfelt sighs of longing for purely creative work. And the products of his creative impulse do express the nature and being of their creator more than do most musical compositions of the time. Talented interpreters should address themselves to the few works he left behind. They show an astonishing internal consistency: Though basically tonal, they lean to harmonic ramification, even to the abandonment of tonality; they express an awareness of the standard repertoire without being derivative; thematically meditative, they are contradictory in the elaboration of themes, but reach for the large forms and frequently fill them.

Returning to the subject of *Figaro*, I confessed to Furtwängler that I was still very inhibited at the thought of singing Count Almaviva in Italian, among such great international names, and in my first attempt at the role! At heart he liked my reservations. In the course of the conversation he told me that he saw in me something like a successor. In my ability to concentrate and depth of feeling he thought he could detect a very special "naturalness." These words have inspired me and given me courage in all the days that followed.

I noticed that Furtwängler frequently contradicted himself, forgetting what he had already said. He often seemed absent. Thus he suddenly told me that when he recorded *Tristan und Isolde* in London, he wanted me to sing Kurwenal; and yet just a moment before he had described the project as completely uncertain. Finally I left, without having refused his offer to appear at Salzburg. I was to think it over for a week.

As I was leaving, he asked me a final question: "What did you think of the Bayreuth *Parsifal?* Surely we have to be a little cautious in our judgment there?" But when he realized that I had no idea, he pulled no punches and expressed the same aversion to Wieland Wagner's approach, stressing abstract staging, that had already been voiced by Hans Knappertsbusch—who resembled him in no other way—during rehearsals ("Where the hell is the dove?"). But when I saw this production, which put its stamp on the festival for such a long time, I found it especially striking. And it was an honor for me to be its Amfortas for two years.

After we had spent a first night in London in wakeful, awed anticipation of the *Tristan* recording, a car was supposed to take Irmel and me and Kirsten Flagstad to the Kingsway Hall. Because our English was still very rudimentary, Irmel and I were delayed slightly in the hotel. When we came out two minutes late, the porter informed us that the car had already left. I thought to myself: The star won't wait even a second. . . .

When I laid eyes on Flagstad soon afterward, I forgot all such prejudices. She suffered as much as I did from nerves before such a recording. Even on the hundredth take she was as serious as on the first. She needed a few quiet minutes before the session to get herself into voice. She was a simple, calm, rather stern woman; the features of this goddess among Brünnhildes and Isoldes lit up only when she was speaking of her grandsons. When she was not singing, she seemed completely concentr ted on knitting. Then she would suddenly rise to her feet and effortlessly produce her powerful sounds.

As always, impressions of Furtwängler were varied. This time he seemed so absorbed in his infatuation with his Brangäne, Blanche Thebom, that he seldom devoted a word to matters of general interest. His relations with the women who surrounded him revealed his basic softness. He found it easier to say no when the person he was turning down was not sitting in front of him and breathing softly. He could not understand music in which breath was not predominant, at least conceptually. In the course of the five years Furtwängler was a major influence in my life, I realized only gradually that breath was the real meaning, the major source, of Furtwängler's perceptions of the world around him. He was constantly the victim of his own breath, precisely because—like me—he had a lifelong struggle with allergies. His breathing was punctuated by barely audible rumblings.

"Sing without much deliberation. Let the music flow naturally!" Furtwängler often used these or similar words to instruct me and other singers. Breath was of preeminent importance here. The term was used to mean a higher naturalness, attainable only by way of creation. This higher nature means musical life, a great stream of slowed tempi, a beginning without tempo, as it were, music that manifests itself only at the proper moment, when the high point of a development has been passed. This "beginning" on a tempo too often elicited a misunderstanding that Furtwängler's tempi were much too slow. But as a movement went on, his tempi could become significantly faster than under conductors who preferred consistent tempi.

"There is only one tempo—the right one," Furtwängler claimed, meaning that the search for meter, which is never exactly the same twice, is, so to speak, experimental. The search began by adjusting to the acoustics of every new concert hall, which were often improved by rearranging the orchestra. And at every rehearsal Furtwängler began tentatively, as if to make the orchestra aware of his personal manner of breathing. He did not speak much in the process. On the contrary: Most of the time he had difficulty verbalizing his intentions, and he was not fond of prose descriptions of his actions (such as I am attempting here)—because he understood that only a little of what has been said can also apply to the next rendition. He spoke to me about the necessity of giving oneself over to the tensions of the symphonic flow, in order to pause at the right moment, and determine the further course. The result of such stringency, previously unheard of, was as a rule a total transformation of both the musicians and the public such as I never experienced under any other conductor. Stylistic considerations played the smallest part in this achievement.

Furtwängler's approach to music determined his method. He did not think much of the technique of the conductor's beat; it seemed to him that each conductor had his own way of eliciting the desired effect in the orchestra. (Georg Solti once voiced similar views when I talked to him about conducting during a break in a recording session.) Though at times details were meticulously discussed and coordinated, these were subordinate to Furtwängler's larger line. His famous-infamous upbeat served among other things to reinforce the tonal weight to the right—among the basses—at first, letting the higher voices enter imperceptibly later—not in an arpeggio or like the "clatter" of old-fashioned pianists, but as an "almost-in-unison." Furtwängler was aware of inadequacies and difficulties in his work. But they applied only to his conducting technique. Those elements that went beyond technique—and they, in the last analysis, were what accounted for his greatness—were quite enough, even in his lifetime, to raise his work above the understanding of most listeners; even on recordings his special quality is evident only to those who were privileged to have heard him in live performance. Be that as it may, no other conductor of the past is assured of as much intense study, especially among young musicians, than is Furtwängler.

In Vienna the rain can be more depressing than it is elsewhere. When I strolled through the narrow streets, constantly buffeted by the strong winds from the Vienna Woods, I found no mental connection to the great books that spoke of the Vienna of long ago. I missed the aroma of life that emanated from Robert Musil's *The Man Without Qualities*, Joseph Roth's *The Radetzky March*, and Heimito von Doderer's *Strudhofstiege*. When as a young man I came to the city by myself, I felt terribly lonesome. Furthermore, on my first visit I had no guarantee of success. Even then I challenged my audience with an all-Beethoven recital, accompanied on the piano by a Herr Zippel. Finally I realized that such a sequence of songs, which could be called more than pure, was not entirely natural. Only a little while later, during rehearsals for the *German Requiem*, Furtwängler, incredulous and somewhat reproachful, brought up the subject to me: "Is it possible to do that sort of program? For no other reason, perhaps, than that the harsh songs would forbid it."

And in fact, the expression and character peculiar to Beethoven's confessional shortest works are unique in the entire history of music; their form is oddly fragmentary and stormy, even wild. The long vocal breath that Furt-wängler was so fond of is rarely found in these compositions. Those backstage visitors at the Mozart-Saal who considered themselves even partly knowledgeable about music took refuge in the remark, "If you sing *that* material, why don't you appear in opera?"—not a suggestion welcomed just then.

A year later I wrote in my diary: "January 1951 was important for me because it introduced me to the Viennese in a recital sung before an audience who still considered recitals part of their daily bread."

Conditions in Germany were no longer quite as favorable. Scarcely any of the outstanding lieder singers from the prewar period were still performing (with the exception of Heinrich Schlusnus and Walter Ludwig). Even worse, a kind of assorted menu had taken over the programs that is still prevalent in many countries today. I countered this trend, mainly for the pure pleasure of shaping a sequence, with lieder having a common denominator; this underlying theme demands concentration from a concert audience expecting sensationalism or distraction. The arrangement also corresponded to a performance style I intended to perfect over time. I wanted to do justice to all the essential characteristics of the form; I wanted to get close to the essence of the lied, to suppress nothing and make no concessions either to vocal limitations or popular taste. The task I set myself was to focus on the age-old struggle between word and sound; every work resolves it in its own way, and every composer places the emphasis differently. I wanted to mirror this relationship faithfully. That my programs could communicate this purpose only with difficulty at first, and that I had to overcome the resistance of many concert producers and had to force audiences to listen, shows what a rut our thinking tends to run in; we find it difficult to free ourselves from tradition because it makes us feel as secure as if we were in the womb. And yet we too often accept unthinkingly what we are spoon-fed by the self-appointed arbiters of current fashion, no matter how low the level of taste has sunk.

Incidentally, my first recital in Vienna had an exciting prelude. Instead of my tails, Irmel had accidentally packed my cutaway, which I have long since stopped wearing and which even then was wildly out of place at an evening recital. Immediately after the rehearsal, therefore, in low spirits and in the pouring rain I took a taxi all over town, checking every possible place that rented costumes or evening wear. The men behind the counter were suspicious: Why should a person like me, who looked not at all like a professional dancing partner, need tails? And furthermore, "We don't got your size."

Finally I had to settle for a garment that could only make me look ridiculous, since its arms were much too short. But not before, in despair, seeking out George London, who was at the same little hotel, staying in bed to preserve himself for the rigors of *Boris Godunov*, which he was going to sing that night. But he cordially invited me in and involved me in a long conversation concerning technical matters of stage procedure. To my nervous question about a tailcoat, he pointed magniloquently to the closet and said encouragingly, "Try it."

Doing so, I was depressed to realize that at that time I came nowhere near fitting into it. Embarrassed, but heartened by his friendliness, I left the great singer, with whom I would soon be alternating in the role of Amfortas

131

in Bayreuth and who always treated me with admirable openness. The last time we met was in a jet over the Atlantic. The poor man had already completely lost his robustly resonant voice as the result of carelessly administered anesthesia. Whispering softly, he conveyed his dream of bringing Julia and me to his production of *Così fan tutte* in Washington. Soon after, George London died.

One of the people who knew Furtwängler best as a friend and wrote about him is the writer Karola Höcker. At one rehearsal of Mahler's *Kindertotenlieder* with the Berlin Philharmonic I saw her sitting in the balcony of the Dahlem Gemeindehaus taking notes. I felt free to go to her and ask her opinion, since we lived on the same street and had frequently acknowledged each other from a distance as she glided by on her bicycle, a beret on top of her short hair. Later we often talked about the phenomenon that was Furtwängler, as well as about her many writing projects, which in my opinion became richer and more beautifully written from year to year. Since all her work, for every age group, is about music, we developed a warm friendship. When either of us is planning a book, the exchange of sources and information is both pragmatic and thorough. Höcker's energy—she is now very old and was recently named an honorary professor—is remarkable.

The *German Requiem* and the *St. Matthew Passion*, both performed in Vienna, meant further happy encounters with Furtwängler. Our farewell to each other was three performances of Mahler's *Kindertotenlieder* at the Titania-Palast during his third-to-last conducting stint in Berlin. Toward the end of his life Furtwängler had difficulty with his hearing after flying, and he had to ask me several times whether the woodwinds had begun to play.

Afterward the composer and conductor Alois Melichar rushed into the tiny greenroom with compositions of his own to show Furtwängler, often and loudly addressing him with the familiar "Du." When he was gone, Furtwängler said, "I dislike using the 'Du' form with anyone but family."

What characterized the conducting of Eugen Jochum was not a beat like Furtwängler's but a tremor of the right arm, which was particularly difficult to decode. He was one of the last of the great old conductors. As probably literally the last, he could afford the subjectivity of movement that not only indicated time with a "bare beat" but also, without using other mobile elements, such as the head or the torso, simply transferred intermediate values of expression or shifts in tempi to his hand.

Jochum gave the impression that he had gone directly to the heart of everything he conducted. He embodied the type of surly southern German secure in his skill, whose harsh speech colored his manner of interpreting music a little bit. He was therefore the right man in the right place after the war when he reestablished the symphony orchestra of the Bayerischen Rundfunk and, with the soloists of the Koeckert Quartet holding the first chairs, made of it a first-class musical organization. He always thought of himself primarily as an educator and fellow musician.

Once again it was the *German Requiem* that first put me in touch with the orchestra and its conductor in 1951, initially in the large auditorium of Munich University and then in the Tonhalle in Zurich. In the train that carried the whole troupe to Switzerland I fell into conversation with the maestro and immediately came to know his warm interest in all the facets of the person he was talking to, his beaming smile, and the ease with which he expressed his mood and opinion.

Before our final meeting during the Berlin staging of *Meistersinger*, we worked together on many other occasions: the "Jedermann-Monologe" with the Concertgebouw Orchestra in Vienna, the *Songs of a Wayfarer* in Berlin, the *St. Matthew Passion* several times, the *Kreuzstab Cantata* and *The Magic Flute* in Tokyo, in Bayreuth *Lohengrin* and (with me singing the small role of Kothner) *Die Meistersinger*.

Although Jochum was usually thought of as the authentic Bruckner conductor, it seemed to me that his special strength lay in more direct, less mystical scores. His amiable fidgeting and his attention darting in every direction could, it is true, get in his way, for the more loudly he issued questions and instructions to one and all, the louder noises and remarks arose all around him. After a session for *Così fan tutte* perhaps, or for Mozart's *Coronation Mass*, I had to draw a deep breath to gather my concentration and inner calm. But Jochum's technical understanding of the works always held out hope of a "better country." And so, with infinite patience, he also opened the way to Hans Sachs, showing me where I should hold back, where to stop, where to move ahead; he steered me safely through the shoals of my first voyage in uncharted waters. His unfailing joy, kindled over and over by the work he undertook, withstood untold blows of fate; he can be a model to all those allowed to work with him in coping with their own dark days.

* * *

In 1951 Karl Böhm conducted a rehearsal for a concert performance of Igor Stravinsky's *Oedipus Rex*. Egon Seefehlner, at that time director of the Vienna Konzerthaus, let me watch from the empty auditorium. At a quiet moment he whispered to me audibly, and Böhm wheeled around furiously. "Please—no talking in the hall."

Although I was completely innocent, I felt a fervent desire to sink through the floor, a sensation that was unforgettable and certain to overtake anyone who had any dealings with Böhm. His rage was so total and punitive that it was impossible to remember how quickly his good mood could be restored, forgetting and forgiving all. When I was introduced to Böhm, he had already heard of me, and his eyes twinkled cheerfully. He was looking forward, he said, to the coming year and *Don Giovanni*, at the Städtische Oper.

At the very first piano rehearsal in Berlin he came up to me with so much warm solicitude that I, a mere beginner in this complicated part, found it easy to sing the role through for him without interruption. He had few suggestions, and at the end he thanked me for my "marvelous preparation." Given "so much incisive characterization," he continued, the premiere could not help but be a success. What conductor who has heard the score sung by world-renowned voices would have such kind words for a beginner nowadays?

Of course on the crucial night the stage devil played a mean trick on me. At that time stage managers did not yet use loudspeakers, and just before the ballroom scene someone, looking stunned, stuck his head into my dressing room. "The curtain's going up."

I was still in my undershirt. At lightning speed I

slipped into my white ball costume and rushed to the stage, only to see Böhm shaking his head in distress. He had had to sacrifice the first two measures of his Giovanni. But all the rest was pure delight.

By the time we were rehearsing *The Magic Flute*, if not sooner, I had concluded that to work well with a conductor means joining him on the same musical level, capturing and feeling his rhythms—easier said than done! The prerequisite is, of course, adaptability, the same quality a good actor must bring to work with a good stage director. As a result, in all the years of working together, I hardly ever received a negative word from the otherwise often grumpy Böhm, although I have seen many nervous soloists and weeping women around me. Though Böhm became somewhat less difficult in his old age, an implicit tension marked his rehearsals to the end.

During the dialogues of *The Magic Flute* I felt once again the chasm that separates contemporary naturalistic theater speech and the technique of singing: Speech strains the muscles around the larynx. My understanding of this difference became acute during spoken passages with orchestral accompaniment, especially when they are as densely scored and orchestrated as in Arnold Schönberg's *Der Überlebende aus Warschau*, where the conductor is forced to improvise if he wants his speakers to be heard at all. The same problem confronts the singer in Alban Berg's operas. In these the lower registers are at a disadvantage, if only because so many wind sections are scored higher than the voice. Böhm showed particular consideration for precisely this situation, and he prepared the premiere of Berg's *Lulu* at the Deutsche Oper with the necessary sensitivity. At the very first full rehearsal—that is, singers on the stage apron, with the orchestra at full strength below—Böhm could be heard muttering to himself, "Whatever he sings he always sings all out." This comment encouraged me to lay aside the score. Of course I had underestimated his meticulousness and his irritability, which he took out on the others. "You can't pass the swimming test so quickly here," I heard his nasal voice say from the podium.

After the relatively hectic premiere Böhm forced his Dr. Schön to take a curtain call alone with him, shaking his hand rather demonstratively. My beloved colleague Evelyn Lear, who was that night's Lulu—and who, after all, had the hardest part to perform—put a charming face on it. Incidentally, she very successfully sang against type.

In 1955 I was scheduled to sing my first Count Almaviva in *Figaro* in Italian at Salzburg. Three years earlier I had been totally opposed to Furtwängler's suggestion, since I did not trust myself with the part on an occasion of such prominence. In the meantime, however, I had sung Almaviva in German under Carl Ebert's baton, and I felt that I had come to know the part well enough to take the risk. But when I saw Elisabeth Schwarzkopf, Irmgard Seefried, and Christa Ludwig romping around in Caspar Neher's serious and dignified stage setting, enchanting Böhm who as usual sat at the stage apron even in the early rehearsals, I was glad of the day or two of reprieve before it was my turn.

The stage director Oskar Fritz Schuh—the "erudite" professor from Austria—was restricted in his movements because of childhood polio, and for that reason he impressed me beyond measure, especially when he acted out a woman's graceful walk to excellent effect. A few clear suggestions about gestures were enough to allow me to mime the domineering but not too bright provincial despot, Almaviva. I followed Schuh's conception, but not with great conviction.

My second *Figaro* production was directed by Günther Rennert, with Böhm again conducting. After one rehearsal, when I had been in pretty bad voice, Böhm invited us to dinner in the garden of his hotel. As we sat under the trees, which seemed to put him in a particularly communicative mood, he gave us a glimpse into the future. Perhaps he was not being ironic when he advocated a change that has by now been implemented: "The main thing is not to burden yourself by repeating the same staging; it's better to keep dialogue (and gossip) going by new productions."

At the time I was shocked by his apparent lack of idealism. Today I realize that in fact artistic achievement of note seems to obey this dubious maxim. Nevertheless, we performed *Figaro* with almost identical casts for ten years—in Vienna as well.

That same summer the Berlin Philharmonic came to Salzburg to play under Böhm. I was to sing Mahler's *Kindertotenlieder.* Once more I suffered from the demands the song cycle makes on the memory, with its insidiously modified stanzas. To sing precisely what Mahler intended requires being as familiar with the directions for the orchestra as with those for the voice, distinguishing the subtly varied repetitions from stanza to stanza. In addition, this cycle always confronts the soloist with a complex of feelings that are almost impossible to master—thoughts of suicide, as the composer Peter Ruzicka once noted. Having happily arrived at the end, I found myself thinking: The Berlin Philharmonic Orchestra is the best. The musicians played with sensitivity, wholly engrossed in the work. That kind of dedication can be felt even at one's back. Böhm directed me confidently and with great mastery, responsive to the variations. The tears began to flow even at the dress rehearsal. And the sound of Mozart's G-minor Symphony, which preceded the Mahler, was very different, and more correct, from the sound produced recently by the same orchestra led by another star of the podium.

Great conductors may occasionally take the liberty of indicating their directions with only slight motions. Lesser talents, however, should be warned against the practice— God only knows why it will not work for them. Böhm followed Richard Strauss' dictums and kept his "packages," as he called them, as tiny as possible, so that at a greater stage distance a singer had to watch him like a hawk. For pianissimo passages he barely pressed his thumb on the end of the baton, so that its tip moved in a very small circle. When he then shouted to a singer on the stage, "Keep up with me, I'm signaling very plainly," those around him probably suppressed a smile.

The mysterious power of minimal motions was demonstrated by Böhm during the recording of scenes from Handel's *Julius Caesar* (with Irmgard Seefried). A short time before, an insignificant conductor had led me in a performance of baroque arias. His rather robust and large-scale beats did not produce any particularly intense sounds from the same Berlin Philharmonic. But Böhm began the Handel with barely perceptible signals, and the orchestra outdid itself in clean entrances and sonority.

When he was younger, even then rather delicate and graceful, Böhm had exorbitant expectations of musicians' ability to follow. At times he seemed to feel that any independence was dangerous, and he would protest. Thus, he might rebuke the slightest rubato in Mozart with "Don't ritard!" although before you could bat an eyelash the tiny change led back to the tempo.

In 1963 the Deutsche Oper of Berlin made its first trip to Tokyo; this was also my first visit to that city. Böhm was to conduct *Figaro* and *Fidelio*. All of us felt groggy after we arrived because of the time and climate change, and we had to contend with jet lag for many days. We all had trouble speaking with one another. People with little self-confidence—and unfortunately I'm one of them when I am a victim of the climate—should not make the mistake of thinking that a silent conductor is dismissing them as "average." When, after minimal remarks from Böhm, Sellner's production of *Fidelio* lay behind us, our reward came from the conductor's lips: "We should have recorded all of it just as it was."

When he was in a reasonably good mood, Böhm was better than most at striking a balance between praise and criticism. I can't think of any other conductor with as fierce a reputation who expressed his approval so frequently and firmly during rehearsals. The only trouble was that his approbation was expressed rather more softly than was his disapproval. A conductor's essentially policelike function naturally leads to constant correction of his players and soloists, a habit that can easily persist outside rehearsals.

During this tour in Japan I gave a recital of Schubert lieder in the medium-sized, acoustically very favorable Nissei Theater. I spotted Böhm in the front row. As always, he visited me in the dressing room afterward and immediately unleashed his critical cannons: "You should have made more concessions to the public."

I was so bold as to reply, "How would that be possible in a program of Schubert?"

At that, Böhm sighed. "Well, all right. And when it comes down to it, you did the right thing."

In fact there had been loud cheering, and one member of the audience had jumped up on the stage—to kiss my shoes.

Sighs were the best Böhm was able to produce when he recorded *Don Giovanni* in Prague. The idea of recording, in deference to history, at the site of the opera's world premiere (which today is in the East and therefore less expensive) was the brainchild of the record producers. They had not thought about the local opera orchestra's lack of experience with Mozart, and its unfamiliarity with Böhm's style. The ensemble had been assembled brilliantly, but the singers were exhausted after restless nights in uncomfortable beds. In addition, two nervous and panicky assistants (one of them had frequently worked with Böhm at the New York Metropolitan Opera and also played the recitatives on the harpsichord) were unable to impose any routine on the preliminary rehearsals with the soloists and with the on-stage musicians. The technicians supervising the recording were also slow, often making Böhm despair. He was unfamiliar with the orchestra. If the musicians had trouble following him, it was due partly to the language barrier and partly to their being unaccustomed to Böhm's sharp manner. As usual, the singers were eager to leave for other engagements as soon as possible. Alfredo Mariotti lost his mother and had to leave at once for her funeral. Ezio Flagello was expected back in New York, as was Martina Arroyo. Accommodating as always, I postponed all my solos to the end of the recording and suffered accordingly. Though Böhm was forced to summon up still more grumpiness in order to keep the television spotlights in check lest they hurt his damaged eyes, he nevertheless handed out generous praise on all sides.

Sometimes Max Frisch looked down at us from the darkened balcony. Once I went to talk to him but found he had already left. He must have been working on his novel *My Name Is Gantenbein* at the time. Reading it nine months later, I came across a passage in which a character says good things about my *Don Giovanni* recording. (Patricia Highsmith has her hero Tom Ripley collect Fischer-Dieskau records.) Frisch is also supposed to have said to one member of the recording team that I did not look at all like a singer.

Following a recital I gave at Carnegie Hall in 1980, Böhm negotiated the stairs to my dressing room with great difficulty and duly gave his criticism: "Is it really allowed to sing so beautifully? And you smoke, too?"

Julia told me later that she had sat next to Böhm in the box and had watched him as he grew increasingly angry at a woman on his other side who was covered with jewelry. Her body moved with the music, and her thick fingers tapped the beat on the railing. Böhm's hand was at the ready to slap at this spongy-white disturbance. Expressing annoyance in this manner seemed to be very good for his blood pressure. Sometimes, it is true, he almost lost control, and then it took an extreme effort to keep himself in check. Such efforts failed whenever he was expected to work with a microphone—a source of constant irritation. He unleashed all his anxiety during the recording of Mahler's *Kindertotenlieder* on a glockenspiel performer who was a little too cautious during the first song. Repeatedly he broke off to ask the hapless player, "Where are you, anyway? I can't hear you!" Eventually the orchestra's morale hit rock bottom. Finally we were ready to listen to the playback. Somehow it must have dawned on the maestro that he had gone too far. He tried to save face by taking my arm and saying, "Look, Fischer, you've got to use psychology when you deal with people. Either you know how or you don't."

Luckily we reached the listening room before I could comment.

After our many joint successes with *Figaro*, I was unable to participate in what was to be Böhm's last performance of the work, at the Deutsche Oper. Just before the first ensemble rehearsal I broke two ribs in a fall on the icy steps outside my house. My substitute was made to suffer Böhm's harassment. After the overwhelming storm of applause, the conductor took the hand of his Countess— it was Julia—to lead her in front of the curtain. With tears in his eyes he whispered, "The only reason they're applauding so wildly is because I am so old."

Only a few weeks before Böhm's death the soundtrack for Götz Friedrich's *Elektra-Film* was recorded. As is the practice, the music was prerecorded, and then the cast (Leonie Rysanek, Astrid Varnay, and I) lip-synched to our own voices. I, however, had to synchronize twice; when I arrived in Vienna, I found that Böhm had taken the precaution of conducting a tape to which I was to add my voice. He sent a touching telegram: "Unfortunately cannot be there, feel too ill."

Though usually I enjoyed synchronizing because it is like a game in which I have to understand and adapt to someone else's vision, this time I kept thinking anxiously about the ailing old man. Later, when, almost at the same time as his beloved Thea, he had left this world—after being selflessly cared for by Jochen Sostmann—I saw the heart-wrenching documentary of his last rehearsals with

143

the Vienna Philharmonic. The gesture with which he laid his baton down on the podium after the concluding measures of *Elektra* could mean only a last farewell.

In Vienna in 1952 I met Mario Rossi, the old master among the Italian conductors. We really began to have a proper "understanding" only after I had polished the miserable Italian I had acquired as a soldier and prisoner of war. During the rehearsal, in the Vienna Konzerthaussaal, for Hugo Wolf's Harfner songs and the *Songs of a Wayfarer*, Rossi glanced casually at the score, then somewhat haughtily at the singer, who was so much younger. People who are far apart in age can probably become close only on the basis of shared activity or philosophy. Rossi was someone who found it almost impossible to work with me owing to our difference in age. Furthermore, he had never before conducted my two solo pieces; accordingly I felt free to express my ideas at the rehearsal. The orchestra eagerly went along; only the conductor showed indifference. When it came time for the concert itself, some terrible technical hitches developed: The violins came in too early, the woodwinds made mistakes, and so on. When we performed the same program in Milan two years later, the effect was still rather unsatisfactory.

It was quite a different story when I sang Rossini's *William Tell* in Milan with Rossi and his RAI Orchestra. Nervous about my first appearance in opera in Italy (even though only in a concert version), I arrived at the broadcasting station half an hour early. Anxiously I alternately sat and stood outside the rehearsal hall, watching the vigorously gesticulating heavyset women and men passing by, whom I supposed to be renowned singers but did not recognize.

Everyone jumped up respectfully and bowed when the slender and aristocratic Mario Rossi entered and, to my great surprise, embraced me amicably. There were three full rehearsals before the opera was performed before a live audience and simultaneously recorded. I am sure that, as the only non-Italian, with my shyness and consequent stiffness, I seemed temperamentally very different from the others. But the public accepted me, just as in rehearsal Rossi said to the others, "This *tedesco* can teach us a thing or two about pronouncing Italian!" I'm sure it was meant as friendly encouragement.

The conductors of the chorus and of the soloists, however, had criticism to spare. They analyzed every word and found passages that required subtle improvements. This opera contains a great many recitatives, which must be spoken rapidly and pronounced clearly.

In spite of my difficulties in Vienna in 1952, I must have sounded natural enough in performance. During intermission Irmel saw Jean Cocteau in the hall; he spoke to her cordially and sent a message that he wanted to see me. Early on I had developed a shyness in the face of "celebrities," fearing that they might turn out to be cold or overly intellectual; many young men who lack self-confidence feel this way. On that day, therefore, I had left long before Cocteau arrived at the dressing room.

The following morning I was sitting in the hall during the rehearsal of Stravinsky's *Oedipus Rex*, which has a text by Cocteau, who was scheduled to read the transitional passages himself. I found myself already liking him for the way he moved restlessly back and forth in his chair before his first entrance, again and again looking nervously at the conductor. Then I heard his voice: melodious and expressive, but full of the emotion that his own stage directions specifically forbade. At the slightest sound his narrow head twitched in that direction of the hall, not as if he were displeased but rather as if he felt ridiculed. This gesture won me over almost as much as the powerful work itself, and now I could happily let myself be introduced to Cocteau, who was graceful, not yet very old, unbelievably vulnerable and sensitive, with eyes that clearly could become sharp and piercing. He held out his arms and addressed me in fluent though incorrect German. I have ever since kept one of his observations in mind as a goal: "You sing as if you had written it yourself!"

And that, he said, was surely the main point in any interpretation: The re-creating musician must also be creative in his own right—he must, that is, move freely in the conscious space between the image communicated by the notes and his own person. Our cordial parting was, unfortunately, for good. Not long after, we heard of his death.

Twice more while I was still young I was fortunate enough to sing with Rossi: Verdi on the Cologne radio—in German, which I regret today, since the public might have been more interested in this excellent production and it might have been repeated if it had been sung in Italian. The *Vespri Siciliani* and *Falstaff* showed Rossi's outstanding familiarity with all the aspects of these works.

Music lovers and performers owe a debt of gratitude to Karl O. Koch for the 1952 unabridged Cologne recording of Hans Pfitzner's *Palestrina*. As head of the music division of the West German Radio, Koch approached his work with untiring joy, a rare attribute today. I remembered him with special fondness from the production of *A Masked Ball* with Fritz Busch. This time too, happy and bustling, he organized the crowd scenes. Among the many renowned singers (the cast called for more than thirty soloists), two made a special impression on me. One was Julius Patzak; I had already seen him briefly at the Vienna Staatsoper as Walther in *Tannhäuser* and had been astonished that he was willing to take on so minor a part. A short time later he was scheduled to sing the Evangelist in the *St. Matthew Passion* with me in Berlin. Pfitzner's resigned yet mellow Palestrina, probably more than any other part, gave him precisely the vocal material he sang with the greatest assurance. But it was also amusing to watch him change in seconds from an aged composer into a rather cynical contemporary who called to me at the moment of highest tension in the Morone scene, "Just don't take it all so serious!"

But I often had discussions with the man who besides being a singer was also both composer and conductor, and if memory serves, we found quite a lot to talk about.

The other singer who impressed me was Hans Hotter, with his friendly, open gaze, who sang the role of Borromeo. In the wake of my shyness I had worked myself up into feeling that an icy river separated the two of us, who were different in age and yet so frequently paired in the repertoire. But a twinkle from Hotter's clever yet amiable eyes melted any barrier around my heart, even in this anxious situation. No other voice resounding next to me had so much volume and inner fullness of tone. I had an opportunity to admire this quality in Bayreuth as well, from the vantage point of the greenroom and of performing alongside him when he sang Gurnemanz or Sachs (although like all aging Hans Sachses, he had trouble making it through the third act—an experience with which I too have become familiar). His way of singing lieder influenced me deeply, as it had in the 1930s, and I can only be grateful to him for all his inspiration by example. By the way, he was the Divine Messenger in *Die Frau ohne Schatten* when, singing Barak, I helped to open the rebuilt Nationaltheater in Munich in 1963.

Richard Kraus was the conductor of the Cologne *Palestrina* recording. Before the First World War his father—idolized by my mother—had been an outstanding heldentenor. His son, a firebrand, was now the principal conductor of the Cologne Radio; a stout man, his blue eyes beamed over a remarkable beard à la Napoleon III. Eager, enthusiastic, and choleric, he was dedicated to his mission of reviving the late romantic to early modern operatic dramas—a mission in which he would have been considerably aided by a more precise beat and greater psychological tactfulness. As it was, there were rebellious shouts and groans from the orchestra—and from me, making my debut as Morone—under his uneven beat and fragmentary instructions. "A little more vig— why don't the violins play more sof— let the percussion section reta— . . ."

But his combination of unbridled temperament and thorough preparation did produce respectable results, still worth listening to. He conducted three of my most important premieres at the Berlin Städtische Oper, though each time he was forced to plead with me to do them. The works were Ferruccio Busoni's *Doktor Faust*, Alban Berg's *Wozzeck*, and Paul Hindemith's *Mathis der Maler*; for all three the stage direction was by Wolf Völker. The climate at his rehearsals, impulsive and loud, was intensified by his hectic manner. Perhaps Kraus will forgive me posthumously for the fact that at one rehearsal, when there was loud whispering in the orchestra, I did not keep my feelings to myself but stepped to the edge of the stage and asked angrily, "Are we having a tea party here?"

In 1952 I was flying from Munich to Vienna, which I was visiting for the second time and which was once more fulfilling its function as a center for musicians. (I also met the very young Jörg Demus there.) Rudolf Kempe and his young first wife were sitting next to me on the plane; he was about to make his conducting debut in *Die Meistersinger* the very next day, a Sunday. Completely friendly at once and fond of storytelling, Kempe spoke of the master ensemble that he had called together for a rehearsal—or at least a run-through with piano accompaniment—in the morning.

The following night I made my way to the Theater an der Wien, which still housed the Staatsoper until its own hall could be rebuilt. I heard a wonderfully transparent and precise rendition of the work, with Paul Schöffler, still in powerful voice, heading the strong ensemble in the part of Hans Sachs. And what did I learn when I went to Kempe's dressing room at intermission? Not a single one of the master singers had turned up for the morning rehearsal—so apparently a run-through had not been necessary.

Kempe had a special talent for surprising himself again and again, flexibly translating new experiences, new nuances of sound into action. His beat had nothing schoolmasterish about it, and nothing routine. He cleverly

149

kept finding new ways of making the orchestra understand him. The performance demonstrated all the characteristic gifts of his conducting, and left the strongest impression by its clarity, unobtrusiveness, and respect for the limits of the singers' vocal capacities. All this is related to Kempe's curiosity about the unexpected, a playfulness that—not unlike that of Dvořák and Hindemith—also inspired him to toy with electric trains. And if, as in our production of *Lohengrin* in Vienna, in which I sang Telramund, everything was in danger of falling apart owing to a singer's hysteria and the necessity of suddenly recasting, he was like a rock of benevolent calm amid the waves of excitement. Because Kempe was familiar with all the manifestations of stage fright, he could calmly reassure me when I made a mistake in the varied repetitions in the *Kindertotenlieder*: "Against the background of the overall artistic accomplishment, it makes no difference whatever."

For the rest, Kempe had a quality rare in his profession: modesty. When we were rehearsing Brahms' *German Requiem* for both live performance and recording, he said something that moved me so much that I have never forgotten it: "If I can make it come out just half as beautiful as Furtwängler did the other day in Vienna, I'll be happy." But what followed was an interpretation that, though echoing its ideal, rejected a highly personal approach in every detail.

The work on the *Kindertotenlieder* was upsetting because at that time Kempe was not in artistic harmony with the Berlin Philharmonic; their playing was never melting and naturally flowing enough for him. He cheerfully made the first and second bassoonists trade places, an extraordinary eccentricity. But the quality of the result, it seems to me, speaks for itself, and there was good reason for so many new pressings of the recording.

Beginning with the text, the *Kindertotenlieder* cycle belongs to the male voice. On the other hand Mahler's alto parts unfortunately do not sound ideal when sung by a baritone, since the balance is affected by the fact that they usually lie below the level of the orchestra. (This is equally true for *Das Lied von der Erde*.) I felt this to be extremely regrettable when the work was performed (the first time for me) in Edinburgh in 1952 with Otto Klemperer conducting. The first rehearsal, dreaded for weeks, was to take place the very morning after my arrival. Before this test, which I was to undergo in the private house of a patron of the arts, I bumped into Hans Gál, the composer and musicologist, who was to coach the singers. "Maestro Klemperer seems nervous to me; he's always unfriendly when he's facing the almost insurmountable difficulties of *Das Lied von der Erde*."

And then for an hour Klemperer, a large man, sat on a small stool at my feet, and when I came to the infinitely touching "Ewig, ewig" that concludes the work, his old man's voice blissfully hummed the orchestral line in accompaniment. The ensuing silence was followed by a lively conversation. We found each other in Mahler's music. His fears—probably about my youth and inexperience—seemed to have evaporated. Asked about the afternoon rehearsal, which he had urgently and repeatedly requested by letter, he exclaimed, "Another time today, with the piano? No-no-no! Totally unnecessary. I'll see you tomorrow at the orchestra rehearsal."

Klemperer's daughter Lotte, roughly Irmel's age and

touchingly concerned for her father, intensified the impression of cordiality this great man among the older generation of conductors made. Nevertheless, as it turned out, the orchestra rehearsal proved that we could hardly expect a piano, much less a pianissimo, from his left hand, which certainly made for a problem. On a personal level Klemperer remained warm, totally without conceit. In fact I got the impression that he was lacking in self-assurance. Once he sighed, "I was young once, too. . . ."

His English exceeded all emigrant extremes, despite the many years he had spent in the United States.

"Die Flöte a little lauter"; "a little breider, gentlemen."

Asked by the concertmaster to give instructions in English, he first grumbled, "What?" Only when the request was repeated several times did he grudgingly admit, "Oh, I understand."

We came to a point where my register could no longer stand up to the wall of sound produced by the orchestra. I dared to lodge a request: "Couldn't you bring the orchestra down a little in this fortissimo passage?"

At once the ambiguous laconic reply: "You'll just have to give a little less."

Only much later did I understand that Klemperer was right, of course, and that he had correctly estimated the orchestra musicians' psychology.

Not long before this encounter Klemperer had to undergo life-threatening surgery. One night as he was falling asleep, an open bottle of cognac spilled over his chest—in itself not serious, but he was also holding a lighted cigarette, and a blaze started. Surgery artfully replaced the skin over his chest. Now, after the *Lied von der*

Erde, Klemperer as usual called to his daughter, "Lotte, dry me off!"

He began to take off his clothes. In Edinburgh's Usher Hall there is to this day only one dressing room. I therefore timidly suggested that the tenor soloist, Anton Dermota, and I retire to the men's room for a while.

"Not at all. Stay," Klemperer insisted in his high-pitched voice. When he stood before us almost totally naked, he beat his newly healed chest, demanding genially, "Still pretty good, huh?"

My own impressions of the old Klemperer were as contradictory as all the stories I heard about him. At the rehearsal of the *German Requiem* in London the huge old man was carried to the podium. He was visibly enjoying himself, and when he reached his chair, he allowed himself to collapse. His signals to the huge apparatus of chorus and orchestra struck me as casual, imprecise, and sketchy. He did not really respond to what was happening around him. At first the tempi were also totally chaotic. After every unavoidable stop he sank back indifferently, as if he had fallen into a lethargy from which he tried to rouse himself by making jokes. He yawned without covering his mouth, sucked noisily on his pipe, and told Jewish jokes moments after "Selig sind die Toten" (Blessed are the dead) had ebbed away. In his sardonic way he tried to play up to my (nonexistent) vanity as a baritone by repeatedly calling me the born Eisenstein in *Die Fledermaus*. (I did eventually sing the part of Dr. Falke on a recording of the operetta.)

Unfortunately a recording of the *St. Matthew Passion* did not proceed happily. Klemperer ended each measure with a ritardando. The orchestra made its way through the notes suffering but cracking jokes. The English chorus sang excellently, without the maestro's cues, with good diction, guided, out of Klemperer's sight, by Wilhelm Pitz. Irmel urged me to confess to Walter Legge how unhappy it made me to be associated with a venture such as this. When I did so, London's music czar and founder of the Philharmonia Orchestra, usually so sure of himself, showed me a side I had not seen before; he was uneasy and embarrassed, nervously gracious—probably because he was feeling guilty. Legge referred to himself as a buffer state; this appellation was not entirely accurate, since he spent a great deal of energy, sometimes with great effect, keeping alive the myth that the old conductor's personality was as forceful as ever. During the recitatives, when the conductor's tempi failed with breathtaking regularity, Sir Peter Pears, who was singing the part of the Evangelist, stood next to me, the picture of serenity, never moved to any sign of anger. But suddenly I heard a strangled "It's miserable!"

For Pears that was an extreme outburst of fury. However, it was the rubato in his performance of the Evangelist that enchanted me—dictated by the text but always true to the music.

As long as Klemperer was still able to walk, he frequently sat in on my recitals. When I met him for the last time, in the stage elevator of the Royal Festival Hall, he was in a wheelchair, pushed by Lotte. At first we had difficulty communicating because he did not recognize me and was unable to take in his daughter's whispered words. But then he asked about my London performance and what I was planning to sing. "Schubert?"

No.

"Schumann?"

No.

"Well then, what?"

Brahms.

"There's no necessity for that" was his laconic response, which took me completely aback.

As we went down the hall, I did not want to inquire further. Perhaps in his youth he had heard his father, accompanied by his mother, singing Brahms once too often. Once I got up the courage to ask him about the lieder he had written, a question he immediately deflected with, "None of them are worth anything!"

As a young conductor, Klemperer had coerced a dream into becoming reality—an opera house with a limited repertory, produced one work at a time, thus avoiding the usual hysterical activity. Klemperer could only tell me about this dream, which I would have loved to participate in; but it came into being before my time, and its life was cut short by the Nazis. In 1927 he was actually given the opportunity of establishing an opera in Berlin that fulfilled every aspect of his ideal. The cultural ministry planned to found a theater wholly independent of the Staatsoper Unter den Linden, using the rooms of the Kroll-Etablissement; this became the Kroll Opera. Here a few selected works were staged, with meticulous, innovative musical interpretations; each could be given a number of consecutive performances. Klemperer was enthusiastic about his co-workers—the conductors Alexander Zemlinsky and Fritz Zweig; the painters Oskar Schlemmer, Laszlo Moholy-Nagy, and Caspar Neher; the directors Jürgen Fehling and Gustaf Gründgens. The competing Staatsoper and the National Socialist bigwigs, who were making their way into government, soon found the new undertaking a thorn in their side. It pained me that Klemperer (not unlike Bruno Walter) had bitter things to say about Tietjen, who had only too soon and too willingly given in to the urgings of Göring, the patron of the Staatsoper, that the Kroll Opera be undermined.

After the war, having had to interrupt work on opera during his years in exile in the United States, Klemperer was unable to find rewarding work on the operatic stage. Though Walter Felsenstein had brought him to his Komische Oper in Berlin's Eastern sector, during his first year there the maestro began to grumble that the conductor "had no say at all."

It was his great good fortune that Walter Legge gave him the opportunity of working in London for the rest of his life, heading the Philharmonia (later named New Philharmonia), with a huge repertoire. When Klemperer died in Zurich in 1973, the crowd following his coffin was far too small. Caught up in obligations, I too was unable to attend.

In 1970 the recording manager of EMI, Suvi Raj Grubb, recalled my hints that though I never got around to conducting, I would enjoy it. When Klemperer became fatally ill and canceled all his recording engagements, Grubb asked me to make my conducting debut with the New Philharmonia, leading the recording of Schubert's Fifth and *Unfinished* symphonies—truly an exciting, if late, debut!

So as not to jump into this venture entirely unprepared, I went to see a relative by marriage who lived in Berlin. Harold Byrns, whose name had been Hans Bernstein before the Nazi era, had worked as one of Klemperer's successors at the Komische Oper in East Berlin. At the time I went to see him, he was deeply absorbed in arranging piano works and lieder for large orchestras. He

---

took a devoted interest in me and later in my son Martin, who became a conductor. We adored the witty, quick mind of this veteran of the Schönberg group in Los Angeles, where he had founded his own chamber orchestra. Our collaboration turned out to be much too short; soon Byrns had to go to the hospital to have a pacemaker implanted, and he did not live much longer.

The four years of conducting chores that followed—always between singing engagements—included all the joys and torments of a new career. I think with gratitude of Zubin Mehta, who generously handed me the Los Angeles Philharmonic and the Israel Philharmonic; of Vaclav Neumann, who allowed me to conduct the Czech Philharmonic; of my soloists Daniel Barenboim (with the English Chamber Orchestra), Jean-Pierre Pommier (RSO Berlin), Alfred Brendel (Israel Philharmonic), and Jorge Bolet (Bamberger Sinfoniker), all of whom gave me their trust. But the physical burden had a harmful effect on my song recitals, forcing me—against my greatest hopes—to give up conducting for the time being.

During the brief period when I did conduct, I tended to leave many nuances of interpretation to the performance. Though a concert reflects the precision with which it was prepared, a good performance on any night will bring out additional elements, which can only be alluded to. To "take an orchestra for a walk," as the misleading expression for this undefinable something has it, puts the performers on the edge of their chairs—and the cutting edge of their talent. Furthermore, a musical "re-creator" turns out to be a new creator at every performance, without in any way distorting the work he is presenting. Karl Flesch, the great violin teacher, once said, "A touch of showmanship is indispensable in conducting."

The maxim does not go to the heart of the matter. It is true that certain conductors do include a bit of showmanship. But what Flesch is referring to is the conductor's ability to clearly project his intention (and of course the intended effect) both forward, into the orchestra, and backward, into the audience. This element may—with caution—be compared to the skill of an actor, who uses his mimetic powers to create a credible character. But a conductor's mimetic or gestural skills are not his ultimate purpose; they merely support him in consistently asserting his interpretation.

Though I never had the opportunity to work with him, my love was always given to one conductor who needed no mimetic supporting effects at all: Arturo Toscanini. He was outstanding not only in the Italian repertoire. Occasionally I objected to the swiftness of his tempi, but it was phenomenal how, despite his speed, he was able to make the score resound in its totality—by which I mean in all its parts. Perhaps it is above all his unsurpassed way of driving the strings to technical perfection that can still make listeners (of his recordings) catch their breath. Toscanini always reminds me of his model, Giuseppe Verdi: his fire, his human warmth, his peasant vividness, his unending struggle with himself—and with perfection.

Over and over again the question has been debated whether or not works are to be conducted from memory. It seems to me that there must be exceptions. First, whether to memorize or not must depend on the temperament of the individual conductor. But as soon as a soloist is added—or, in opera, the singers—it is always advisable to have the score at hand as well as in one's head. Soloists are not members of the orchestra.

Neither subjective nor objective reproduction should predominate. The vocation of conducting must include both an absolute grasp of the material and a strong individual personality. In no instance is it enough to allow another insignificant performance of X to run its course— but neither can the true aim be achieved by the conductor's self-importantly interfering between the composer and his intention. To the extent that performers are human beings with hearts and nerves, there can be no such thing as an "objective" rendition—among other reasons, because we do not have a direct telephone line to the composers of the past. Though taste and knowledge are both necessary, they are not sufficient to bestow grace on the performance.

A frail Bruno Walter walked into the lobby of Edinburgh's George Hotel in 1953. Brahms' *German Requiem* was on the program in two days, and I, all of twenty-eight, was to be initiated into Walter's holy rites. Since he was not carrying a piano reduction, I naively offered him mine for the rehearsal. With his usual expression of extreme suffering, he uttered a gentle "I know the piece!"

And then I began to sing confidently but softly, as if I were praying. After the first syllable—"Herr!"—Bruno Walter lifted his fingers from the keys as if struck by lightning. "No! A thousand times no! It has to sound world-weary, as if it were being sung by a high priest who seems indifferent to everything around him."

Though I did not share this opinion, I darkened my voice appropriately, and the maestro was satisfied. The following day I saw him struggling with the festival chorus, mainly to elicit the expression appropriate to every measure of the work. The result in the concert itself was an unimaginably wrong intonation—almost the entire work sounding a quarter-tone lower in the chorus than in the orchestra. Wilhelm and Elisabeth Furtwängler were sitting in the front row of Usher Hall, and from my soloist's vantage point I could hear him whisper to his wife during a soft passage, "Those tempi—much too swift. . . ." The sentence included enough sibilants to make its way unintentionally to the conductor's ears.

A reunion of the two idolized conductors was scheduled to take place after the concert. The two had not met since Bruno Walter had emigrated while Furtwängler remained in Germany—a decision for which he was much criticized. Some were looking forward to the meeting with trepidation, others with suspense. The worlds of enforced exile and inner emigration, burdened by old rivalries and personal animosities, encountered each other in an electric forcefield that could not have been more explosive. Nevertheless, Furtwängler did not avoid the occasion but faced up to the confrontation, thus towering over Walter, who, perhaps withered by the exertions of the concert, had collapsed in an armchair.

In answer to Walter's question, "How did you like it?" Furtwängler made no mention of the Requiem, responding instead to the Brahms *Haydn Variations* that had preceded the major work: "The finale might have been somewhat more majestic!"

Because the meeting was kept short, the tension in the air did not ignite into an explosion. The tragic histories of both men could not help resulting in animosity, and it soon became clear that neither Walter nor his close friend Thomas Mann was able to summon up any sympathy for the conductor who had chosen to remain in Germany.

Mann expressed his feelings to Walter von Molo. "How much apathy does it take to listen to *Fidelio* in Himmler's Germany without covering one's face with one's hands and rushing from the hall. . . ." To which Furtwängler replied: "Does Thomas Mann really believe that in Himmler's Germany one should not be allowed to play Beethoven?" And in fact, during the Nazi period Furtwängler trod the thinnest possible tightrope in using his music to console people amid the general disaster.

A year later Walter conducted his mentor Mahler's *Songs of a Wayfarer* with the London BBC Orchestra and me as soloist. He followed it with the related First Symphony.

I was meant to be flattered at our first meeting by such remarks as "I've heard many good things about you." But the ploy did not work. When it came to my approach to the Mahler lieder, which had in part been defined by Furtwängler in Salzburg, Walter urged me to double my tempo, arguing that Mahler's intentions could be conveyed only by a kind of nervousness that betrayed no hint of assurance. And in this he was only too right. Since that time I have been more inclined to agree with Walter's forward-rushing interpretation of the song cycle, especially because at the time the frail old man's conducting of the First Symphony convincingly brought out the specific themes of the songs it contained.

Once again the astonishingly rejuvenating influence of music on old men was to be marveled at. Walter dragged himself to the podium, where as soon as the first notes sounded, he was transformed, infused with fire and dynamism.

I never saw him again. Only a year later he died in California.

Of all the lions of the podium I have encountered, the melancholy Pole Paul Kletzki was the one who projected the least sense of power. But he was free enough to act upon his feelings. Thus in 1960 in Paris there was a great to-do about the worldwide broadcast of a UNESCO concert held in the Salle Pleyel. I was singing Goethe's *Harfen-Gesänge* in Hugo Wolf's setting and unfortunately awkward orchestration. When some members of the audience were still arguing about the seating well after the first notes had sounded, Kletzki stamped his foot on the resonant planks of the stage floor—the stomp heard round the world—to restore quiet.

Although before it was rebuilt the hall had been a tasteless eyesore, something of its unbelievably rapid transmission of sound to the rearmost seats was lost to the renovations. And this loss meant forfeiting at least some of the acoustical quality.

Kletzki suffered from the occupational hazards of compulsive perfectionism. It sometimes happened, for example, that in the night between two recording dates, at four in the morning, he would call from his room at the London Savoy to mine, complaining in a weepy voice, "I simply don't know how to attack this damned quintuplet!"

"Why don't you bear down once, then the other four will automatically follow," I would reply.

And when after awhile I had calmed him down, he

would be comforted: "Well, if someday I'm playing with Mahler in heaven, I'm sure he'll forgive me."

When the *Harfen-Gesänge* was scheduled in Geneva after Kletzki had taken over the Orchestre de la Suisse Romande from Ernest Ansermet, the news broke that he had suffered a nervous breakdown, and the concerts were canceled. Some time later I received a touching letter of apology, and this was followed by his obituary. I hope Mahler is telling him now about his own way of conducting a quintuplet!

Günther Rennert had inherited the conductor Joseph Keilberth for the Bavarian Staatsoper from his predecessor, Rudolf Hartmann. During the war Keilberth had led the German Philharmonic Orchestra of Prague, before attracting attention at the Dresden Staatsoper and the East Berlin Opera.

That is where I attended what must surely have been the only performance of *Meistersinger* without the principal singer. Jaro Prohaska had not canceled his engagement for that night until nearly two o'clock in the afternoon, and it was impossible to find a replacement in time. In the first act, instead of Sachs, an insubstantial figure mingled with the masters, and from that moment on the audience had to be content with this helpful but entirely unsuitable stopgap. The old chorus singer must have sung the part ages ago with some provincial company, but he remembered only fragments of the text and music. Keilberth was constantly raising his left hand, signaling to slow down or speed up—a sign of anxiety without parallel. One thing did become crystal clear that memorable night: Wagner had constructed his work so well that even without its center a certain impression of its consistency remained; a convincing union of form and content could not be destroyed. My admiration for Joseph Keilberth's calm and thoughtfulness was boundless.

The musicians of his Prague orchestra reassembled in the Bamberger Sinfoniker, with whom he remained connected until his death. It is hard to imagine an odder couple at the head of an opera company than Rennert and Keilberth. Rennert was inspired by romantic interpretation and nimble playfulness; Keilberth tended to the broader German tempi. He had profited from Furtwängler's energetic support. Furtwängler told me that he considered Keilberth the most significant of the younger conductors because, among other reasons, he was able to work up effectively to a climax.

Keilberth seemed to me to conduct more phlegmatically and with considerably less subtlety than Furtwängler, but his personality charmed those around him; he was a serene man, almost meditative (his favorite reading was the German philosophers). He was at all times considerate of his soloists, and he brought to his work so much experience and preparation that the singers were always able to shine. Once when our conversation came around to the "directors' theater," he immediately dismissed it: "Give me a couple of spirited singer-actors and a good stage designer, and with four or five rehearsals I'll give you a sensational premiere!"

Keilberth had given concerts with me in Hamburg and Montreux when I received an invitation from Bamberg to perform Mahler's *Lied von der Erde* with him. The Bamberg symphony thus responded to my suggestion to tour with this work one more time. Bamberg received me sleepily; it seemed a miniature version of Prague. During the rehearsal in the church, which had lost much of its beauty when it was renovated into a concert hall, the overheated, dry air bothered our throats. Since Keilberth accompanied softly but with great liveliness, I managed pretty well all the same. But then the question loomed, Will a cold inevitably follow? My answer to myself was: not if we were all constituted like the bright and cheerful Fritz Wunderlich, who was singing the tenor role.

The work itself was still not completely familiar to the orchestra, whose German members had mostly been trained in Prague. Their derogatory remarks about orchestral details troubled me exceedingly. We had a cozier time at dinner at the Bamberger Hof, where Keilberth held forth about other conductors, mercilessly pulling them to pieces. No one, not even tenors and sopranos, and especially not cellists, takes so much pleasure in gossiping about his colleagues as a conductor: "Just the other day, in the middle of Mahler's Sixth, Bernstein whispered to his New York Philharmonic, 'Keep on playing, I have no idea where we are.' . . ."

The following day Keilberth told us anecdotes about the life of Bamberg's "ghost," E.T.A. Hoffmann. Though I had a vague memory of having heard them before, I enjoyed them all over again in his version. Soon afterward, just around the corner, I examined the idyllic house in the fake-medieval style that was part of the legend. Then, suddenly, in the magnificent cathedral, I stood before the familiar outline of the Horseman of Bamberg, whose plaster head our art teacher had displayed before us for two years so that we might draw it painstakingly and accurately. Anyone who fell asleep or tried to talk to the boy next to him was given a hearty blow to the back of the neck: "Work, my boy!" I had imagined the sculpture to be much larger. The image was imbued with the vestiges of an eerily righteous autocratic age.

When the "Ewig, ewig" of the second concert in Nuremberg had died down, Keilberth embraced me and wept.

In Stuttgart (it was not long after Irmel's death) I walked alone for the first time in the garden of the Villa Berg, sad because the peaceful section with the ginkgo trees was being dug up. Barracks cut the sight of the hill in half. The weather was cold and drizzly, as if determined to break once and for all with past pleasures. The asymmetrical Beethoven-Saal in Stuttgart, with its acoustical tricks, contributed to lowering the concentration of the performers, not to mention the rather sleepy audience.

Bonn made up for these disappointments by a promenade along the shining Rhine. The president of the Federal Republic, Heinrich Lübke, attended the performance of *Das Lied von der Erde*. He had decided that after the concert the three of us (Keilberth, Wunderlich, and I) should meet him in the lobby. He appeared affable and told me at once that the newspapers were treating him shabbily when they claimed that he had received thirteenth months' worth of salary a year, a situation that had now been rectified. He never went in for that sort of thing, he assured me. Not a word about the Mahler.

Keilberth fell victim to his diabetes, which he had neglected. The singers who were there told me about it: In the second act of *Tristan*, as the love duet moves toward its climax, he collapsed over his lectern, and the performance had to be stopped. About fifty years earlier, the great Felix Mottl had had a stroke at almost the same moment in the work and in the same place.

During the memorial service in the filled-to-capacity Nationaltheater, I thought of my various moments with Keilberth. Especially my debut in Bayreuth in 1954, which took place under the bad omen of a conductor's cancellation. Igor Markevich—suffering from nerves and ill health even then—had successfully guided rehearsals from the piano. But when he found himself in the pit of the Bayreuth theater, which extends far under the stage and in which the instruments are grouped in a pattern different from that of most orchestras, he took leave of his senses. Markevich could not get used to the fact that in the Festival Hall the singers and the chorus could not be heard well, and sometimes could not be heard at all on the conductor's podium, of all places, no matter how splendid the acoustics in the auditorium. During the orchestra rehearsals Markevich kept sighing and saying imploringly, "Gré [Gré Brouwenstejn, who was singing Elisabeth], Ramon [Ramon Vinay, who was singing Tannhäuser], *aidez-moi!*"

But they could not help the conductor with so little stage experience. On the contrary: They collected signatures on a petition to have him removed from the premiere. I could not agree to this request, though it meant breaking solidarity, since I myself had no problems with following Markevich's original idea of the music for *Tannhäuser*. Before the dress rehearsal, however, Wieland Wagner announced that owing to illness, Markevich had given up the job. Joseph Keilberth was to take over.

He steered us carefully and without any problems through our stage fright during the premiere. Bayreuth rewarded him poorly for this and other good turns that, almost free of charge, he enthusiastically offered up to the master, Richard Wagner. After almost ten years of work he was shown the door without comment, and to his death Keilberth could not come to terms with this affront. Whenever the name of Bayreuth arose in conversation, his face clouded and he seemed withdrawn.

Joseph Keilberth conducted the two works, rehearsed simultaneously, that were to open the rebuilt Nationaltheater in Munich in 1963; both were staged by Rudolf Hartmann. Before it rose on *Die Meistersinger*, the curtain opened on *Die Frau ohne Schatten*. My Barak was suffering from a cold as late as the final rehearsals, but Keilberth reassured me by remarking, "Actually, I prefer indisposed singers—they pay three times as much attention to their vocal cords as do healthy ones."

Nothing was as congenial to Keilberth as Richard Strauss' broadly executed cantilenas, of which Barak was given a generous measure. Given the leisurely tempo set by Keilberth's baton, the singer retained enough freedom to spread himself out economically, without forcing. Thus after the premiere even Herbert von Karajan went so far as to say, "I never heard you sing better than in this part."

When we were all forced to accept the fact that we would never have Keilberth again, our hearts were heavy. Gerhard Stolze sat next to me at the memorial service. A musical actor of the first rank, my screamingly funny Bardolph in Verdi's *Falstaff* and my opponent Loge in Karajan's *Rheingold* in Salzburg, Stolze was weeping uncontrollably.

The friendly, witty conductor Hans Schmidt-Isserstedt was just as casual as Keilberth. In 1955, shortly after its world premiere with Paul Sacher in Basel, Wolfgang Fortner's solo cantata *The Creation* was to be performed in the Hamburg Musikhalle. I had become familiar with the appearance of the cool, prudent principal conductor of the Nordwestdeutscher Rundfunk through some films of the Nazi period, in which he must have been the staff conductor used whenever symphonic concerts had to be shown to serve some dramatic function or other.

How differently interpreters think of new music nowadays is shown by the following event at rehearsal: Fortner, who was present, rushed to the podium of the Musikhalle after Schmidt-Isserstedt stopped the musicians for the first time; Fortner, well known for his moist speech, sprayed the conductor while he also, somewhat more loudly, shouted instructions to the orchestra. This procedure was repeated perhaps four times. Schmidt-Isserstedt listened calmly. Finally he turned to his orchestra and said with an amused smile, "Gentlemen, you heard: We should play the piece as if it were music."

Today such a remark would be unthinkable, especially applied to a composition such as the *The Creation*, hardly one of Fortner's atonal works. Fortner's first trip to Berlin to see me in the early 1950s gave us an opportunity to discuss several problems raised by the new tonality. Little has changed in the musical world since then, although Fortner saw that world perhaps too much from the point of view of his own place in it. At that visit he arrived hastily and very late, and after apologizing over and over, stayed a mere ten minutes. He played songs from Shakespeare and lieder from Hölderlin for me (later I often sang them in public). As I had noticed with other composers, his playing did not reflect precisely what he himself had written down, especially in tempi and volume.

One can count on the fingers of one hand the composers who are also satisfactory pianists. Best that they do not play at all.

In 1958 Irmel and I were touring the United States. In Cleveland the sight of the rotunda in front of the hotel struck us as a deliverance. Flowers and open vistas, and proximity to the arena of our trial, Severance Hall, lightened our mood. Our first quarters, in downtown Cleveland with all its ugliness and gloom, had deeply depressed us. The walls spewed out noise day and night, and no request was filled promptly, let alone accurately. Now that we had moved, we could see the outline of the fabled Severance Hall through our window, and only a short walk brought us to the door.

My anxiety at my first meeting with George Szell was not relieved by remembering my cancellation the previous year—a result of the Cuban crisis, a time when I was reluctant to cross the ocean. "Extremely sorry and disappointed" was Szell's reply to my letter; but he had closed with an understanding "cordial greetings," approximating the customary German closing.

Now the maestro wished to go over the Handel aria and the *Songs of a Wayfarer* with the piano before laying them before the orchestra. He was sitting at the grand piano in his small office, his face with its rimless glasses stuck deep in a score, scarcely seeming to take any notice of the newcomer, whose tongue was beginning to stick to the roof of his mouth in anxiety. But after the aria came a brightened face and the remark, "I can see that we can do the Mahler straight with the orchestra."

So there it was, the site of so many extremely sensitive

and smooth recordings that had long set standards for the avid collector: a not very large theater, converted into a concert hall, that immediately explained the forced, quick orchestral sound (not unlike that of the Philadelphia Orchestra). In the front rows sat some of the students and assistants Szell had gathered around him, turning Cleveland into a mecca for budding conductors. And then began a sensible rehearsal—not a bit hot-tempered, as gossip had led me to expect. When it was over I felt that a natural merging could not help but occur. The man who had so proudly unlocked these magic sounds insisted that on the three nights of performance, quite contrary to my custom, I sit in the last row of the auditorium on the little jump seat, done up in my tailcoat, and listen to Dvořák's Symphony in G-sharp. It was very important to Szell to demonstrate his special relationship with the orchestra. "You'll see, every night I take the people for a walk somewhere else."

And in fact, I was astonished at the possible variations in this music played by 120 musicians. After the final concert one of the women's clubs that play such a significant role in America held a reception. It was one of those occasions on which the conductor and the soloist had to suffer through all the characteristic unpleasantness of such gatherings. After about an hour of noisy chatter by 200 guests, while I held a drink that I never raised to my lips, Szell vehemently and angrily pulled me into an adjoining room, where delicious food was still patiently waiting to be tasted. "I'm sure you're hungry. Let's start." And silently and undisturbed we ate our fill, until I grabbed Irmel and we left before the wave broke over us.

The first year I was singing opera, Heinrich Schlusnus, who for the last time was alternating with me in the part of Posa in *Don Carlo*, said to me in the waiting room of an otolaryngologist, "Young man, never go to a post-performance reception!"

His wise warning has echoed in my ears ever since. And every time I did not heed it, I was sorry afterward. Who among the guests is humane enough to understand that after the exertions of a performance the artist needs to relax and eat something? He surely is not eager to tax his patience listening to the compliments of people who have already had a good dinner. What rich hostess ever thinks about how wrung-out the concert singer or opera hero feels after a performance? As for the strain on the voice, I need only say that standing around with a glass in one's hand, trying to make oneself heard over many competing voices speaking all at once and through clouds of smoke, produces hoarseness—for even singers cannot be so rude as to remain silent in the face of any and all questions.

On the second day of our stay we were cordially received in Szell's home. The inside of his house, at the center of the white ghetto, was unbelievably elegant. We immediately fell into examining the many Postimpressionist paintings lining the walls, rare examples of the pointillists and Nabis. We were so absorbed that we did not notice that our hostess had come into the room. She may have been in her fifties. Her head was that of a smallish predatory animal, velvety, with reddish hair. She was beautiful, and though her voice was soft, it was so penetrating that one stood to attention at once. Without my realizing it, she had her claws in me. The impression probably arose because she contradicted Szell and I felt compelled to make eye contact. He uttered hardly a sentence that she left uncontested. He no longer noticed. After dinner we took leave of the women and retired to his paneled study. Each of his remarks made me feel that he was now eager to "initiate" me into new areas, into his way of programming, into works new to me. "You absolutely have to sing Mozart's 'Mentre ti lascio'; just listen."

Szell played any score wonderfully softly and with crystal clarity. Naively and unthinkingly I relaxed and chattered away freely. I could not conceal my immense ignorance. Perhaps to amend it, but surely also because he wanted to express a liking for me, as we left he gave me a gift of a first edition of Eduard Hanslick's *Vom musikalischen Schönen*. When I read it I understood which beauty it was that Szell and Hanslick loved in common—the "resounding moved form."

There were the most wonderful results when we performed, and then immediately recorded, Gustav Mahler's *Wunderhorn* songs with Elisabeth Schwarzkopf in London's Festival Hall. Even Szell's nervous obsession with speed, which usually led to time-consuming rehearsals, his compulsive need always to have an opinion different from others', and his considerable paranoia when it came to the orchestra's ill will—none of these could prevent me from appreciating his ability and his warm, even enthusiastic, praise of my contribution. During a break in the rehearsal he called me back to the podium to confess to me in a low voice that he had never before encountered a singer in whom the internal and the external coincided to such a degree. "Your commitment and musicianship are admirable."

Vulnerable as he was, Szell protected himself against disturbance and confusion. To make music that is clear and transparent is not an automatic skill that, once acquired, is never forgotten; it must be striven for over and over again, endlessly. A man like Szell must have the strength to say: "This is the way I want it. And to make it that way, I must reject anything that might prove damaging." The tension between the enormous wealth of individual musical experience and all the additional knowledge and feeling that might still be added to it was intense. Everyone who carries this world inside himself is constantly faced with the decision of what to reject. And the judgments of those who have no inner world at all are invariably presumptuous and petty. Szell was always prepared to go on either the attack or the defensive—something he shared with Karl Böhm, as he did the compulsion to choose as quickly as possible a lightning rod from among the musicians in front of him, who in the end served to keep his working spirits up. His attitude was determined first of all, by confidence in his manual skills, which he did not use as armor but as his shell, as part of himself. He saved emotional language for special occasions; he was suspicious of anything that was merely polite. He deeply mistrusted unintentional confusions of sound and disturbances in the purely musical aspects of a composition. He was even capable of denouncing a master such as Hugo Wolf for insufficient musicianship, rejecting the composer's declamatory style and his way of through-composing. After a Mörike recital with lieder by Wolf in Lucerne, Szell rushed into the dressing room in great excitement. "How can you sing anything like that, Dieter, that isn't music at all!"

Perhaps he can be called a chemist among conductors, able, as was almost no other, to keep the sounds of the orchestra pure and distinct. That judgment should not tempt us, however, carelessly to pigeonhole him as one of the "analytical" conductors; when he worked he brought music to life, breathing, inspired. Recently a well-known conductor demonstrated on television alterations Gustav Mahler had made in Schumann's symphonies, mentioning also George Szell's changes, which at times went even further than Mahler's. Then he gave musical examples, but unfortunately he never went beyond theory, since there was in them nothing that could be recognized as Szell's sound, and even less of his breathing musicianship.

Only when he was dealing with Beethoven did Szell come off stiff and overly correct in some passages, deferring to the idea of the "classical." And instantly the Americans called him the classicist, in comparison with whom no other star of the art of conducting could dare hope to be accepted as an equal. His Cleveland Orchestra, a jewel he cut and polished personally, was set adrift by his sudden death after twenty-four years of increasing solidarity.

To see the maestrissimo Herbert von Karajan acclaimed from afar is quite a different experience from being near him. Up close he is the picture of relaxation and kindness, showing an interest in every detail of people's lives, never stinting on helpful hints for those working with him. Toward the end of our performances of Brahms' *German Requiem* in Salzburg, I let slip my wish that after such an experience we should not have to take bows. Karajan immediately forbade any further curtain calls.

When he was still doing stage direction as well, I admired his highly practical system of rehearsal; it saved the voice by relying on a previous recording. Karajan's left hand held a small cassette player, which he rewound as he felt the need, allowing us to act according to his musical and stage vision, free from the always time-consuming arrangements with the rehearsal pianist. He had an inimitable way of making clear to me, still a young singer, trait for trait the character of the Father of the Gods in *Das Rheingold*, from the way he was to hold his spear to his furious resignation at the end. Among directors Karajan was a truly professional guide for performers.

The recording of *Rheingold*, however, was not made under a lucky star. Both of us were somewhat physically handicapped—Karajan by the back pain that had already become severe, and I by a plaster cast on my left foot, having broken a bone during the dress rehearsal for *Otello*. Respectively crippled, we greeted each other with laughter when I arrived at the Jesus-Christus-Kirche in Dahlem. He politely helped me up the steps to the singer's podium. And then the smooth, bewitching sound of the Berlin Philharmoniker ran along my nerve endings, compelling me to the utmost intensity of which I was capable. Though unfortunately we could record only a few scenes during these winter rehearsals, we had prepared the entire part with the piano in my apartment, to which Karajan was happy to come. The rest was recorded during two synchronizing sessions when, quite alone in the dark, storm-lashed church, I conjured my contributions onto the prerecorded tape. The result was a wonderful recording; in a letter Karajan recalled all the obstacles in the process, while at the same time congratulating me on successfully realizing "the Renaissance man such as I imagine him."

After Fritz Wunderlich died, Karajan got the idea of

entirely recasting a recording of Haydn's *Creation* that was already three-quarters finished. And so I stepped in for Walter Berry, and for the first time I experienced this splendid work in the maestro's spacious, grandly arranged interpretation.

Britten's *War Requiem* and the *St. Matthew Passion* were two other works I was privileged to sing for Karajan, the latter in the baroque manner, letting the soloists set the pace. And then the ten years of my contract were up. This was the maestro's custom with most singers—he dealt with the relevance of newly emergent names.

But though this custom might be hurtful, the memory of special musical experiences more than compensates for the pain. Herr von Karajan, by the way, tended to reveal the extent of his power rather indirectly: At times the halls or studios are out of bounds to mere mortals because he has chosen to use them just then, sometimes on the spur of the moment; it did not seem to matter that scheduled rehearsals had to be canceled, no matter how urgent they were. But the maestro shares this attitude with many others similarly invested with absolute power.

When at Oxford University Harold Macmillan handed Herr von Karajan and me honorary doctorates, conferred on musicians for the first time in many years, the sun was streaming through the upper windows of the hall. And when the doors opened so that the solemn procession in medieval headgear and gowns might start its way through the cheering throngs of passersby, trumpets joined the organ. Karajan was walking next to me, the two of us silent as befitted the solemnity of the moment. Suddenly I heard his deep bass voice: "Don't walk in time to the music!"

I flinched and made an effort to catch a syncopated step between the beats. Of course a man so used to com-

manding and staging was driven to direct even these proceedings. And I, lost in distant thoughts, had paid no
attention to my marching step. . . .

At times an American conductor, with quite a different
temperament, was promoted, especially by the Viennese,
as a rival to the Austrian. In the 1950s and 1960s few men
represented the United States so distinctively and so "personally" as Leonard Bernstein. On a flight to the United
States I was given a brochure about the country that featured a portrait of Bernstein. It was taken for granted that
he represented America. He still brings his entire artistic
being to whatever he does, imbuing it with love for the
work—a phenomenon that has become all too rare.

It was characteristic of Bernstein's Mahler series, an
overwhelming experience I was privileged to share. He
brought a fiery intensity to all of Mahler's important
works. His versions were faithful though marked by in-
terpretive freedom. The studio recordings that Bernstein
produced concurrently led to the rediscovery—even a
popular revival—of Mahler throughout the world, a result
no one could have predicted. Bernstein shared with "his"
composer an absoluteness, a will to hear in new ways, a
will to discovery, to suffering on the way to success; and
this success can never be wholly achieved by any genius.

But of course bias was not in his nature. He conducted
everything there was for a musician to conquer. Without
abandoning the famous American orchestral perfection,
he brought to European stages new qualities of ecstatic
expression, visible in the person of the conductor and
made audible by his performers. Young people profited

for life, older ones in a rut were startled out of their routine, like-minded spirits felt that they were understood. Many people held it against Bernstein that he always aimed at the most popular effects, utilizing all the media and embarking on new and successful methods. But they forgot their petty concerns when they heard the results.

In his early years conducting opera in Milan, Bernstein met Maria Callas and never forgot her. I don't think I ever felt more handsomely acknowledged than when in the 1960s he said that "Maria and Dietrich" were his favorite singers. To have Bernstein behind you in the concert hall at the grand piano or in front of you in the recording studio means not "accompaniment" in the usual sense but something more like the "Tiger Rag." Between his hands and the keyboard something like an electrified zone is created; it seems as if he were advancing into a dangerous area that gives him no choice but to fight or flee. When we were recording the Mahler lieder in New York, he had five concert grands set up in a circle, and he moved—more or less outraged—to the next instrument as soon as he found something to dislike in the mechanics of the previous one. During a concert, as if reluctant to start playing out of the blue, he will always let his hands glide silently across the keys while the audience is still applauding. But then there is one electric shock after another—continually paraphrased rubati, always surprising coloration, something exceedingly intimate and yet extending far beyond the edge of the stage— and the singers must prove themselves a match for these if they are to succeed. During the intermission of a lieder recital in Carnegie Hall, in which he was not my accompanist, Lenny sat down in my dressing room, sunk in

_____

thought and taciturn. Only when he was leaving did he say, "I just wanted to hear singing of this quality one more time."

After I had appeared with him many times in New York, Bernstein and I also took part in a memorably difficult Carnegie Hall concert. The venerable hall, where Tchaikovsky, Dvořák, and Toscanini had performed, was to be sold and razed. Unless . . . The then president, the violinist Isaac Stern, and his right-hand man, Julius Bloom, wrote to me asking if, along with other prominent musicians, I would be willing to participate without pay in a benefit to save Carnegie Hall. Vladimir Horowitz was to "accompany" me.

So one afternoon Julia and I arrived at Horowitz's apartment on New York's East Side. It seemed to me a gloomily furnished cave, in which purple and black predominated. Wanda Horowitz, née Toscanini, entertained us for an hour until her husband, refreshed by his customary nap, came into the room, beaming, wearing a dressing gown with a flashy handkerchief in the breast pocket. After a short chat, during which Horowitz searched, seemingly with great difficulty, for a name— "Wilhelm K—, Wilhelm K—, Wilhelm Kempff,"—we got down to work. We went straight through the *Dichterliebe* without repetitions or closer examination. "Forty years ago I played the cycle with a soprano," was his only comment.

The following day the dress rehearsal was held in Carnegie Hall. Representatives of CBS, the company committed to recording the live performance, were also at the rehearsal. It gave me enormous pleasure to sing with Horowitz, and if a tape had been running, we would have a truly remarkable document today. But unfortunately, as always happens on such occasions there was no technician to be seen. Lenny sat in the empty auditorium, visibly moved.

The following night the house was filled with all the stars of the American musical world, from Rudolf Bing to Eugene Ormandy, from Luciano Pavarotti to Marilyn Horne. Just before we were to begin, Mr. Bloom told me of a change in the program: I was not to appear until nearly midnight, the next-to-last act. You cannot imagine what it means to sit within the cardboard walls of a dressing room, hearing Rostropovich to the left, Horowitz to the right, Menuhin behind me and Isaac Stern a little farther off, all practicing, for hours. My *Dichterliebe*, my mood, and time ran out.

When my moment finally came, I had nothing left but a reedy little voice. Filled with utter repugnance, I nevertheless acceded to Horowitz's request to take him by the arm and lead him to the piano. In his three hours of rehearsing, the old gentleman had used up much of his strength, and his hand was trembling in mine as he repeatedly muttered, "I am always with you. I am always with you."

Well, this prophecy did not come entirely true, as can be heard on the recording made that night. Nevertheless, the phrase kept coming from his lips like an incantation: "I was always with you."

Scarcely had we reached the safe port of the wings when stagehands rushed up to us to hand us scores for the improvised finale with chorus and orchestra, the "Halleluia" from Handel's *Messiah*. The soloists arranged themselves somewhat timidly along the stage apron; I was standing between Yehudi Menuhin and Mstislav Rostropovich. We all sang our hearts out, even Lenny and Isaac

Stern, but in all my life I have never heard so many wrong notes.

As I made my exhausted way out of the building to go home, I met Bernstein on the stairs, going up as I was coming down. He smiled slightly as he called out to me, "I know, I know!"

Between 1955 and 1980 I toured the United States fourteen times. Though my impressions varied, for all the continent's youth and size I could never think of it without recalling the witty comment of Erwin Chargaff, the biochemist: "America is exactly as little Moritz thought it would be."

Each time New York presents a different face, and it is a shocker for the visitor who likes to look around. Strange, and more intense than anywhere else in the United States, are the sounds and noises, the neurasthenic pulse of a city that never sleeps but never seems fully awake. It displays an intelligence both uneducated and arrogant, unbridled violence, extremes of filth alongside the kind of fake luxury that cannot get enough of glitter. Then there is the purchased praise that must be part of any political or commercial career (the two are related), which ends in imprisonment or obscurity. The confused, grammatically distorted language, the constant misuse of superlatives that makes it almost impossible to go on believing in any kind of future. The consequent drug addiction and alcoholism. All these achievements of "progress" have since been exported to Europe, even the canned cheerfulness, the smirks and grins, that has made the country and its people ever more ill-tempered. It will surely not be long before the rest of the world reaches the same condition. It seemed therefore almost a miracle that the "old-fashioned" subjects of my recitals were accepted, even loved! Their principal theme is tragedy, which Americans reject or despise as immoral. But New York audiences were so insatiable, and my manager (Ann Colbert) so cheerfully inventive, that it became possible to produce subscription series of lieder recitals in Carnegie Hall that were sold out and loudly acclaimed. Later I performed such serial recitals in Frankfurt am Main, Berlin, and Munich. They give the audience an opportunity to listen their way into the style and program of one interpreter, achieving a better understanding and more objective judgment.

Another conductor friend was very German, deeply rooted in Munich. Wolfgang Sawallisch showed the absolute falseness of many mistaken judgments by his deeply committed manner, inspired by piety, that newly unlocked Schubert's masses not only to the public but also to me, a participant. Time and again he cleared the way for such novelties as Paul Hindemith's oratorical works. Hindemith's choral composition *Das Unaufhörliche*, on a text by Gottfried Benn, and his requiem *Als Flieder jüngst* (When Lilacs Last . . .), based on Walt Whitman, with me as the soloist under Sawallisch's baton, sounded much more convincing than was the case when the composer conducted. It seems only right, too, to emphasize the power of persuasion with which Sawallisch shaped the taut strains of Brahms' *German Requiem,* and at the same time allowed the harsh rhythms of Dmitri Shostakovich's Fourteenth Symphony to contribute to the emotionally moving effect of the work, even if they were elicited from an opera

183

orchestra quite unaccustomed to performing in concert. Julia and I witnessed a number of such performances.

A life spent in helping others to become effective in their own right, having to instruct them in what they are to do or not do as instrumentalists or singers, has its own difficulties. And it is unlikely that there is a conductor whose secret or overt love is not for solo appearances; most of them began their careers that way, after all. Wolfgang Sawallisch took what amounted to fiendish delight in occasionally taking the "more passive" role of someone who is merely inquisitive about his soloist's intentions, letting them, without much ado, become reality. Whether the soloist in question was a string or wind player from the orchestra—all of whom, thanks to their conductor's initiative, regularly had a chance to stand out—or one of his singers, who cared as much as he did about art songs, Sawallisch always honored the code of the chamber musician. The fact that at times a glance suffices to resolve a problem of ensemble playing or that a verbal hint is enough to reveal the essential element of an interpretation explains why Sawallisch usually does not bother to make notes on his conductor's score, any more than he feels it necessary to mark up the full score. Whatever he has absorbed of the wealth of the repertoire and has amassed in practical experience enter as a matter of course into a reading that also recognizes everything important in a score, grasping it as a whole even as it respects each detail. In this too lies his very crucial difference from those conductors who only conduct, without really having mastered an instrument at concert level. Their scores are usually dotted with so many marks and colors that the notes can barely be discerned.

As both conductor and pianist, Sawallisch has a genius

Bologna 1944.

With Wilhelm Furtwängler,
Salzburg 1950.
ELLINGER/SALZBURG

With Irmgard Poppen,
Berlin 1961.

With Gerald Moore,
Berlin 1969.
SIEGFRIED LAUTERWASSER

With Karl Böhm, Berlin 1963. DIETHER WARNECK

With Benjamin Britten,
London 1963.

Rehearsing *Don Giovanni*
with Ferenc Fricsay,
Berlin 1961.

With Herbert von Karajan, Berlin 1972.   SIEGFRIED LAUTERWASSER

With Elisabeth Schwarzkopf
and Julia Varady, Munich 1985.
FELICITAS TIMPE

With Sviatoslav Richter,
Tours 1977.   DG/KNECHT

With Eugen Jochum,
Munich 1985.
FELICITAS TIMPE

With Harmut Höll,
Salzburg 1985.
SCHAFFLER/SALZBURG

Eighty-fifth anniversary of Carnegie Hall, May 18, 1976.
Yehudi Menuhin, Dietrich Fischer-Dieskau, Mstislav Rostropovich,
Vladimir Horowitz, Leonard Bernstein, Isaac Stern. CARNEGIE HALL ARCHIVES

As Macbeth,
with Grace Bumbry, Salzburg 1964.
PRESSEBÜRO SALZBURGER FESTSPIELE

Dantons Tod, Berlin 1963.
ILSE BUHS

As Lear, with Julia Varady, Munich 1978. SABINE TOEPFFER

With Julia Varady
in *Arabella*,
Berlin 1977.
JÜRGEN KRANICH

Below left:
As Hans Sachs,
Berlin 1976.
SIEGFRIED LAUTERWASSER

Below right:
As Falstaff,
Vienna 1966.
FAYER WIEN

In his garden in Berg at the Starnberger See. WOLFGANG HAUT

for accompanying; he does not sacrifice his individuality, whether he is applying himself to the fairly problematic orchestral songs of Hanz Pfitzner (and not forgetting to eliminate typographical errors) or cleanly and clearly performing Richard Strauss' piano intricacies as if they were the simplest thing in the world. There are long stretches of an opera performance during which the conductor's attention is focused more on the singers than on the orchestra. It has happened to me that while singing a major role I saw before me a very clearly mimed expression from the conductor; at that moment such an instruction was more confusing than helpful, since the director might have insisted on a quite different way of acting out the moment. Sawallisch saw the truth as dwelling in what was simple, free of artifice. Of necessity this attitude means that great sentimentality is not in his nature, and this leads to a combination of personality traits unusual in a conductor of Wagner and Strauss. Only rarely have I met a conductor who could resist the temptation to let conductor's music (the only way to describe Wagner's) turn into a conductor's monument. Sawallisch opposes all sentimentality to such an extent that even phrasing in a long line might appear to him too pretentious, so he tightens them in order to avoid any subjective emphasis. In this he may be comparable only to Leo Blech, who in the past purged Wagner astonishingly, and at the same time opened up such "conversation pieces" as *Die Meistersinger von Nürnberg* to the point that the words were crystal clear.

When Sawallisch is conducting, the listeners are spared the burden of overly narrow preinterpretation; they are free to listen along actively. This is related to Sawallisch's rejection of any intellectual observations based on nonmusical considerations—not because he is incapable of reconstructing such an interpretation or conveying it to his musicians, but because his way of working simply has no use for it. He looks only for appropriate expression—that is, nothing that would falsify the composer's text—without subjective slant.

I first worked with Karl Richter in 1958, on the separate recording of the four bass arias from the *St. Matthew Passion.* With forced cheerfulness I tried to break through the somewhat stultifying atmosphere. The quiet, shy man on the podium and the new, not exactly quick-witted recording team all seemed determined to maintain a mute hauteur. Although I did hear criticism on details, which were immediately remedied, there was not a single encouraging or helpful word. I felt that my pleasure in the work was arousing suspicion. Secretly I was annoyed with the "slowpokes" who were aware only of the difficulties but took achievements for granted, without comment; they seemed complacently asleep.

This recording, along with that of Bach's Mass in B-minor, is one of my favorites. It reflects fairly accurately my idea of what aria singing in Bach should be: resembling a leading instrument that nevertheless is given the most concise expression through the text and does not merely sound along with the music. Having heard only recordings, at that time I could only guess at the brio of Richter's concert performances, combining as he did the force of his intellectual temperament with coldly distant calculation. Nor had I yet learned of the apocalyptic mood, which might easily be called panic, that overcame him frequently—caused, of course, by the onset of his progressive eye disease.

Only when he came to the Hotel Vier Jahreszeiten to invite me to work with him in his London debut did I realize how much Karl Richter actually thought of me. For this, his most important concert, we agreed on Handel's *Apollo e Dafne*. The performance was made very difficult, almost spoiled, by the equipment made available to us in London.

Like so many "specialists," Richter was eager to step outside the customary sphere of liturgical baroque music and conquer opera. This ambition began to be realized when we recorded Gluck's *Orfeo* in Munich. The occasion proved that Richter's conducting was marked less by virtuosity than by inspiration, the reverse of his harpsichord and organ playing. If he did not master the musical material immediately, he held the failure against himself, and he could spread about him a good measure of ill temper, so that any attempt to clear the air was more or less ineffectual. But one could always rely on the accuracy of his ear. And when the work came to an end, there was a charming postperformance chat over champagne; Dr. Farese, the immensely important language coach, who had carried out his task with gentleness, joined us.

For a long time Richter, shy and awkward as only a German can be, addressed me as "Herr Kammersänger"—the latter word denoting a title awarded to outstanding singers by local or federal authorities—until I begged him to call me by my first name. The respectable collection of cantatas we recorded within the Bach edition with the Hamburg Archiv Produktion brought us together repeatedly in Munich's Herkules-Saal, where Edith Mathis and Peter Schreier joined us. On these occasions, and in concert performances of the Passions, I admired Richter's ability to draw upon his deep religious feeling. During the party following the final recording session for the cantatas he proudly announced to Julia that just the day before he had had laser surgery on his eyes but had experienced no pain and now felt wonderful.

I have rarely seen an artist whose job it was to capture and move large audiences from the podium practice his craft so masterfully and with such continually surprising novelty as this Munich "Thomas Choirmaster." A motion of the baton that was both precise and unconventional, only rarely losing itself in wide sweeps of the arm, allowed him to reconstruct the smallest emotion, immediately and freshly felt, and offer it to his audience.

One recital, which presented all three of Bach's solo cantatas for bass, also permitted me to appreciate his skill as an accompanist. And the *German Requiem*, which I was privileged to sing with him in Baden-Baden, promised a great deal in the direction of the romantics—especially in opera. Nothing that this arch-musician did was pedantic or narrowly choirmasterish. After his death in 1981 it took a long time for Munich to find a successor to the student of Karl Straube and Günther Ramin who dedicated himself to nurturing Bach. Hanns Martin Schneidt eventually took on the role, most felicitously.

The name of Rafael Kubelik elicits in me the memory of several unusually relaxed events, evenings "given over" to making music in the Herkules-Saal in Munich: Golo in Debussy's *Pelléas et Melisande*; and the precious oratorio around the Sermon on the Mount in *Les Béatitudes* by

César Franck, in which I sang Christ's words in Latin, surrounded by an excellent group of singers headed by Jessye Norman. Meeting this large black queen, who dominates place and space and who has the voice of a young girl, always set my heart fluttering. Once, it is true, in a performance of *Figaro* in which she sang the Countess, both she and I found the part where she has to sit in my lap so awkward that some of the audience snickered.

Rafael carried us above all the floods of Franck's score like a true St. Christopher.

We also did some recording in the Herkules-Saal. At the very beginning of our friendship we recorded the *Songs of a Wayfarer*; Rafael never lost a second in translating into action whatever I whispered to him in the way of my wishes, which derived from Bruno Walter. He had clearly done his homework by making himself familiar with Furtwängler's much broader interpretation. After we performed the song cycle, he grew momentarily angry at Irmel's reprimand, "Don't indicate each entrance so blatantly; Dieter knows the work!" But his good nature would not let him hold a grudge.

He was much troubled by backaches, and the recording of Paul Hindemith's *Mathis der Maler* was delayed again and again. At long last it was done, a marvel of sound.

When Kubelik and I visited La Scala in Milan for a recording of Verdi's *Rigoletto*, our hearts were beating hard. Whenever non-Italians dare to produce this national treasure in its own country, they must, understandably, count on absolute suspicion. Thus during the choral scenes I could clearly make out mutterings behind my back about what right "questo tedesco" thought he had to perform this work. By that time, though, the orchestra had already gone through the rehearsal of my first monologue with me and had vociferously cheered me. Whenever Kubelik and I ran into each other on the street after a recording session, we would commiserate with each other. The orchestra gave him the same kind of grief I had experienced with the codirector for the soloists, who reprimanded me frequently for insufficiently aspirated double consonants, closed or open o's, and other sins of pronunciation. The only trouble with these instructions was that nothing learned earlier in, say, Rome was valid for Milan.

Apparently I did not do too badly, however; the Italian newspapers were the first to praise my interpretation. To this day Italians—such as, just recently, Giuseppe Sinopoli—occasionally let me know that they are particularly fond of my Rigoletto. At my last visit to Milan the bellhop at the hotel volunteered his opinion: "Il più grande Rigoletto del mondo."

The Milan cathedral stands almost exactly across from La Scala, and once I went in to offer up a fervent prayer for the following day's recording session, which was to include several difficult passages. Inside the cathedral there was just as much chaotic activity as there was out on the streets. At the center a mass seemed to be going on; a few people, either lost in prayer or sleeping, sat in the darkness of the pews. Tourists in bright clothing that stood out against the gray walls were trotting down one of the side aisles behind a man pointing a finger into the air. The height of the nave and the smell of dust made me feel slightly ill. There were the irritating smells common to all old churches: candlewax, incense, the stale odor of the grave without refreshing coolness or stillness, old clothes, old wood, sweaty crumpled lire notes, and blending them all together, the overlying aroma of human breath and human bodies. I'm sure that some of the people had come there for a little creative thievery; a sign outside the portal warned visitors in Italian and English to beware of pickpockets. It was impossible to forget about money, since wherever you looked you saw poor boxes with little signs asking for contributions for children, for the poor, for maintenance of the cathedral. Each was protected by a strong lock, so as to keep the very poor from taking what belonged to them just as much as to anyone else. Outside the door a man was selling popcorn from a pushcart. Children ran around playing noisily. Men loitered and chatted and smoked in the entryway, where little boys sold Chiclets and candy.

6

"Sanfte geistige Gewalt"

During his years of exile Carl Ebert, once Leopold Jessner's Faust and trained as an actor by Jürgen Fehling, had developed into one of those operatic stage directors who broke new ground for the musical theater and illuminated the dramatic truth of music. In 1953, when he began his second (postwar) term at the Städtische Oper in Berlin, succeeding Tietjen, I worried that since I was not yet fully trained as an actor, I would have to step aside and would not have another opportunity.

Just the opposite happened. Ebert paid me a visit and announced to his skeptical listener that I was to sing Verdi's Falstaff. As always when faced with something new, I was reluctant at first. But after we agreed that I would think about it, I said yes; I really wanted to learn more. Since I was still totally unacquainted with comedy, I had high hopes of that undiscovered country.

The rehearsals were wonderful. Ebert had just rehearsed the work in Glyndebourne with Fernando Corena, a pure basso buffo, who apparently was not entirely satisfactory in the upper-register role. Because Ebert's concept involved bringing out the basic nature of the character, he worked on precisely controlled gestures, the most telling facial expressions, differentiated coloration. All I cared about was bringing the shapes he established to life. He gave me time to develop the character, and once we had determined the outward mask of Falstaff—for whom I was actually too young and smooth-faced—he gave me an almost entirely free hand. I quickly realized that even the most highly skilled makeup artist could not produce the simple "picturesque" effects with which I planned to equip the good-natured braggard, such as the apple cheeks that had to be made to leap out from the face by shadows and highlights. So I took on the job myself, happily painting away for the next five performances. I also arranged some of the basic movements for myself (such as the toddling walk, the finger gestures, the swing of my hips). Ebert was overjoyed at the tuft of baby hair I fixed to the center of my bald pate. The success I had with this figure (resident somewhere between England and Italy) is three-quarters due to Ebert.

Shakespeare, like Cervantes with his tilter at windmills, turned his fat knight into a figure of flesh and blood and nerves. When the character was created, it amused the royal theater patron, Queen Elizabeth, so much that she asked the playwright to serve up at once another play using Falstaff—though he was still not at the dramatic center. It was left to Antonio Salieri, in his opera *Falstaff*, and then to Otto Nicolai, in his *Merry Wives of Windsor*, to give the old Lothario the position due him. Arrigo Boito, an Italian of Polish descent, introduced some ideas and phrases from Shakespeare's *Henry IV* into his libretto, greatly enhancing the character and its effectiveness. Giuseppe Verdi's music clothed this arch-British figure in southern sensibilities, bringing him closer to the heart of Europe and raising him to a first-rate artistic creation—truly to what may arguably be the most compelling operatic character of the twentieth century. For we should not forget that "il vecchio" Verdi—after years of indecisiveness, inhibited by Nicolai's genuinely droll predecessor—wrote his opera at the beginning of this century. Much nonsense has been written about the harmful influence of Wagner on *Falstaff's* specific declamatory style, about the thinness of the melodies, and about any number of other prejudices. In reality in this work Verdi was bringing the style he had always striven for to perfection—even to a foreshadowing of the operatic theater that was to come. The brevity of the musical phrases, the syllabic singing style—none of these should blind us to the fact that we are dealing with absolutely pure Verdi. It is true that any director with ambitions of his own will find himself handed some hard nuts to crack. Not only did Verdi sketch out his ideas of how the work was to be staged, he also specified all details, down to finger movements. I was lucky enough to work with a director who had engraved this score on his heart and mind and who taught me to reconstruct it. At first, when I was still a young singer, some elements of my performance may have seemed too loutish or clownlike; these deepened into telling character traits, however, under the influence of Luchino Visconti and Günther Rennert.

In 1966 in Vienna Visconti was already deeply absorbed in preparations for his next film. He appeared under a great strain. Before the first rehearsal I bounded up on the stage to introduce myself; he and all the young Italian "retainers" surrounding him stared at me in astonishment. After all, I was a lanky, dark-haired, relatively young man. The master was used to casting his movies according to physical type rather than, as was the case in opera, respecting the prescribed vocal register.

"You are . . . my Falstaff?" Visconti whispered, already resigned. It was my privilege to change his attitude. He saw the action in the opera as rather subdued; he intended to create an integrated effect. I took a childish delight in the fact that he followed my exuberant escapades with lively interest, egging me on to even more of them. There was no longer any sign of the tired director we had met at the start, of whom Leonard Bernstein, the conductor of the production, remarked, "Uncle Luchino is asleep again!"

As rehearsals progressed, the gentleman from an ancient, esteemed Milanese family (La Scala has always been partially financed by a branch of the Visconti family) worked himself into ever more lively gestures and facial expressions, until finally at high points of exuberance he seemed to be one single uninterrupted motion.

Visconti will also remain in my memory as a great artist because of his films *Death in Venice* and *Ludwig*. Film was a medium in which he felt more confident than in opera. To omit nothing and to add nothing—I have been guided by Visconti's maxim of interpretation in the service

---

of truly great works of art ever since, whenever I had to embody Falstaff, whom Verdi was kind enough to place not in a deep bass but in a high baritone (Victor Maurel in the world premiere). And thanks to Verdi's allowing the aging drunkard to be both a knight and a senile baby (in his walk as well), shifting from somber melancholy through bursts of anger to Homeric laughter, the role is a gift to the performer. Verdi, whose own life was anything but pure delight, permitted himself shortly before his departure from this world not only a skillful fugue, of the sort he attempted only one other time (in his sole string quartet) but also built it on the text "Tutto nel mondo è burla"—Everything in the world is fun.

An important part of the success of the first night at the Städtische Oper also belonged to the conductor, Alberto Erede. Mariano Stabile, the legendary protagonist under Toscanini, had previously sung Falstaff with Erede, who told me he remembered bits and pieces of Stabile's interpretation. Erede, who lisped slightly, was altogether lacking in showmanship, and in his subsequent career he would not rise above repertory conductor, aside from his brief tenure as general musical director in Düsseldorf. Erede once came to my hotel room in Amsterdam and complained about problems of conductors, with which I was already familiar—the record companies remembered him only sporadically, the managers rarely kept their promises. He thought of producing *Falstaff* in Italian for Prague, Florence, and Rome, and I suggested that he engage Visconti as the stage director. This last idea was offered to me subsequently in Vienna by Leonard Bernstein. The impression of self-critical objectivity predominated in Erede, even if on occasion he gave way to tearful complaints about not being given his due. As a genuine Italian he knew how to flatter outrageously, without pretending to truthfulness.

Ebert realized that I could be successfully cast in the so-called problem operas. His principal director, Richard Kraus, confirmed him in this opinion. Kraus mounted a new production of Ferruccio Busoni's *Doktor Faust*, a work that had long gone unappreciated and was almost forgotten. To help me in preparing the title role, he gave me his friend Wolf Völker, a jack-of-all-trades and skilled artisan, to act as my director. Helmuth Melchert, the singing actor, came from Hamburg to sing Mephisto. The success of the opening night was such that the work could be performed fourteen times more in the next two seasons.

One night Igor Stravinsky, an old enemy of Busoni, was sitting in the stage box; when the performance ended, he came on the stage. Behind his thick lenses his wide-open eyes glowed with excitement, as he said, "I never knew that Busoni was such a good composer! One of the most important evenings I've ever spent at the opera."

Not much later Sir Adrian Boult got in touch with me from London to ask me to suggest possible cuts for a concert performance in Festival Hall. I sent my ideas to him by return mail, and eventually I had the great pleasure of singing in a successful performance with this ever-young champion of new music in England.

After Ebert rediscovered Verdi's *A Masked Ball* in the late 1920s and presented it with overwhelming success, he thought of staging it again. I had sung Renato under Fritz Busch's baton as early as 1950 in Cologne, in a concert version performed during Busch's last visit to Germany. It took place in the large broadcasting hall of the West German Radio, which at the time was still under construction; the soloists had to get to the stage by climbing over planks. It was winter and bitter cold; in the hall we could see our breath as we sang. All the members of the ensemble suffered from colds. Thus I was not able to give my full attention to the single run-through with piano. Busch himself was at the grand, and when at one point I began to sing nonexistent notes, he shot a glance at me over his glasses and called out, "Don't compose, young man!"

It was under Busch that I learned for the first time the true meaning of Italian brio. His temperament swept us all up, and the performance was justifiably preserved in a recording. Unfortunately none of the great plans Busch and I forged (including *La Forza del Destino*) became reality because after the subsequent concert in Hamburg he was granted only one more public appearance, in Copenhagen, his beloved home-in-exile, before his death.

Almost ten years later, when Wolfgang Sawallisch was conducting *A Masked Ball* in Berlin (the stage director was Fritz Busch's old companion, Carl Ebert), I could finally present my Renato on the stage. It was a success for Sawallisch that was something like a breakthrough; it was also the beginning of our long friendship, which stood us in good stead whenever we worked together on Italian pieces. Today, for reasons unknown, people begrudge German conductors any success in the Italian repertoire on international stages. *Don Carlo, Falstaff,* and *Macbeth* under Sawallisch became high points of my operatic career.

In the late 1960s I met with Erede again, when we produced Giacomo Puccini's *Gianni Schicchi* in Cologne with Karl O. Koch. I had to send the outraged powers that be a telegram to let them know that I had a cold but would nevertheless be there. As happened frequently, the cold disappeared during my flight to Cologne, so that I had no hesitation in recording the complicated role of Gianni in two days.

Erede, the conductor—a charming man and a charming conversationalist—relied on others. "Bon voyage," he would call to the musicians when an unrehearsed ten-minute take was about to be recorded. Of course this method necessitated corrections, which were all the more awkward. Since in addition Erede sat fairly far away from his soloists, I took my bearings more from the movement of his glowing white beard than from his baton.

After *Doctor Faustus* I felt much more severely challenged when Ebert hired me for Alban Berg's *Wozzeck*, based on the Georg Büchner play. The 1959 revival had sets by Theo Otto, direction again by Wolf Völker, and musical supervision by Richard Kraus. The production stimulated other houses to stage the opera. Berg's music naturally led me deeper into the style of the new musical theater. In order to reveal Wozzeck's animal suffering, I had to call upon all my powers of dramatic expression in singing and acting, perhaps precisely because *Wozzeck* tested the limits of my ability vocally, psychologically, and musically.

Conversely, *Mathis der Maler* by Paul Hindemith— normally an extremely demanding role—seemed almost child's play. The Spanish soprano Pilar Lorengar was making her debut in the role of Regina; her beauty and the splendor of her voice enraptured the entire ensemble. Though she spoke only broken German, her animation contributed greatly to our success. Ebert loved to have such beautiful creatures around him. On another occasion he would not rest until he had translated into theatrical pluses the problems posed by Da Ponte's libretto for *Don Giovanni*, which never really gives the hero a chance to be a conqueror, while presenting him only dimly as a lover.

The new opera house on Bismarckstrasse was inaugurated by Ebert—though only to witness his almost immediate departure, since Gustav Rudolf Sellner had already succeeded him as manager. The rehearsals for this last premiere under Ebert's aegis began with a great deal of praise for my conception of the role and a completely uncharacteristic faith in my success. It seemed to me that Ebert was far less malicious than formerly. I had had high hopes of him for the technical details of my second Don Giovanni. But Ebert seemed entirely concerned with the musical arrangement; at first he was mischievous, then nervous. His departure and replacement by Sellner no doubt had a detrimental effect on our work. The way rehearsals were structured was anything but helpful.

In her direct way Irmel risked a kind of reproach one day when she attended a stage rehearsal. She suggested that Ebert ask someone to bring him a cup of coffee or a snack now and then. The old gentleman, who was not devoid of vanity, interpreted this remark to mean that Irmel had succumbed to his masculine charm, promptly earning us a place in his good books.

Once I had a "black Friday," when Ferenc Fricsay tried for an hour and a half to impose his dramatic ideas on me. Perhaps because of the advanced stage of his illness, Fricsay behaved overbearingly; there was no way I could reconcile his ideas with Ebert's. But at least this instruction was delivered in private, and I was grateful for that. Nevertheless, it left me feeling quite insecure. Because the premiere was to be taped for television, Ebert had called in a fencing master just before that evening, so that the opening scene could be worked out telegenically in close-up as well. The professional trainer lashed out at Josef Greindl, who was somewhat corpulent and no longer young, and me, who had little aptitude for athletics. Whatever we might have achieved in rehearsal up to that point was lost under the sergeantlike barks of the trainer. Terrible visions arose of a new barracks discipline. A rebellious word of protest had no effect whatever, and so we crept away, soaked with sweat and scorned, like poor sinners. This ordeal was followed by four hours of exhausting orchestra rehearsal, during which Fricsay seemed to have a very good time issuing his suggestions for changes. As far as I was concerned, the last straw was the many stairs in Georges Wakhevitch's set that had to be climbed backward, with my muscles already stiff from the afternoon's exertions.

I made a mental note for the future: In such cases it's a matter of quietly overcoming anxiety, screwing up all your self-confidence even when it seems impossible to find any, not listening to anything said to you but knowing in yourself what you are doing, relying on your own artistic judgment, even—and especially—when there are a lot of people who have a say. This holds true as well whenever you feel yourself harassed by unfair reviews. Like apparitions from a better world, my two sons, Mathias and Martin, stood backstage and waved at me.

As the opening night drew nearer, the humanitarian in Ebert awoke to such an extent that he called it "adorable" when I made a mistake in a couple of steps of the choreography. And the only result of all the fencing practice was that during the second performance Greindl drove his sword into the back of my hand with such zest that blood spurted. I grew dizzy from shock and weakness. When, two scenes later, bright stage lights glared over the rearranged steps and illuminated the arena of the realistic battle, I stared at the tiny puddle of blood I had left behind. Fortunately the theater physician merely gave a mocking smile as he bandaged my hand.

After Ebert had actually done what he was given to threatening—resign—he suffered from feelings of abandonment far away in his home in Pacific Palisades near Los Angeles. Once, after giving some concerts, I visited him in his home, which was hidden behind lush espaliered roses; I was appalled at the uninterrupted marital battles of the old couple. With all his screaming, Ebert managed to reminisce with me only for a few minutes. Always "something came up." Shortly thereafter I wrote to him suggesting that he accept free-lance assignments as a stage director.

"Yes, I'd rather return to the prison that is Berlin than dry up intellectually here," he replied. But his last work in Berlin, a new mounting of the Glyndebourne production of Stravinsky's *The Rake's Progress*, did not really succeed. In 1972, at eighty-five, he wrote me, paraphrasing *Tannhäuser*, "I look up at only one of the stars—and the period of shared struggle, refining the right, the true expression, the search for perfection stand before me once more."

Ebert had called me FiDi; soon I was known by that name all over the building on Richard-Wagner Strasse, and shortly after that, elsewhere as well.

In 1954 I was given a glimpse behind the rosy curtain I had mentally placed around Bayreuth when I was young.

Winifred Wagner, director of the festival during the 1930s, honored an old custom by inviting the singers making their debuts at Bayreuth to tea, along with old friends. Some years before, she had moved into the "Führerbau" next to Villa Wahnfried, where she lived surrounded by magnificent pictures and priceless manuscripts from the Wagner period. Wieland Wagner, her son, stayed next door in the main house, in a somewhat self-consciously furnished "modern" apartment, very colorful and with windows that could be opened and closed electrically. He had not once set foot in Winifred's rooms in all those years—surely more from outside coercion than from conviction. As we left, we saw him say good-bye to company of his own outside his front door. Mother and son exchanged not so much as a glance. No sooner had Wieland disappeared from view than Winifred, without the least embarrassment, began to rail at the "lack of style and arbitrariness" of his productions. Her steely eyes impressed me as those of someone who is both hot-tempered and obsessed with herself. She surreptitiously pulled my cigarette pack from my jacket pocket, only to offer me cigarette after cigarette from it. Then she pointed to one of the guests, the daughter of the once-famous conductor Arthur Nikisch. To the young woman's great embarrassment, Frau Winifred inevitably spoke of her as "resembling a noble steed." The evening sun shed its light on the banister and on the Lenbach paintings on the walls. Winifred revealed that one of these, a portrait of Siegfried Wagner, was a "youthful mistake" by Wieland, though it seemed to me a very successful imitation of the Lenbach style. While we were still looking at the picture, the lady of the house uttered such pearls of wisdom as "Picasso is an incompetent" and "Art must bring joy." This was enough to destroy my pleasure in the young man's work of art.

This must be the way monarchs speak. I thought of the laudatory references to Hitler in the course of the conversation, of his relationship with the lady in the very early Nazi days, when, she claimed, she brought him blankets and food to the Landsberg Fortress when he was imprisoned there. Twice the monomaniac asked for her hand in marriage. But the daughter-in-law of the prince of music put him off—anyone worthy of courting the young widow of Siegfried Wagner could not possibly hold a rank lower than that of Reich Chancellor. Would it have fallen to the lot of a Frau Winifred Hitler to help prevent the catastrophic course of events? Not until 1940 did the friendship between the two break completely, when Hitler stopped visiting Bayreuth. We listened in silence as she made all these statements.

Sometimes an astonishing light can be shed by a lack of comment as well. In a television interview, discussing Syberberg's film about her, Winifred Wagner sought to defend it against her son Wolfgang's outrage over the "revelations" disclosed in the film. Consciously or unconsciously she confirmed, even glorified, those elements that were allegedly to be glossed over. Is it necessary to draw a mystical veil over these events that are not so very far in the past?

Without a doubt Wieland Wagner's 1954 production of *Tannhäuser* opened up new perspectives of simplification and stylization and introduced new arrangements for the chorus, which were related to the choreography. The difficulties caused by the scarcity of material goods helped realize what Richard Wagner may have had in mind, a stage almost bereft of props. But precisely here it is appropriate to conjecture what Wagner really intended. The grandiose visual effects were beginning—and the process is far from complete—to take on independent life.

Our first stage rehearsal took place late at night, under the backdrop of the imposing sky of the interim Temple of the Muses. When I had finished singing the "Abendstern" aria to the accompaniment of the tinkling piano, a graying man who moved gracefully came up on the stage to me. Wieland Wagner embraced me, saying ". . . the fulfillment of what I wanted to achieve."

This cordial welcome (in Bayreuth I never met the powers that be until after I had already sung; the same thing happened with Hans Knappertsbusch, whom I did not meet until after the dress rehearsal for *Parsifal*) was to be followed a few years later by my abrupt dismissal, simply because I was unwilling to put on a hunting hat that was designed in such a way that I could not hear and thus adjust my voice. But I learned the reason only years later, through a third party.

Wieland invited us to eat with him, and we spent the afternoon on the terrace of Wahnfried in a long conversation, during which neither Irmel nor I managed truly to exchange ideas with him on even the smallest point, let alone on substantive issues. It was as if he were speaking another language. I did notice one thing: At heart he—like many other producers—was not interested in music, especially not in his grandfather's. On the contrary; if a performer wanted to use a particular bit of stage business, he had only to say that the Master had not meant it to be that way, and immediately it was made part of the production. Wieland focused on concepts that could be communicated by symbols, and the conductor was therefore bombarded with wild suggestions for cuts to be made in the music; fortunately these were rejected. The idea that music is the most suitable means for explicating the ideology of a music drama is one that occurred neither to the people involved in the production nor to the press. I was therefore never quite happy with my great personal success there as singer and actor.

Amfortas did not have an easy time of it in Bayreuth. Not only did he have to spend the whole second act and half of the third far from the solemnity of the stage, he was also made to wait an hour between each act. Once, in 1955, I decided to spend the opening of the third act on the stage. I pushed my way through huge crowds to the left front stage, which was beyond the audience's line of sight. Of course there was hardly any room in which to sit, but someone did make a little corner available to me. Behind me two firemen, standing next to the theater physician, were yawning. To my right a dancer from the flowergirls scene, wearing her robe, leaned flirtatiously against the wall. She was watching not the stage but a reporter who had just arrived, garlanded with cameras.

Parsifal was singing, "Heil mir, dass ich dich wiederfinde," with a bored face, while good old Ludwig Weber was animating his role of Gurnemanz, reacting with gestures and facial expressions. The wife of Wilhelm Pitz, the choral director, nudged me gently and, holding out some photographs of me, asked me to return them to her after the performance with my autograph. Martha Mödl was washing Parsifal's feet, as far as I could tell from her gestures. Hermann Uhde, who was in Bayreuth to sing the title role in *The Flying Dutchman*, came up to me and angrily reported a conversation he had just had with Wieland, which completely demolished all the plans he had made for the following year. Then a dutiful stage manager pushed his way to the lighted switchboard next to me and pressed several dressing-room buttons, including mine. (On other evenings I was already backstage, concentrating on my entrance.) I rushed back to my place, lay down on my sick man's pallet, and was carried in a rocking motion from the fascinating depths of the rear of the stage behind the chorus toward the orchestra. Wilhelm Pitz was standing on a chair next to the curtain, his flashlight moving to the beat, while his eyes slanted sideways to Hans Knappertsbusch. At this point I could clearly hear a penetrating whisper: "That's too bright, the audience can see it."

But then, recognizing that it was Pitz on the chair, Wolfgang Wagner patted him benevolently on the back, rather far down. After the curtain had been closed for several moments on the final tableau, I, still in character, was lying on the steps to the Grail, exhausted in body and soul. Ramon Vinay, who was singing Parsifal, came down the stairs laughing; he poked the holy spear into my side: "Hey, you finished now!" I heard, and I looked up at his face, his ordinary, everyday face. Next to me Ludwig Weber slowly unclasped his hands, stared quietly into space, and then shook my hand. "Kna," whom I had only seen once so far, after the dress rehearsal, came up on the stage from the orchestra pit and patted my shoulder, muttering some words of praise. It took the stagehands only seconds to clear the scenery, as if by magic; they set up a piano in the background because now, at ten-thirty, there was still more singing to be done.

If a singer takes the precaution of canceling rehearsals because he has a runny nose or his throat is sore, the director is quick to accuse him of shirking. When in the early 1960s rehearsals were held for the revival of *Tann-*

häuser, I experienced these symptoms, arousing Wieland's suspicions and calling them down upon my head. The panic culminated on the eve of the dress rehearsal. Cautiously and politely I asked what they thought of getting another Wolfram for the following day's exertions. My condition improved overnight, but by the next day Wieland had already concluded a "contract" with George London. Perhaps he saw the incident as a god-given opportunity to get rid of me. He must have preferred a personal, unshared triumph.

On the opening night I managed to forget all intrigues, even the conductor's flippancy ("In my orchestra two oboists are fighting over who gets to play the performance") and my sore throat. However, this lasted only until just after the beginning, when the added tension made me forget the thread of the text; I found my place again only after a line of the piano arrangement.

At the end we took individual curtain calls, most of them in pained embarrassment; we were received with measured, muted applause. When it was my turn to take a solo bow, Wieland characteristically hesitated to let me go in front of the curtain, giving me clearly to understand the actual state of affairs. But there was no way he could stop me altogether, and the shouts and applause made me happy, most of all because they could not help annoying this genius of defamation who had quietly leaked to the press a story about my "dislike of work," just the sort of thing the papers were always hungry for.

I did not suffer quite so long as Joseph Keilberth did from the abrupt firing from Bayreuth, which sent me away in the midst of a great triumph. Although my contract covered the following year as well, Wieland Wagner—prudently in a private meeting—announced to me that the next year's Wolfram had already been assigned to a Viennese colleague. Later, much later, I learned that the true cause of my dismissal was the scorned hunting hat. It was no surprise, then, that I never heard from Bayreuth again until Wieland's premature death. Every year Christmas cards dutifully arrived from the site of the Festival, putting me into a slightly melancholy frame of mind. There is no question that under Wolfgang Wagner's leadership some aspects have been democratized. But what matters most is that in spite of all opposition, the festival has not lost its courage to experiment. Nowhere else in the world is Wagner's work given so much new life as in the Temple on the Hill.

Gustav Rudolf Sellner's management of the Deutsche Oper, Berlin, as this major house was now called, conformed more closely to the "way of the world" in every possible sense than had Carl Ebert's term. It was Sellner who initiated the large-scale tours abroad of the entire company. Thus in 1963 I flew in a plane filled with members of the ensemble to Tokyo (and not for the only time!). There we stayed at the Imperial Hotel, which had not yet been renovated, so that it was reminiscent of those Japanese imperial structures that have by now been entirely replaced by the faceless glass fronts typical of American architecture.

What was important was not only that these flying visits brought in money; but, more usefully, that the Germans were tilling a soil that had already been irrigated by Italian companies, and that merely remained to be made completely fertile. The Japanese had become intimately familiar with European culture only in the 1930s, and they were avid to learn still more about it. The various (though sometimes disastrous) ties the Germans had already established with Japan were to be extended and reinforced. The opera's first appearance in Tokyo was preceded by three years of preparations. More than once it looked as if all our plans would have to be abandoned because of financial difficulties. But then the Japanese stood in line for tickets for hundreds of hours, some sleeping outside the box office for three nights.

It was only reluctantly and in order to cut down somewhat on the enormous expenses that the Berlin contingent decided to have the scenery redesigned and rebuilt in Japan to fit the somewhat smaller Nissei Theater. Everything went off without a hitch. The scenery sacrificed only a little of its depth; our hosts spoiled us with green tea during rehearsals. Because of Tokyo's great distances the stage crew camped out in the theater on sleeping mats. I can still see Sellner, sucking on his pipe, patiently supervising the technical details in *The Magic Flute* and trying out for himself the trap door through which the Queen of the Night was to disappear.

Anyone who still doubted the Japanese eagerness to study German music had only to turn on the radio. The first morning we were in Tokyo I heard an arrangement of Schumann's "Die Beiden Grenadiere," sung by three male voices with heavy vibrato; though the rendition sounded odd to me, I found it strangely affecting. From every other display window on the Ginza my image stared at me, since my records had already made the rounds here in generous quantity; soon interviewers were making me tell them again and again why in 1955 I had sung a particular measure in such a way, and in 1960 had sung it differently, and in 1961 had added such and so a detail.

There was a lot to see, to experience: the imaginative and colorful neon signs; the minor earthquakes, occurring with admirable regularity, that never failed to send a shudder of fear through us; the venerable Kabuki Theater, with its didactic masterpieces of dramatic art, performed entirely by men (I once witnessed with admiration a solo performance in which the actor gave a virtuoso presentation of crying, from the first sob to the moment when he actually broke out in tears, a feat that took three-quarters of an hour). The audience may spend as long as eight hours in the theater; in the more expensive front rows they may lie on mats, noisily expressing their encouragement and approval; then there are the Takahasuka Girls, a company in which, conversely, all the parts are played by women; and a hundred more entertainments.

Whenever we encountered Japanese hospitality, the women remained in the background. At official parties and during interviews the only women visible were interpreters. That situation has changed considerably since then, though the changes also mean that today far fewer kimonos are to be seen. It was only in the teahouses, where I cheerfully tried to stretch my long legs under the low tables, that there were women to entertain the customers; with a directness assumed for the benefit of American tourists, they talked constantly, stopping only when they sang songs accompanied by a plucked instrument.

As soon as our ears had become accustomed to them, we were vouchsafed a multitude of musical sounds; they testified to the Japanese joy in concentrated lyrics and explained at least in part that nation's pleasure in German lieder. On that trip I heard the most beautiful Japanese music in the Imperial Palace, and on a subsequent visit in one of the hidden temple shrines of Tokyo, when the imperial band played Gagaku, magically spacious, mysteriously constructed out of nearly imperceptible gong rhythms, and always accompanied by the sound of mouth organs, with their celestial sound that transforms the soul.

During the three visits the Berlin opera paid to Japan, all performances were taped for television, with no additional lights and no special rehearsals for the singers. At that time private video taping had just been invented, so that no one was really concerned about preserving the tapes. Today there are no souvenirs of those performances; all the tapes have been destroyed.

I am sure that in all the world there are no more cunning autograph hounds than the Japanese. They discovered and occupied all the escape routes after performances, and they persisted all the way to the elevator doors or the haven of the hotel room. At that time in Tokyo—and of course in all the other cities we visited in the southern and northern sections of the country, all of which are blessed with outstanding massage parlors—I experienced the wonders that shiatsu, Japanese massage, can perform when combined with acupressure and acupuncture. Mr. Nakayama, who took care of us with untiring enthusiasm on our later visits, became for us a symbol of well-being in the Far East. All attempts by Europeans at imitating his ministrations fall short of the original.

It was in the Imperial Hotel—high up in the Rainbow Lounge, where we had to get and replenish the dishes ourselves from the steaming buffet—during our third visit that Sellner asked me to go with him to a more isolated table so he could tell me that he was considering me as his successor in the job of manager; everyone trusted me implicitly, he said. I asked for time to think it over, only to learn from colleagues that very night, in my dressing room before the performance of *Falstaff*, that I had already and definitely been named to the post. I nevertheless turned the offer down, since I did not believe that my talents lay in the direction of more diplomatic and administrative activities as head of an opera company.

I associate two Verdi roles with Sellner. The first is Giorgio Germont in *La Traviata*, a fiery character but also one who is given melodious songs—a good opportunity for me to master the Verdi style quite deliberately and more thoroughly in Italian and under a conductor such as Lorin Maazel, who was our general music director at the time. Sellner's *Traviata* impressed me as somewhat inhibited— possibly he was intimidated by Filippo Sanjust's lavish, realistic sets. During his term in Darmstadt Sellner had created a seminal form of abstract modernism that was hard to reconcile with this splendor. Only in Schönberg's *Moses und Aaron*, which he gave a new and very successful production, did Sellner fall back on his "primal style." But we singers managed to take a number of little suggestions and cobble them together into a performance that transcended the dictatorship of the scenery.

In studying many different recorded versions, I came to realize to what an extent the usual method of singing Verdi was arranged schematically and misinterpreted, with a wrongly applied "italianità." The kinship with Schubert is overlooked, giving rise to a distorted and tasteless evaluation of Verdi's style. True, the "grido" and the brilliant acuti should not and must not be ignored. But just as we would refuse to listen to an unvaried fortissimo coming from the dramatic stage, we cannot allow the refined Verdi type to be reduced to the broadest entrance of the voice for its own sake.

Next came Macbeth, surpassing all my previous Verdi roles in its wild, primeval dimensions, though it is marked by long drawn-out cantilenas as well as by broken, choppy lines. I handled the role better in Salzburg, partly because of the reverberating acoustics of the Felsenreitschule. What use is the most imaginatively spare scenery (by Michael Raffaelli in the Berlin production) when there is no resonance in the hall, making voice control unnecessarily difficult?

I imagined Macbeth as a blond giant with a dull melancholy, susceptible to the witches' nebulous magic, then raised to exalted brutality, eaten alive first by ambition, then by remorse. The vision of the dagger had to be made palpable entirely through my own bloodthirstiness. The recitative of the monologue had to be shaped to lead to the outcry, followed by the toneless whisper of "Tutto è finito," babbled as if by a guilt-ridden slave in thrall to the cold, power-hungry woman. In the magnificent aria in D-flat major the soul of the damned thane must be imbued with a dark lyricism, must dedicate itself to destruction. This is preceded by outrage, fury, and fear interchangeably, sometimes without transition; here you could breathe Italian cantilenas, declaim recitatives so that they had dramatic presence, to bring to life a northern, uncanny internalization and allow the weight of the murderous impulse—to bring a world theater to real life.

The next visit to Tokyo included my first Italian *Falstaff*; Maazel performed it the first night we were there, after a mere half-rehearsal on the morning of our arrival. Television taping was included. There were no additional spotlights. The entire quite complicated stage process had

215

been so minutely rehearsed by the Japanese in advance, using stand-ins, that the transmission with synchronized subtitles in Japanese could take place at once.

The Berlin production of Alban Berg's *Lulu*, in a black-and-white staging intended to be reminiscent of silent movies, was, in my opinion, not nearly enough appreciated by the press. The idea was new, and the production did full justice to the subject. Perhaps the most successful was Sellner's premiere of *Dantons Tod* by Gottfried von Einem. During the rehearsals, which he attended, the composer, beaming, expressed his approval most of the time. The witty Austrian-by-choice became a friend; I performed three of his works for the first time: the cantata *An die Nachgeborenen*, written for the United Nations and given its world premiere in New York; the lieder cycle based on poems by Hermann Hesse; and the series of lieder with texts by Hans Carl Artmann, *Rosa mystica*, for voice and orchestra, which I sang in Vienna under Karl Böhm's baton.

When Sellner left, Berlin lost not only an eloquent conversationalist; the courage to tackle unfamiliar works and stage them successfully also vanished into thin air. The somewhat timid mounting of specimens of legitimate "modernism" failed to arouse any real pleasure at the particular season's schedule. But this was an approach the Deutsche Oper shared with many other companies.

I associate the name of Rudolf Hartmann primarily with the opera *Arabella* and with its staging, which, though conventional, was in part determined by the ideas of the composer, Richard Strauss. The work began in Salzburg in 1956, when Hartmann, together with Stefan Hlawa and

Joseph Keilberth, laid the foundations for a number of performances in Munich and later in London.

At a rehearsal Hlawa asked me, "Are you Slovakian? The way you speak is just the way German is butchered where I come from." Actually my idea was to achieve a Walachian or otherwise Hungarian rustic sound; all the same, I was pleased to be taken for the "real thing." When the stage designer learned that I came from Berlin, he was truly disappointed.

Lisa Della Casa, who at that time was at the height of her vocal and dramatic powers, and the fresh young Anneliese Rothenberger were wonderful partners. It is true that Lisa must have been wearing very complicated clothing, since in most of her scenes she concentrated on standing comfortably and not tripping over her hems. And during the love scenes, of all times, she remembered the old stage rule (not worth adhering to) to look at one's partner's forehead as much as possible rather than in his eyes, in order to avoid any distraction. Too bad! But we got along pretty well for ten years; as far as the looks went, I made up for what I had missed with Lisa when I performed with Julia in Peter Beauvais' staging of *Arabella*.

In London Hartmann, Della Casa, and I experienced a musical sea change when instead of Keilberth's calm Germanic beat, Georg Solti's lightning bolts descended on us. Let there be no mistake: Making music, especially *this* music, with this Hungarian, whose Magyar training had so prepared him for it, was absolutely marvelous. It is true that the stage of the Covent Garden Opera House looked more like Paris than Vienna. But the production was wildly successful, and it gives me a certain pleasure to note that to this day revivals of the time-worn staging evoke nostalgic memories of the original cast.

217

The following year the production was repeated six times, and as always in such cases, the performers had a hard time of it, perhaps particularly because Lisa was not among them. The weather had just turned, and my pleasure in making my way to the daily rehearsals past the market stalls among the scents of vegetables and flowers, thinking of all the lovers who had come here to send their declarations of love in floral form, was almost at an end. Too many rehearsals with a new Arabella had tired me unnecessarily.

In connection with the premiere there was an enjoyable party. As so often before, in the Munich Prinzregententheater and then in the Nationaltheater, I had spied Dr. Franz Strauss among the audience. At a distance his head so resembled his father's that it seemed as if Richard Strauss had come back to life. Now he had made a special trip to London to celebrate this Strauss spectacle. He took me aside to express his cordial interest in my welfare. No sooner was I back in Berlin than I was holding a generous present, taken from a package with a Garmisch postmark. I was delighted to be able to augment my collection of holograph scores with two pages from the love duet from *Arabella* in Strauss' elegant pencil notation.

When I wrote to Dr. Strauss to thank him, I added that I had two letters from his father to mine. They revealed that by a hair the son, when he was still called Bubi, would have moved into the school supervisor's home in Zehlendorf as a foster child. At the time my father refused, because of the extra work it would have entailed—a decision he later, understandably, regretted.

Shortly after this exchange between Strauss and myself, I had to regret not having accepted sooner his cordial invitation to visit him in Garmisch; I kept putting it off for lack of time. As it was, he died before he could show me his treasures.

Rudolf Hartmann once more proved himself a virtuoso of planning when he brought Hindemith's *Cardillac* to the stage of the Munich Nationaltheater. Everything was predetermined down to the last detail, including every emotion and every movement, so that the performers could, as it were, lie down in a made bed. This sort of planning must also have helped him in realizing his pet project, the resurrection of the opera house on Maximilianstrasse, which we still might be waiting for had it not been for his efforts.

I tried with all my artistic means to present Cardillac as a special case, a man who felt totally committed to the creative task imposed upon him. Hartmann made every effort to stage the work so that the material was not expressed in purely abstract expressionistic ways. This left me with the task of making my audience believe that the demonic nature of this romantic-pathological figure, corrupted by the magic of manmade gold, was realistic.

The first time I met Günther Rennert, in Salzburg in 1958, we immediately trusted each other. Nevertheless, it was long after the festival summer before we got to know each other better as artists. To this day I can feel nothing but regret for my shyness and reserve. There can be no doubt that when Rennert did his new staging of *Figaro* in Salzburg, my chubby-cheeked, rather plump Count Almaviva presented a problem for many members of the audience. And today I can understand why just before the dress rehearsal, of all times, Rennert came to my dressing room looking fairly troubled (which was unusual for him, since normally he seemed elegant and self-assured) and announced, "Let's try to shape the role in a totally new, totally different way."

During rehearsals I had made a more than usually good impression by my excited efforts, and I had garnered more than one expression of praise from my colleagues. This left me standing there all the more bewildered at such unspecific criticism. I doubt that I changed much during that dress rehearsal, since I could not make rhyme or reason of Rennert's suggestion. Only much later did I realize what he could have meant.

I believe that it was while watching a movie by that expert Theo Lingen that I understood that uncontrolled roaming glances necessarily impede the clarity of a performance. Every look, the direction of every glance, should be true to the content of every event, every action, once that has been understood. When this harmony has been achieved, command is automatically transmitted, not only to the audience but also among the performers themselves. I had been taught as much by Marianne Hoppe (although she sometimes went too far, using a fixed stare). If the performer is economical and terse in his mimetic expression, this steadiness of gaze gives added support. As far as the Count in *Figaro* was concerned, this could mean cutting down on everything that was hectic, throwing all ballast overboard. In this case only command could conjure up spontaneity. Nor is this meant to encourage the director's possibly misguided ambition to turn into uncontrolled absurdity what was once seen as appropriate. Exaggeration is embarrassing in that it exposes something of the effort that went into achieving the effect.

Years later I participated in a Rennert staging of *Figaro* that had been on the boards for years. I was pleased when he praised my virtuosity in adapting myself to his intentions in a minimum of time. Whenever the work was revived, for festivals or tours, he never failed to tell me, "You've remembered an awful lot"—the highest praise possible from a man who stinted on praise.

Following an incredibly bad review of my performance as the Count, Rennert sent me a note: "Carissimo Conte—you must not dignify this idiot by letting yourself feel bad for even a moment. We and all Munich are so happy that you are back here. And again next year? It would be such a help to us."

I must admit that I neither forgot this—nor did I really learn from it. Time and again the paeans of hate composed of prejudice, envy, and sensationalism swell the critical columns of newspapers and magazines. The preferred arenas for critics in this field are the newspapers in Austria and in Frankfurt am Main. What makes these matter is that the preconceived opinions spread far and wide. And this, to be blunt, bothered me a lot. After all, it is not only theatrical people—who are frightened by any kind of printer's ink—who fear the press; others who perspire in the heat of the spotlight are equally affected. Unfortunately many critics are also influenced by the performer's age. If a singer is over sixty, he is assumed to be too old to be practicing his profession. I remember that when I was a young man, I too always felt about older people: They're already on their deathbed. All my life I have never lacked friends—nor did I have to work at making enemies; they were there ahead of me, anonymous and unrestrained. . . .

Significantly, Rennert cast me in *Il Tabarro* and *Gianni Schicchi* by Puccini in contrasting roles. Performing both in one evening was not easy.

221

Whenever I arrived at the Munich Nationaltheater, Rennert, the ubiquitous manager, greeted me: "Welcome to our troop of strolling players. How are your worries about Kristina?" My young wife, whom I had married after my divorce from Ruth Leuwerik, was an alcoholic, and long ago I had had to have her institutionalized.

Of course the roguish Rennert had his own thoughts when Julia Varady and I began to rehearse. My courting of the blond singer surely exceeded somewhat the ardor indicated by Puccini, though the lovely tale that during performances I pressed notes into her hand is a total invention. Warmhearted and spontaneously emotional, while blessed with a wonderful sense of humor, Julia radiated warmth and an inner empathy. When she talked about her childhood in Romania, about her kind parents and the pranks she played with her brothers and sisters, visions of a simpler life opened to me that I thought I had completely forgotten. And of course I was devastated by her inimitable voice, the sound of stormy passion, a triumphant glow in the high notes that made even the Queen of the Night easily accessible, a powerful mezzo timbre at the bottom of the voice, both reinforced by a zest for acting and a talent for it rare among opera stars. Her graceful bearing made the ailing Traviata as believable as the youthful Tatiana in the first part of *Eugene Onegin*; she moved across the stage with a dancer's buoyancy.

Rennert cannot have been ignorant of the fact that Julia and I spent a lot of time together even after rehearsals. Shortly before opening night, when we thought everything had been discussed and there was nothing to do but wait calmly for the performance, we were surprised by a telegram from Rennert: We were to have a good rest, not overdo, and if at all possible, stop in at the opera house the following morning to reassure him that we were in the best of health.

Rennert also made sure that others who were facing a major singing challenge took good care of themselves. At the slightest mention of a cold or other symptom Rennert gave them time off or admonished them to spare themselves. Wiry, agile, and tense himself, he served as a lightning rod for any nerves during rehearsals. The waves of excitement were soon calmed. This particular evening, playing two such divergent characters, meant a great deal to me, not only personally but also on an artistic level.

For *Il Tabarro*, a tale of poverty with the charm of the working class and the tension of a mystery story, Rennert worked up a special set of gestures for the shadowy life on the Seine barge. He taught us to walk like predatory beasts on the boards of the ship, to move like animals, in the way the feet of seagoing people seem to cling to the planks. Every detail had to be naturalistically correct, growing out of tension in order to produce tension. I had to present both a man disconcerted by love groping his way through life and a barge captain traversing his little realm; the same gait was appropriate to both.

In *Il Tabarro* Rennert had built the role on the nuances of body movement; he achieved a total transformation during the short intermission. In the burlesque *Gianni Schicchi* I was given a different nose and directed to achieve an effect of exaggeration, of acid caricature, in depicting a satiric portrait of hereditary underhandedness. Around me as the "intelligent center" Rennert created a comedic but choreographically precise set of actions. I can still see how he demonstrated for me the bizarre gestures of the big solo scene. Tito Gobbi's later "restaging" of the work, with the same sets but a different cast, resulted in an incomparably paler, duller picture.

Rennert, who was a favorite of the stagehands as well for his quickness, lent a willing ear to everyone under his care whenever the need arose. Ita Maximovna was the stage designer most compatible with him. She had an assured taste and yet was always flexible, a consultant working to realize Rennert's ideas. With her he created a totally secure atmosphere for the performers. The most telling example: the unbelievably dense and therefore convincing production of *Così fan tutte* in Salzburg in 1972. I knew at once that he saw Don Alfonso as crucial to the balance among the six singers. He was to be neither a mere intriguer who took pleasure in human failings nor purely a voyeur of the amorous goings-on; responding to the other characters, he was a philosopher, a grand seigneur who understood the human soul and played a resigned yet enjoyable chess game of cheerily and diabolically manipulating everyone's seduction. As the performer, I had to stage a psychological game of provocation that enmeshed the others to the point where they lost their identities. To keep the action flowing, to establish a smooth sequence of movements, Rennert seemed to be everywhere on stage at once (he was the first director to wear gym shoes). He never insisted on anything that had already been decided; he did not care about being right. What was important to him was the "notion of the human heart"—and this was just as true in his private relations with his cast. In all the years when, unfortunately, I was no longer singing with him, he visited me regularly during the Salzburg Festival, traveling the short distance between his apartment to mine. We sat over our teacups and discussed a variety of problems of direction and operatic singing. Rennert's last production at the Bavarian Staatsoper was *Falstaff*; it was my third staging of the work in Munich, and I was able to satisfy Rennert in it. "It really was great fun. Thank you for this Falstaff," read a note after the opening night, which was also his farewell.

For Rennert, everything concerning my character turned on one pivotal sentence: "This little pile of middling mankind," an expression of Sir John in his tirade against his tormentors. When everything seems at an end, when the genuine marriage has made way for the farce of the masked revelers, Verdi begins his final fugue, which is generally sung on the stage apron, in oratorio style. Rennert gave to this stormy finale, cued by Falstaff, the staging that expressed Verdi's musical architecture. As the characters joined in the fugue one by one, they stood, thus visually emphasizing a crescendo that gradually drew all the singers into its vortex. During the final infernal laughter everyone left the stage, after casting off their masks. Sir John remained alone for a moment, separating himself from the mass of "middling mankind," to gravely—and solitarily—stride from the field of the merriment that had been.

Rennert's versatility in matters of style distinguished him favorably from the purists of minimalism of the 1950s. He could counter the theories of those permanent demolition experts with a living theater. When a retirement party was held for him on the large side stage of the Bavarian Staatsoper after the premiere of *Falstaff*, all eyes expressed gratitude, but many were also sad. I shared a table with three great Brünnhildes of two decades—Martha Mödl, Astrid Varnay, and Ingrid Bjoner; all three had tears in their eyes when Rennert took his place in front of the orchestra to conduct the overture to Mozart's *Ab-*

duction from the Seraglio, for the fun of it, with spare, elegant movements and more persuasively than many a professional hand. As he worked—quickly and without ceremony—so did he leave this world. Such a "luxury death" was what he had wished for. Long illness and aging were not his way.

I met August Everding briefly when I sang Germont in a revival of *Traviata* in his staging. During the rehearsals I was happy to find that the protagonist I was paired with was a performer of the highest rank, whose voice also fascinated with its unique timbre: Teresa Stratas, an American of Greek descent, like Maria Callas. The second of the two scheduled performances had to be cut short in the middle. During the first scene Stratas fell to the floor in a dead faint, fortunately without the hemorrhage that Sarah Bernhardt suffered in the 1890s at the same passage in the play. But we—the unimportant remainder of the cast, waiting and listening in the wings, fully costumed and made up—saw only the curtain closing and Everding stepping through it to ask the audience to leave.

When, after Rennert's death, Everding moved from the Kammerspiele to the Nationaltheater as manager, he told us the news and invited us to visit him in the Grünwalder Castle, where he had had a handsome apartment restored for himself on one of the floors. The rooms were decorated with a tasteful economy that allowed each object to be seen to its best advantage. The lady of the manor gave an impression of balance and calm, the precise opposite of her husband's mercurial nature. Not long after we arrived, Everding was bombarded by interviewers; he also had an appointment he could no longer postpone. All this put him in a panic, but his wife, the embodiment of calm, let nothing distract her from listening attentively to her guests. I noticed small collages and sketches on the walls that seemed to me done by a professional; the artist was Everding.

I never saw Everding in a bad mood or without his sense of humor. Once, just before a performance of *Meistersinger*, the chorus, in order to reinforce (illegitimately) their union demands, announced that they would be boycotting the performance by merely whispering. Everding responded with at most a slight uneasiness. His constantly active imagination never deserted him; liberating laughter dispersed the black clouds of threat. When we rehearsed *Meistersinger* with him, the atmosphere was pleasantly relaxed, though even at that time his relationship with his general director of music, Wolfgang Sawallisch, was ominous. It is a special peculiarity of the Munich cultural scene that such contrasting types and attitudes as Everding's and Sawallisch's can flourish side by side and tolerate each other.

We were enchanted by Everding's approach to details in *Meistersinger*. There were so many psychological subtleties in Eva's second-act entrance and the duet with Sachs that it was unlikely the audience could perceive them all. And Beckmesser, sung by Hans Günther Nöcker, an extremely likable man because of his intelligence, became trapped in such complex technical problems in miming in the shoemaker's room that the resulting lack of self-assurance alone was fascinating. Jürgen Rose's open street set, which showed Sachs sitting beside bare wooden struts plying his trade, made me understand once again how precisely Wagner knew how to evaluate his acoustic supports and tonal conditions, and I realized anew that we would always pay dearly for any repudiation of his detailed directions for both characters and stage space.

It is probably not a misinterpretation to call Everding a director who likes to be surprised and who welcomes any new detail, provided that what has been amassed before is not overwhelming. Everding had no better opportunity of making his ideas felt than during a backstage postperformance party in 1983, when *Lear* was retired (and, secretly, my opera career), and the speeches were frustrated by an insurmountable obstacle: The microphone went on strike, and the words of the speaker for the Friends of the Nationaltheater became an incomprehensible mutter lasting about half an hour. The chorus and the orchestra were clearly uneasy, and hecklers shouted from the crowd. In the ensuing embarrassment Everding, unshaken, set the unfortunate microphone aside and improvised a charming tirade against the press and its divergent opinions on particular new productions of the recent season, bringing tears of laughter to the listeners.

In the 1950s Oscar Fritz Schuh used his remarkable talents to turn the Berliner Volksbühne into an internationally renowned theater. He was helped by excellent performers, many of them from his native Austria. I enjoyed particularly close friendships with Aglaja Schmid and Leopold Rudolf. (The performances of both in Hugo von Hofmannsthal's *Der Schwierige*, directed by Aglaia's husband, Rudolf Steinboeck, were wonderfully revealing and charming.) I have the impression, though I may be mistaken, that his years in the theater on the Kurfürstendamm (not yet squeezed in among shops and still surrounded by old trees) were Schuh's most productive and fulfilling period. The people of Berlin, in any case, must have thought so, since their "Volksbühne," formed in the 1920s, failed to meet their expectations before Schuh's tenure and seldom met them after.

When I expressed my enthusiasm in writing, Schuh invited me to sing a second part (after Almaviva)—Macbeth in Salzburg in 1964. As always, I had reservations, among other reasons because of the unwholesome damp walls of the Felsenreitschule, where the performance was to take place. But Schuh was good at reassuring me, and he spoke of his "enormous pleasure." I therefore enjoyed the incredible acoustics of this auditorium, was pleased to be partnered with Grace Bumbry, and sang one of my favorite Verdi roles. Of course the colossally wide stage demanded all my energies—and there were few moments when Schuh did not use the entire area in his staging; he rarely allowed me to remain in one spot. But when the Bavarian Staatsoper staged *Die Frau ohne Schatten* by Richard Strauss some years later, we both happily remembered the earlier event. Part of my satisfaction came when Schuh wrote me, "For the first time in the world of opera I have truly felt connected to a singer."

Later, in Munich, when Schuh was weakened by illness and old age, he often repeated himself. And whenever he sat apart from the others in the half-light of the auditorium, he was likely to doze off. If someone stumbled over his knees trying to get past, he would start up and call out, "Oh, excuse me, I wasn't asleep."

But he followed the theatrical events of his time with a clear mind, and he saw to it that the high standards of the past were maintained as long as possible.

_____

229

* * *

Actors seldom write long letters. Too much of their time must be devoted to rehearsals by day and performances at night. But I came to know some actors when they were in the audience at my recitals, through mutual friends, or when we shared a concert stage. Thus Judith Holzmeister, Sebastian Fischer, or Wilhelm Borchert recited Ludwig Tieck's novella whenever I sang the related romances from *Die schöne Magelone* in Berlin and Vienna. One of the players did not rest until he got to know me better, and subsequently wrote me interesting letters.

There was a heavy thunderstorm in Berlin on the summer day in 1955 when Walter Franck telephoned me. He said that he and Leopold Rudolf were at a café and were just then singing my praises, without ever having met me. "Why don't you join us? Come on, do it."

Thus the friend and brother of actors and directors hooked me, and I enjoyed my conversation with the President and Kalb in Ernst Lothar's staging of Schiller's *Kabale und Liebe*. Though both performers shone in their roles, they did not have a good word to say for the director. I was glad I had overcome my shyness and accepted the invitation; while champagne was poured inside and rain poured down outside, we were soon deep into a discussion of acting problems, punctuated by Franck's hearty, ringing laugh. When we parted, he said in his deep, slightly Frankish-tinged bass voice, "Actually, I just can't talk to anybody but artists anymore."

I was soon to understand that Walter had a passion for music and that, furthermore, he knew my recordings. In his apartment in the Schmargendorf section of Berlin I also discovered veritable treasures of rarities on shellac.

Berlin was the city where Walter had become famous, the city whose fame he had contributed to for forty years. Broadly built, with a resonant voice, he had no difficulty filling the spacious stage of the acoustically problematic Schiller-Theater; the smaller boards of the Schlosspark-theater and the Werkstatt-Theater elicited from him quite different tonalities, more like chamber music. After 1948 Walter Franck appeared almost exclusively on the public stage: His special art was in realistic portrayals in works that had been dropped from the standard repertoire. Very early on I wrote in my diary, "Ibsen's *Masterbuilder* with Walter Franck in the title role: It reopened old wounds and set the rusty wheels of my theater craze to turning again."

Since Walter was the friend best suited to artistic adventures, I profited from his selfless advice as I prepared the parts of Wozzeck and Mathis. As Hanns Lietzau said at Walter's memorial service, "An actor who did not indulge himself in virtuoso repetitions of his skills, an interpreter of human beings who took into his being on the stage the seriousness, the melancholy, the misery, the dark melody of our current, present-day being. Truth, truth was his ultimate goal. Wherever this goal was applied, this actor was large and significant. To lie, if only to please a little more, was not possible for him."

In 1959 Walter wrote to me from his beloved Flims, "The only thing they gave me this time for the Festival Weeks is the 'world premiere' of a one-act play by Beckett, *Krapp's Last Tape*. It is the half-hour monologue (nobody on the stage but me, myself, and I!) of an old man, down-at-the-heels, who plays and listens to—tapes from his younger days. The whole thing will be a one-time studio performance."

231

He could not know that this daring venture on the part of his manager, Boleslav Barlog, was to be the start of a worldwide success, that he would repeat his interpretation countless times. (Later on the fabulous Martin Held played the role in a quite different, but no less valid, register.) Further impressions in Berlin: the morbid fervor of Walter's Philipp in Schiller's *Don Carlos*, the coldness, to the point of emotional emptiness, of his Götz von Heidenstein in Sartre's *The Devil and the Good Lord*; his waiting like a beast of prey as the Commissar in *Raskolnikoff*, Leopold Ahlsen's dramatization of Dostoevsky.

He remained loyal to Berlin, where immediately after the war he acted as the district mayor of Schmargendorf for a few months. Around the time the Wall went up, he wrote me, "Our Berlin gives us something to worry about. No acute fears, but the prospects are not rosy."

Twice he gave readings in my music room, regaling our guests first with Schiller and then with Hemingway, who was a particular favorite of his because of the terseness of the language.

One day in 1960 an announcement took me by surprise: "You may be pleased to learn that in February, during the first plenary session, you will probably be elected to membership in the new 'Academy of the Arts.' " I am sure Franck's vote was a resounding *aye*.

Franck liked to listen; he was not given to monologues as so many actors are. One day I gave him and Dagny, his wife, a caricature rendition of the dialogues from *Freischütz*; he laughed so hard that he cried ("Schiess nicht, Max, ich bin die Taube" was one of the passages I included). A short time later, on the occasion of a concert, he sent me, instead of flowers, an engraving with scenes from the opera in question and a portrait of Weber. On a trip through Swabia he sent me postcards. One, signed "Eduard Mörike," read, "Am devastated to learn that in Berlin you sing only songs by that old Olympian and bearded Heyse, when *my* songs are the best ones Hugo Wolf ever put to music." Another one, from Weinsberg, informed me, "I am in my house, with wine and old friends. I was astonished to hear from you that you stubbornly refuse to sing my poems—set to music by Schumann—in Berlin. If this situation does not change soon, I will have to begin to haunt you. Yours, Justinus Kerner."

Franck was particularly fond of the song cycle based on Kerner poems; he played my first recording of the song "Auf das Trinkglas eines verstorbenen Freundes" over and over.

He was not always happy about his appearances in Vienna. In 1961 he wrote, "I dislike Vienna more each day. Though my reviews for Krapp in his *Last Tape* were sensational, the Viennese don't seem to like this kind of play. Most of the time only half the seats are filled, and the applause is downright pitiful. Unfortunately I'm obligated to perform daily until the end of March. The opening of *Dance of Death* is scheduled for April 5. I can't wait to find out how it will go over with the public."

Well, he was acclaimed, as he had been shortly before in Berlin, for his part in the Strindberg play, which had never seemed to me nearly so penetrating and disturbing as in this production.

One morning in August 1961 Irmel innocently telephoned Dagny in Garmisch, where the Francks were on vacation, to inquire about Walter's health, since he had not come to Bayreuth for *Tannhäuser*, as we had expected him to. There was a long silence on the other end of the line, then a voice like stone: "Walter died at ten o'clock last night."

All our attempts to take in the news were in vain. Our anticipation of "Franck Day," which we had planned to spend together, was at its height; after all, it had been a long time since we had had anything of the sort to celebrate. And now—unalterably—this! Suddenly I was aware that time and again I had unconsciously noticed that Walter's face had become hollow; I had seen him marked by death.

He was always sensitive, and one of the few who truly cared about us. He liked having us near him, in his care, perhaps even under his influence. Sadly, because of time constraints, there were far too few of these occasions. When we learned of his death, I felt as if a pillar of my life had crumbled, emotionally and artistically. In every departure there is so much that is incomprehensible. We are almost ashamed of going on living, eating, sleeping, loving. Perhaps the most bitter aspect of the loss is having to call a friendship incomplete for the rest of one's life.

Dagny Franck survived her husband by ten years, during which there were many occasions for mutual support. In 1968 I was experiencing a deep emotional crisis. After Irmel's tragic death at Manuel's birth, I could not manage to give my life and the children's lives another focus of love. Irrationally I decided to cut short my career in opera. Dagny responded by writing, "Remember Walter's statement when he was asked at a press conference who was the most promising among the younger actors: 'Gentlemen, there can be no doubt that the greatest genius among the younger generation is not an actor but a singer!' But you can't have forgotten."

* * *

I met Heinrich Schnitzler and his family through Dagny, who stayed with them whenever she happened to be in Vienna. The son of the writer-physician and temporary director of the Josephstadt, as the Viennese called their wonderful theater, lived in a magnificent mansion that boasted one of the most handsomely housed private libraries I have ever seen. The lord of the manor extended a courteous invitation to me to inspect it.

Once Ernst Deutsch was at our house. Walter had wanted to be the first to bring him to Berlin after his exile; there his Nathan the Wise was a triumph. Deutsch was quickly able to dispel the initial somewhat unpleasant feelings of distance. He related anecdotes about Karl Kraus, Peter Altenberg, and Adolf Loos—the first as a monologuist, the second as a fool, and the last as someone who pretended to be deaf when he became impatient with the conversation. Thus all the characteristic Viennese ingredients were present—the intimate surroundings, the intelligence imported from Prague, the carping tone, and the names that the city boasts of as its own.

As a general rule actors present human beings more imaginatively and completely than it is possible for singers to do: Actors must compose their own verbal music and can adapt precisely to the imagined human model they are to project. Nothing, not even a strictly determined musical framework, comes between the character to be created and the audience. But actors envy singers for the music that creates an atmosphere from the outset and prepares the audience for the work they are about to see.

Some actors frequently attended my recitals: Erika von Tellheim and Gisela Matthishent, Erich Ponto and Theo Lingen. Gisela, an actress and a woman left on her own, felled too soon by the most fatal of diseases, had experienced mixed feelings when, sitting in the dark auditorium surrounded by my whole family, she saw and heard my first *Macbeth*. Perhaps she saw the performance more than she heard it, since her eyes, assuring her of a standard of experience, took in more intensely what was occurring than did her ears. Conversely, she judged her own work more by her hearing, and probably too one-sidedly. She therefore never quite made it into the first rank of actors. Television, too, kept offering her the roles of mysterious or evil women that ceased to attract her once she had reached a certain fame.

On opening night, which she lived through in torment as usual, her opportunity came. We were sitting together in my music room with friends, going over the details and events of the evening. She really, she said, had not wanted to interfere. But she could not let the matter rest, and she bent her long torso over to whisper in my ear, "It is an old stage truth that we must learn over and over. No performer may make jerky movements when the play seems to call for them if they are only externally assumed. Because naturalness lies precisely in soft transition and, besides, the throat is grateful for them."

I had to agree with her although, as always, I did not see myself as quite so culpable. Why is it that our own impressions generally remain partial and incomplete? I constantly need others to evaluate and correct all the things I overlook. Once I understood this, I also stopped being afraid of telling artist friends what I thought was amiss in their performances. And since I have developed some skill at this, my students can only profit from it (to the extent that they are willing and able).

Happy to have rid herself of her observation, Gisela left the gathering.

I find it difficult to speak about teaching, since it is an art that has to be tailored individually to each student. This truth immediately became clear to me many years ago, when on a beautiful day in late summer Hans Chemin-Petit asked me in the name of the Berlin Akademie der Künste to revive the series of master classes that Edwin Fischer, Wilhelm Kempff, and other famous artists of the concert stage had conducted before the war. It was doubly difficult for me because it was important from the start to create an atmosphere that was both comfortable and conducive to concentrated work for my pupils, who were being watched by a sizable audience. Most recently I had to do this for the music festival in Kassel, which was limited to an even briefer period. Here I was further burdened by the presence of a number of singing teachers.

The master classes in Berlin had two deeply satisfying consequences, which shaped the further course of my life. I heard Hartmut Höll accompany his highly talented wife, Mitsuko Shirai, a soprano, and I persuaded him to become my partner in recitals; both of them became dear friends as well. Second, the music academy became aware of me and, through Johannes Hoefflin, asked me to join the faculty to teach song interpretation. Here I assumed a responsibility that in many ways was like walking a tightrope. For it was not only a matter of addressing the technical weaknesses of each student without running counter to the work of the particular singing coach; it was also important to help the students, whose time was already pretty much booked, prepare a large concert repertoire so that it was ready for performance and worth listening to. At first I had to rely almost exclusively on the skills of the so-called repertoire pianist. As the years passed, I managed to persuade the piano teachers to send their most talented students to my courses, so that I might be able to gather as many students as possible around me.

No two voices are exactly alike. It is up to the coach to examine the shape of the face, the manner of breathing, the size of the chest, the posture while standing, the movement of the lips, and inner commitment—apart from the presence or absence of musical talent—and to make a diagnosis of the singing condition, which results in the appropriate "treatment." In this process the part of singing that is invisible from the outside—full use of the resonating area, breathing, the formation of the palate, and the use of the diaphragm—play a far more important role than the obvious attributes. What becomes important are feeling and sensitively hearing the resulting sound, so as to be able to influence it appropriately. But if in addition we consider that all this serves at most a preparatory purpose, that only insight into the secret of interpretation—that is, of translation—can have a significant effect on the student's ability to feel, we begin to appreciate the magnitude of the teacher's task. As a performer, I approached many things in my profession intuitively; only when I began to teach did I penetrate to the ramification of details—not without making sure that I could return to the trunk. And for me this trunk was curiosity; many of the young people had no real concept of it, it had to be awakened. It may be that this "aha" experience cannot be achieved in three school courses; but there is hope that after some years it will break into consciousness.

Gisela Matthishent played the role of the Signora in Max Frisch's new play, *Andorra*, under the most feared of directors, Fritz Kortner. After the war and his return, he worked more as a director than as an actor in Germany and Austria. He spent much time in looking, in critically or happily receiving. He never tired of looking at people. One of his favorite observation points, when he was directing at the Munich Kammerspiele, was the lobby of the Hotel Vier Jahreszeiten. If we happened to be staying in the city at the same time, I could see him in the mornings, still disheveled from late-night rehearsals, sitting on a flimsy chair next to the hotel's revolving door, absorbed in the passing parade. An impassioned reader of Freud, Kortner managed to include almost everything he had seen in his very psychologically oriented productions. Once, after I had passed him without acknowledgment for about three weeks, he suddenly rose to shake my hand vigorously. "I know you and venerate you," he called out in his well-known nasal growl. Then he sat back down to concentrate once more on his observations.

In Berlin the opening night of *Andorra* was imminent, and thanks to Gisela I was able to attend the dress rehearsal. The Schiller-Theater filled with theater experts, and those who considered themselves as such. Shortly before the curtain was to go up, an usher approached me in my seat and said, "Herr Kortner would be pleased if you would join him in the front row."

So I ran the gauntlet through the packed auditorium.

Arrived at last, I found Kortner collapsed in his seat, his expression sinister. He ran his fingers through his short stubble of hair and after a brief handshake muttered as though to himself, "I merely wanted to tell you that this performance isn't final."

I could not help smiling as I remarked, "Is anything ever final?"

He smiled back.

That morning I was most impressed with Klaus Kammer's and Martin Held's performances. But the actor Ernst Sattler later told me about terrible problems. Once again Kortner had been prey to suspicions about possible anti-Semitism (after all, anti-Semitism is the crux on which the action of *Andorra* turns) and to fear at his own daring as a director. He vented these feelings by engaging in annoying buffoonery. And many of the actors in his company found it hard to accept the slow, hesitant, meditative manner of speaking that he insisted on as the only true one. I assume that up there Kortner is still carrying on rehearsals far into the night, and complaining that not nearly enough time has been allowed for preparation.

On a stormy afternoon in December 1967 Ruth and I visited Harry Meyen and Romy Schneider in their apartment in Grunewald. Little David Christopher had just been born. There was as yet no sign of the unlucky star rising over this marriage and the lives of all three. (The parents committed suicide several years apart; the boy had a fatal accident while playing.) Meyen, a cool man, the marvelous director of so many new plays in Berlin, retreated behind a wall of disapproval. Romy, who was outstanding and wonderfully unpretentious, especially in her French films, was the embodiment of naturalness and warmth, without makeup or movie-star affectations, a human being through and through.

I became obsessed with finding out what it was that united the two of them, since clearly an abyss yawned between them. I also gave a lot of thought to the conclusions that might be drawn about a relationship from the way physical harmony is expressed or hidden. Meyen had furnished the apartment; it looked as if no one lived in it, as if it were merely a picture cut from a magazine. Later I saw Romy once more, at Orly airport, at the center of a group of men who looked very much like movie moguls. She was laughing, almost bursting with good humor. No shadow signaled her imminent death.

It was also Ruth who brought me to Helmut Käutner's peculiarly designed home in Grunewald. The conversation naturally dwelled on actors and their affairs. Whenever members of any profession get together in a group (and there were some ten of us around the elegant pool), the exchange, always centered on one topic, cannot help seeming somewhat puerile to the uninvolved listener. There was laughter about things that did not seem at all humorous, conversation monopolized by people who needed to be at the center of attention, and undisguised rivalries. I always felt something of an outsider whenever I had to listen to this backbiting for any length of time, although some genuinely witty things were said too. Käutner's films *In jenen Tagen, Film ohne Titel,* and *Der Hauptmann von Köpenick* are masterworks that have become classics; once at my house in Berlin he hinted vaguely that he wanted me in a movie for a specific role. But this was shortly before his final illness, and nothing came of it.

* * *

In 1955 I received a letter on delicately scented airmail paper, signed "Lilli Palmer." She wrote enthusiastically— making me feel wonderful—about my first recording of Schumann's Eichendorff lieder. She explained that she came from a highly musical family—who incidentally had lived just around the corner from my Westend home. She mentioned that only now, after her return from exile, she was trying to read German poetry without resentment.

At the time I had not seen any of her movies. I made up for the lack as quickly as possible and immediately became a fan; she had so much feminine charm, she was so extraordinarily beautiful, and her acting had an awesome austerity. I could have wished her better scripts and more British directors.

For a long time there was silence between us. Then one day in Salzburg I saw her sitting way up front at one of my recitals. After that she attended regularly and, together with her husband, Carlos Thompson, made sure that I was aware of their enthusiasm. I learned of her success as a painter, saw reproductions of her work, and agreed with the paeans of praise it had received. I read her autobiography *Dicke Lilli, gutes Kind,* admiring her style and the power of her language—which she never quite achieved again in subsequent books. I wrote her something close to a love letter, but she politely did not respond to my overtures; she was a well-brought-up lady, clad in an "iron suit of armor" that she had acquired in the hard years of working her way up from chorus girl to Broadway star.

Not quite a year before her unexpected death the

great moment was finally at hand: Our neighbor and friend Siegfried Fischer-Fabian and his wife Ursula, a painter, had Lilli Palmer staying with them, as so often when she visited Munich. Siegfried telephoned me and asked me to come over; Lilli was there, he said, and was looking forward to talking with me. She came down the stairs with a youthful step, willowy, wearing a pants suit, cordial, and ready at once to engage in a lively conversation about painting. Of course we named our favorite painters, learning with astonishment that Gustave Moreau, the symbolist with his own Paris museum, was high on the list for both of us. She spoke of her admiration for Orson Welles as a performer, and complained about a forthcoming trip to Russia to do location shooting for *Peter the Great.*

Shortly before she left for California for the last time, where she intended to spend the winter writing her new book, she telephoned Fischer-Fabian once more. "Would you ask Fischer-Dieskau to send me one of my favorite records, a very particular one?" She specified the lied in question: " 'Ich bin der Welt abhanden gekommen.' Lyrics by Friedrich Rückert, music by Gustav Mahler." The final stanza contains the lines, "Ich bin gestorben dem Weltgetümmel und ruh' in einem stillen Gebiet! Ich leb' allein in meinem Himmel, in meinem Lieben, in meinem Lied" ("I have become dead to the hurlyburly of the world and rest in a serene place! I live alone in my heaven, in my loving, in my song").

I sent her a compact disc that contained this selection, and she thanked me: "I have acquired a small CD player just for this recording."

A bare two weeks later the papers printed the news

that Lilli had died. Fischer-Fabian told me that she had confessed to him, "It doesn't look good. I've got to go under the knife. Cancer."

The "good chance" she had believed in was no longer a possibility. One of her last statements was, "Actually I've lived long enough. If I have to go now . . ."

7

"Schöpferischer Lüfte Wehen"

More than once I found myself agreeing with Frank Wedekind, who treated the composer in his play *Kammersänger* with great disrespect, having him snort as he plays selections from his latest work on the piano— and plays badly at that. Winfried Zillig, whose opera *Troilus und Cressida* Tietjen produced in 1951 (with Elisabeth Grümmer and me sharing the title roles), called attention to himself during rehearsals more than once by arguing, "I studied with Schönberg, and that's why my music shouldn't really be resounding. . . . But since it is anyway, they think I'm a romantic imbecile."

The day after the premiere, which was only moderately well received and where I was terribly hampered by my short Greek skirt, Zillig came to my house to play his songs for me. Perspiring, he tackled the piano exactly as Wedekind described; he also "sang" along. The sound swelled and ebbed floridly and bombastically—that is how I remember it. To sing the lines or produce them on the instrument—apparently he did not care about this. And yet no one could have been more convinced of his own versatility. He may have been most talented at conducting. The press, as might be expected, told him what it really thought, and this criticism seemed, if anything, to increase his self-esteem. How often I witnessed similar scenes at my grand piano!

Throughout the Brown years I guarded the forbidden treasure of the *Mathis* symphony, recorded on three shellac discs as conducted by the composer, Paul Hindemith. I played them often—secretly and at low volume—for my friends from school, and thus we gained a first, shadowy idea of what is called contemporary music. We had not been allowed to hear any of the new music written before and during the Nazi period.

An accidental witness, in the winter of 1948 I was standing next to Paul and Gertrud Hindemith when, after years of living abroad, they registered for the first time at a hotel in Frankfurt. Earlier, Hindemith had already visited his mother and Willy Strecker, the publisher, in the city. The hotel was across the street from the main Frankfurt railroad station, one of the few of the many dark houses that was still habitable. The short, stout, bald gentleman with the rapid speech entered his name in the hotel register in an almost calligraphic hand, and then the couple quickly went to their room.

246

It would be many more years—not until 1957—before I would meet him again. It was on one of the occasions when I was singing his wonderful Requiem based on Walt Whitman, mourning the war dead and the murdered Abraham Lincoln. Hindemith himself had skillfully translated the words into German. To test out this version we met in the Berlin Hochschulsaal with the Philharmonic and Diana Eustrati, the solo alto. Hindemith tackled his chore with enormous zeal, giving the orchestra no quarter, and he was generous with his Frankfurt invective; he was so bold as to remark, "And you call yourself the Berlin Philharmonic Orchestra? I'm used to something quite different from the old days."

It is true that for Hindemith such crude boastfulness was tantamount to a confession of affection and trust and was intended merely to elicit their superlative best. I have said it before: No other orchestra has given me so much admiring pleasure as has the Berlin Philharmonic. And of the countless conductors with whom I stood in front of these musicians, Hindemith was by no means the greatest. Actually, he was one of those conducting composers who, though they are skilled at the craft, do not give outstanding performances of their own works, owing to overly hasty tempi, sound that is too dense, inadequately differentiated motions. Frequent repetition, of course, allowed at least a synchronization, and at the performance itself I must have sung with special joy and expressiveness, because before he left the podium, Hindemith said, half critically, half in praise, "You're not a singer at all, you're a bard."

Incidentally, the city paid astonishingly little official attention to his visit. After all, before Hindemith had been forced to emigrate, he had lived there and had exerted extraordinary influence through his teaching at the

Hochschule. And the Free University of Berlin had bestowed an honorary doctorate on him some time ago.

In Vienna I saw and heard him conduct his *Mathis* opera. Once again it seemed to me hasty and insufficiently modulated. When we met again in Berlin for his oratorio *Das Unaufhörliche*, I had long since sung *Mathis der Maler*, though unfortunately without Hindemith's having been able to conduct this part, which was my favorite. Sections of it had already appeared on records. Once again, as he conducted, every part of his energetic short body was in motion, spurring singer and instrumentalists on in a somewhat unseemly rush. He correctly identified himself as "actually only a reasonably trained podium horse." There can be no question that the performances he conducted were not as authentic as they were thought to be by some conductors, who refused therefore to take on the works. But I truly enjoyed singing Gottfried Benn's splendid lyrics, inspired by his friendship with Hindemith during the early 1930s and written especially for this work; I was equally struck by the music, which occasionally—especially in the choral passages—became intensely inspirational.

One long night served to reveal Hindemith's talent for storytelling; he clearly felt at home in a crowd. When I asked him if he would write me a song cycle that would extend through a whole recital, something like the *Marienleben*, he thought it over for a moment. Then he said, "Well, yes, if I live that long. It may be that soon I'll be taking a long train trip. It's possible that I'll think of something then."

But this circumstance, which seemed to be the condition in which he preferred to work, seems not to have occurred. After a year a package with notes arrived—*Mo-*

248

tets, written between 1940 and 1960, based on Latin biblical texts relating the life of Jesus up to the calming of the storm. I was forced to write to Hindemith and tell him that the work was unfortunately too high for my voice, and I sent it back. I believe he passed it on to Ernst Haefliger, my beloved tenor colleague, for its world premiere. The motets were published "for soprano and piano." Paul Hindemith died in 1963.

It is greatly to the credit of Rudolf Hartmann, the manager, and Joseph Keilberth, the chief conductor at the time, that they were the first after the Brown period to produce *Cardillac* in its original version at the Bavarian Staatsoper. I was entrusted with the title role. Gertrud Hindemith, who attended rehearsals, was deeply disappointed that no effort was made to use later revisions and expansions. Since I never did become familiar with these changes, I am unable to evaluate them; I only know that the work called Op. 39, the original much tighter version, felicitously sums up Hindemith's compositional work of the 1920s, being based on the prototypical movements of his instrumental works: light music, nocturnes, concertinos, passacaglias, basso continuo, and so on. The libretto, by the expressionist Ferdinand Lion, gave clear evidence that in some sections it had been adapted to the music afterward; this was typical of Hindemith's attitude to words. I did not consider this a failing; rather, it seemed to make the work that much more attractive. The inward emotion is composed with reference to the music of Bach and not so much to the individual words, especially in the lyrical passages. The staging, by the skilled craftsman Rudolf Hartmann, whose work had already been tested on many occasions in the same theater, favorably displayed this opera, with its constant latent tensions contrasted in the orchestra by simpler expression. Though Gertrud Hindemith objected that in Cardillac's duet with his daughter I treated her with too much coldness and cruelty, the situation and the music in this instance demanded just that.

Winning the approval of composers' widows is a special kind of problem. Once while I was in Tokyo, Frau Schönberg telephoned me from Los Angeles to demand that I sing Moses in Boston three days later. I had never studied the part, and of course I had obligations in Japan. "That hardly matters," was the reply on the other end of the line. I was unable to persuade Frau Schönberg of the impossibility of her plan. . . .

I should add that the kindness of Dieter Rexroth, the head of the Frankfurt Hindemith Society, enabled me to perform the world premiere of a number of Hindemith songs. These had been composed between 1930 and 1947 but never published. Aribert Reimann and I worked from manuscripts. The recital was followed by a recording and publication of the score. Novalis, Claudius, Brentano, and Nietzsche were among the writers Hindemith set to music in these compositions; the songs give an insight into the richness of his tone color and movement.

I have thought a great deal about the attractive figure of Hermann Reutter; he was one of those whom we might call "silent in their own country"—so silent that it took some time before we became close. What brought us together was thinking about the way a new creative idea might come into being and be developed. Before a musical concept can be thoroughly and successfully formulated, many prerequisites must be fulfilled. A literary education, practical effectiveness in concert, and a teaching function must become synchronized in a very specific way.

While we were both on a concert tour, I felt that Hermann Reutter was the right man asking the right questions. This coincidence of prerequisites, though it may appear rather haphazard, occurs more frequently than we realize. On the other hand, in music it may not always be possible to achieve such confluence. What is less a matter of serendipity is that the musician must find his public—that is, he must publish and appear in public. Young Hermann Reutter, with his songs set to poems by Theodor Storm, understood that superbly. But he was less successful when he dedicated the *Winternachtskantilene* to Irmel and me and attempted to be somewhat lightweight both in theme and treatment.

Time must be ripe both for the creative question and for its answer. Reutter understood this most especially in regard to the radio-opera version of *The Bridge of San Luis Rey*, with a libretto based on Thornton Wilder's novel, which he gave its world premiere with first-rate singers on the Frankfurt radio. In this event I had—unfortunately for the only time—the opportunity to share the microphone with the highly regarded Martin Held, who was reading the part of the Speaker. It amused and comforted me that even an actor of such eminence often misspeaks— Held followed each mistake with a loud obscenity. But even this opera by Reutter showed that there is a time during which the public takes the works of a writer such as Wilder to its heart, only to let them die with their author. It might be fair to say that it is a sign of their lasting value that during his long life Reutter's works (he traveled the world as teacher and accompanist until he was eighty and almost blind) found so little acclaim.

251

I first encountered the music of Zoltan Kodály in Fricsay's rehearsals of the *Dances from Galanta* and the *Háry János Suite*. They strike me as a curious mixture of entertaining effects and a fanatic determination to unite Hungarian folk melodies with his own individual music, each enhancing the other. In Vienna a friendly journalist (such people do exist there!) told me vivid stories about the shrewd old master Kodály, who once, after a full year, returned a composition sent to him with the remark, "Bad." In his relations with me Kodály was never anything but extremely kind, though he was known to be cold as a rule. After the debut concert in Budapest he telephoned me at my hotel; after the *Dichterliebe* he even wrote to me; these were said to have been absolutely unique acts.

Budapest, its "Margaret Island" with the couples freely embracing in the Parisian manner, the theater with the audience bursting with emotionality—these were always a feast for me. Hungarians love to sing, and they are mindful of the richness of their heritage of folksong; they never tire of keeping it alive.

Kodály and I met again when he conducted his last major symphonic concert in London. Of course the program included his own works, and I was expected to sing ballads in Hungarian for three-quarters of an hour. This was quite an uncomfortable situation. The old gentleman with his flawless command of German sat beside me for two days, his elegant boots sticking out in front of him, trying to teach me the proper pronunciation. If he had to make me repeat for too long a time, he would remark softly but with determination, "Let's at least pretend that you understand what you're singing."

Well, the fakery worked more than adequately in the Festival Hall, before an audience that filled the house. The almost four thousand listeners, half of whom were Hungarian exiles, responded with tears of joy. I can still see the heavy golden laurel wreath that was placed around Kodály's neck at the end of the concert. A happy fate later gave me a Hungarian wife, who made me a little more familiar with the language that has absolutely nothing in common with ours.

When he was eighty years old, Kodály remarried. He proposed to his very young assistant and pupil with the words, "How would you like to be my widow very soon?"

The "young" couple attended the Bienniale for contemporary music in Venice, sitting among the few listeners who dotted the auditorium of the Teatro Fenice. The performers on the stage—a larger group by far than the audience—were struggling with works by Hans Werner Henze. With Ettore Gracis conducting, I sang selections from the *Elegy for Young Lovers*, and the applause was as frenetic as could be expected from so few hands. Kodály and his shy wife came to my dressing room to ask me with a friendly smile, but pointedly, "You actually sing this sort of stuff?"

I am sure Henze was too dissonant for his taste.

Hans Werner Henze and I often and happily—for his part as well, I think—performed together in world premieres of his works. Our long series of collaborations ended abruptly, in a way I found totally unnecessary. It was in 1969, when Henze was self-critically calling on composers to take music to the streets. His previous compositions, he claimed, were counterrevolutionary, overly aesthetical, courting establishment approval. He was looking for a way that musical language, no matter how corrupt and tattered it might be, could reach people who needed to be awakened by music.

Today Henze has largely moved away from this form of art directed to the people; he wants more than simply to shake people awake politically and synchronize them ideologically. On television he has indicated that creativity appropriated to political purposes could no longer claim the name of art if it prostituted itself on the streets. Where has art that is dominated by party, state, and society led us? It has resulted in reduction to the lowest common denominator and to cheap flattery, as we have seen in fascist and communist dictatorships.

Of course such a misunderstanding of art does not occur by chance; in every case it results from the helplessness of artists who for decades laughed at their paying listeners, who in turn stared in incomprehension. While art must not be allowed to establish itself in a vacuum above the heads of those for whom it is intended, neither may it exist solely in opposition to society.

The world premiere of Henze's oratorio, *The Raft of the Medusa*, took place in Hamburg's "Planten un Blomen" hall. In spite of its "Ho, ho, Ho Chi Minh" ending, the work was impressive and persuasive. Ernst Schnabel, the author of the libretto, brought along a troop of students from Berlin's Free University, so that they might plant the red flag next to the conductor and shout provocatively, to give the performance its ideological flavor. Schnabel was not entirely easy with his plan, as his nervousness made clear. Henze too looked somewhat paler than usual. He said, "It's going to be an exciting night." And yet in his new work he had not drawn artistic conclusions from his own self-critical remarks. He did not reduce his demands on the audience one whit. But they were never allowed to be made, since—for the only time in my career—not one note of the work was heard by the assembled audience. The world premiere failed because of much ado about nothing. *The Raft of the Medusa,* dedicated to Che Guevara and sold to the Norddeutsche Rundfunk for 80,000 marks, only made it as far as the dress rehearsal and the recording of it; Henze refused to conduct without the presence of a red flag. Like myself, the orchestra and chorus had come from West Berlin, and they were not a little astonished that they of all people, who owed their freedom from the Red threat to the Allies, were expected to demonstrate in favor of Communism.

After a wait of about twenty minutes, while the police, like extras in an operetta, marched in noisily to take their stations in front of the conductor's stand, the chorus had had enough. They began to leave the stage. My patience equally taxed, I joined them. Some of the audience began to applaud to indicate that they were unwilling to tolerate a political demonstration.

But even this debacle, and a long letter I wrote to the offended composer, could have had little to do with the fanatics abandoning their determination to restructure society. All of us are hopelessly enmeshed in material existence. The experience of supertemporality, as revealed by the great works of art, should mean all the more to us.

In 1952 Erwin Stein, the head of the largest British music publishing company, got in touch with us at our London hotel and came to pay a call with his enchanting wife, a member of the royal family. At first it was not clear what was on his mind. Stein, who himself composed prodigally and had been a student of Arnold Schönberg, was not trying to persuade me to do more to advocate the second School of Vienna. Rather, he eventually spoke out on behalf of his protégé, Benjamin Britten. Britten's new opera, *Billy Budd*, was to be performed soon in Berlin, and they had me in mind for the leading role. It pained me more than I can say to have to reject such a flattering offer. The engagements Tietjen and my concert agents had loaded my calendar with were already too much to handle. How happy I am that one day I could make up for this refusal! Not until nine years later did Britten write me a letter that included the following passage:

Coventry Cathedral, like so many other wonderful buildings in Europe, was destroyed in the last war. Now it has been most remarkably reconstructed, and there will be a large festival to inaugurate the new building the end of May and beginning of June next year (1962). I was asked to write a new work for this event, which touches us all. What I am writing will probably become one of my most important works. It is a major requiem for chorus and orchestra (commemorating the dead of all nations during the last war), and I am inserting many poems by an English poet, Wilfred Owen, who fell in the First World War, into the Latin text. These splendid lyrics, filled with hate of the rage to destroy, form a kind of commentary to the requiem. Of course I am using them in English. The poems are being

---

scored for tenor and baritone, accompanied by a
chamber orchestra placed among the other instrumentalists. They require singing of the utmost beauty, intensity, and seriousness. I am
asking you with great timidity if you would be
willing to sing the baritone part.

At both the end and the beginning of the letter Britten
apologized for disturbing me.

When Irmel and I arrived in Coventry in May 1962,
we were greeted by rain and cold. As was so often the
case, the hours before the first rehearsal, and afterward
as well, were made more difficult by the hotel, where the
wind blew through the tiny rooms, meals ordered from
room service failed to arrive, and the nonfunctioning electric sockets could be made to work only after endless efforts by workmen dripping with perspiration. When we
stepped into the fairly modern-looking cathedral, we were
met with penetrating cold. When I begged the furnace
tender for a little more steam for the sake of our health,
he laughed contemptuously. "Just practice hard, that'll
make you warm."

But then there was the sound of Ben's music, in which
I was to sing one of the two soldiers. The male solos were
contrasted to the liturgy (soprano and chorus). The work
seemed to breathe great seriousness and was chock-full
of new melodic ideas. Various stylistic influences were
evident. I heard Auerbach, the photographer who was
snapping away during rehearsals, jeer, "I thought we'd
already had the premiere of Orff's *Carmina*." And the
most fortissimo passages reminded me of William Wal-
ton's excesses of this kind. But the work as a whole was

imbued with Britten's highly personal expression; it was remarkable how often he managed to engage the emotions and occupy the mind at the same time. Meredith Davies, the conductor, who directed the larger company, approached his task with zest, but his interpretation seemed to me somewhat too athletic for this particular work.

The rehearsals were long. The British are hard workers, sometimes excessively persevering. Furthermore the cold defied all description. My birthday tea party took place in a merciful stray sunbeam on the street, where we fled during the break, escaping the refrigerator temperature in the hall.

The first performance created an atmosphere of such intensity that by the end I was completely undone; I did not know where to hide my face. Dead friends and past suffering arose in my mind. And of course singing with the gifted Peter Pears was also a moving experience.

The soprano part was not taken by Galina Vishnevskaya, as programmed. She was detained in the Soviet Union, although the reason for her trip was a very special event. As she herself tells in her book, the minister of culture Irina Furzeva talked some kind of drivel to her about West Berlin and all the enemies of the Soviet Union lying in wait. It is also quite possible that Moscow interpreted my participation as a "provocation," since I was and am a West Berliner. So instead of Galina, the marvelous English soprano Heather Harper sang the part. Benjamin Britten knew her well; she had proved herself more than once in his works. I can still hear her triumphant silvery sound.

The following day we lunched with Britten, and he asked us to call him Ben. He told many stories about Shostakovich and about the somewhat isolated Paul Hindemith, who was overjoyed when his "young colleague" Britten asked him for advice.

The scheduled recording of the requiem was delayed. Shortly after the Coventry performance Britten wrote me, "The truth is that I was pretty sick and had to spend a lot of time in bed on doctors' orders. A sad state of affairs! Because it means that for three months I have to cancel everything."

I therefore urged a competing record company to make available time already set aside for me for the Britten recording—"Because," Ben wrote, "I consider this recording as testimony to what so many of us honestly feel, and no one is able to make this testimony as crystal clear as you, dear Dieter."

I did succeed in persuading the company, and Ben's joy was great. During this recording each of us was suffering from some kind of minor complaint, and more than once I had to comfort the tormented composer. I also tried to distract him with other matters, and that is how we came to talk of my old dream of an opera of Shakespeare's *King Lear*. Ben seemed interested at once, though he sighed that such a project would take years and years of preparation. And there was no time to waste, he thought, since just as I was the only one who could sing Lear, only Peter could be considered for the Fool. And not much time was left before Pears would have to stop performing—at the time Peter was enjoying the idea of retirement, though he went on performing for more than ten years after that. But Ben did not live long enough to do *Lear*. I am grateful to destiny for granting me the most valid setting of this material, through Aribert Reimann.

During the recording of the *War Requiem*, Ben and Peter turned up unexpectedly at our hotel for dinner. The *Lear* opera I had proposed was very much on their minds. The shadow of Verdi, who had tragically failed in his projected setting of Lear, hung persistently over our discussion.

We also talked about other topics. Ben wanted to write a cantata for the Dieskau Consort, as he called my ensemble that gave yearly chamber-music recitals. The result, Ben's revision of Purcell's cantata *When Night Her Purple Veil*, was not what I had expected. Once again Ben proved that he rejected the iconoclasts without tradition in music, and that he was thinking of the recent German first performance of the cantata based on Giordano Bruno by Henze. Peter could not find a comfortable role for himself in this music, no matter how hard I tried to explain to him that it was not because of a lack of tradition. I gave Ben my own attempt at translating the baritone sections of the requiem, which seemed to me to catch the rhythms and rhymes of Wilfred Owen's difficult poetry more felicitously than had been done in the other sections by Count von Hesse (who used the pseudonym Ludwig Landgraf).

The lyrics for a song cycle Ben wrote for me after Irmel's death—*To Dieter the Past and Future*—were made up of aphorisms and poems by the English painter and poet on the edge of romanticism, William Blake. We must thank Peter Pears for the choice of texts. I was especially taken with the terseness, the British understatement, the intellectual concentration, and the enigmatic smile of these dense, linguistically original sayings. I came to value them truly later on, when I had an opportunity to see this early surrealist's watercolors in the Tate Gallery.

I am glad that you have made friends with the idea of the "Blake Songs." Because I am fond of them and worked hard on them. Peter organized a wonderful arrangement for me—six or seven songs, interspersed with very dramatic statements, wonderful to declaim (sung—not spoken). Very serious! It is hard to capture such weighty words in music; so far I am not entirely dissatisfied. I'm sorry that the score is arriving so late, but for a long time I could not come up with the proper idea. Now I feel that it is right for you.

After we had given a world premiere of the songs in the small town hall in Aldeburgh, there was a recording session in London that for two days took us to the same Kingsway Hall where we had already met many times for memorable recording sessions. In between there was a day of painting all alone in my hotel room while a picturesque storm roared outside. As expected, the taut recording gave the lie to Ben's fears that the four hours I had allotted for it might not be sufficient time. Though after the intense concentration I urgently needed two hours of midday rest, we were nevertheless finished an hour early—almost the norm for me.

The very next day saw the London premiere of the songs. Fairfield Hall in Croydon introduced me to an astonishing cultural center at the edge of the city. A number of important people had made the hour-long pilgrimage by car just to be there. Unfortunately the weather had seen to it that I was in a weakened state, especially after the concert was over. Ben touchingly apologized for his bad playing, and I admitted his errors in precision. But we were nevertheless happy about the outcome—for which we were, after all, responsible—and the audience's shouts of approval.

Ben found it difficult to deal with the world. Though he was careful never to let anyone see that side of him, darkness reigned all the more frequently in his music, speaking of the shadow side of life. Time and again Ben was driven to express his personal suffering, especially in his works for the stage. This moral aspect also discloses his musical understanding. He never ceased searching for innocence. Although he hated quarrels, he had no trouble asserting himself against opposition.

Of course the time soon came to sing the requiem for other conductors, with widely varying temperaments, which meant that the music too showed itself in different lights. An element of fussiness might become evident, or one might notice a certain stickiness. But on occasion, and in relation to the formal concept, even these contributed to the work's fascination. Since the early romantic period composers have understood that repetition of whole or partial themes can enhance understanding and memory. This holds as true for Wagner's Saxon urge to tell stories and make an impression—an urge that repeats elements of the action in the form of reminiscence—as it does for Liszt's early works and for Dvořák's later symphonic poems, in which trenchant musical phrases are emphasized by repetition, to such an extent that the audience is overcome by yawns of understanding. If, furthermore, the repetitions are of simpleminded ideas, the listener can easily feel insulted. Such banal simplicity never occurs in

Britten's work, and since the listener is thus spared, the composer always wins complete approval.

It is certainly a matter of concern: For a creative musician it is extraordinary to have an audience of millions in his lifetime, and Britten was cordially envied as a result. Britten's popularity confirmed for me once again that for a composer it can, paradoxically, be essential to be rooted in the intonation and sensibility of his own landscape in order to be recognized all over the world.

Anyone burdened with grief—as I was when in 1963 Irmel fell victim to eclampsia at Manuel's birth, leaving me alone with three sons—is simply not able to withstand the emotional onslaught of such music. The afflicted listener is condemned to temporary Philistinism. A time of testing began. As in the ancient Romans' willingness to die, I was overcome by a desire to follow Irmel, sharing her death rather than simply enduring it, like an avalanche of sterile sorrow. Until that time I had lived my life with an inner confidence, almost without questioning it. Now doubt reared its head—I doubted everything. The ground under my feet had moved so violently that nothing seemed in place any longer. Black despondency took possession of me. Even before I knew it, life had become hateful. Anxious and frightened, I faced the road ahead. Internal disorder paralyzed me, and when I awoke from the initial numbness, I saw clearly the power that had been inherent in Irmel, her ability to maintain her partner's being. A few pages beyond the passage where she had laid aside the book she was reading at the end, E.T.A. Hoffmann's *Die Elixiere des Teufels* (she read in solitude, as if reading were a sort of suspect activity), I found a passage that touched me most deeply; to this day I do not know whether I ran across it by accident.

When he leaped up in fright and, holding a lamp, went looking for his wife, she had given birth to a little boy. He took the child from its mother's lap, but at the same moment the woman gave a terrifying, penetrating scream and, as if seized by powerful fists, writhed. The midwife and her assistant came in, followed by the doctor; when she went to help the woman, she recoiled in horror, since the woman had stiffened into death.

For a long time Hoffmann's novel preoccupied me, with its breakneck chase of the self through the character of the principal figure, Medardus, and that of the author. Content, form, and language unsettled me to such an extent that I was startled awake, and wept.

During the period of unconsciousness, before my feelings were grounded again, there were many unsolicited attempts to comfort me that seemed to assume that the person to be comforted was no longer capable of thinking. But there were also long conversations with many patient friends—Erich Riebensahm, Günther Weissenborn, Wolfgang Strich, and others. I owe special thanks to Jörg Demus for teaching me, and not only through his playing, to tolerate music once more. On his own initiative he came from Vienna with the intention of getting me to open my mouth to sing without my throat's constricting. He demonstrated thematic comparisons on the piano, perhaps between sonatas and certain lieder passages, and quite unaware I hummed along. The matter-of-factness of this friend who was serving as my accompanist freed me for action.

And there was the difficulty of suffering through repeated visual memories of the children and, instead of the quiet I needed, having greater worries. When the children said good-bye to Irmel's "last Christmas tree" right after her death, it was the touching gifts Ben and Peter sent from Aldeburgh that pulled me back to the surface of the slough of despond.

As a consequence of our way of life, Irmel had become almost the sole point of stability for the children, no matter how often she traveled with me. I had only a very peripheral sense of what children mean or need. Public persons who travel a great deal should think deeply about the question of children. Nevertheless, we had looked forward to the new arrival with the greatest joy and curiosity. But all unaware, the crescendo of life's zest had been lost in the darkness. The only thought that consoled me was that their early life and music had given the children a number of positive influences.

Having followed Irmel's coffin along with Mathias and Martin—one on each side—I paid a great deal of attention to their questions and their search for something to cling to. We achieved a closeness that comforted me more than anything that reached me from outside.

I was largely spared a father's helplessness in the face of his sons' rebellion, except for moments when the boys were not yet adults and my own crises in the years after Irmel's death. Of course the heritage of the name makes for additional burdens, since all three boys chose artistic careers close to the area of my endeavors. I am certain that even if they had chosen different fields, the name would have represented a target that could only with effort be reconciled with personal demands.

A father can scarcely hope for more than a trusting friendship with his children. And I am glad that my sons, unlike those in Thomas Mann's family, do not need to jot

down notes for future conversations in order to make sure
that the flow of words is not dammed up too embarrassingly. We never lacked for things to talk about, especially
when there were artistic experiences to be shared. And
when we all took our places for an evening of chamber
music, we always felt the greatest intimacy, such as non-
musicians can only guess at. Whether Manuel is discussing questions of interpretation in the cello literature with
me, or Martin, the conductor, brings into the discussion
the interpretation of one or another orchestra leader, or
Mathias, the stage designer, raises questions of stage
space, or my own experiences on the concert stage serve
as a negative or positive model, the exchange is always
lively and fruitful. The success all three sons have earned
makes my heart glad.

Not long after Irmel's death I inevitably had to resume
my concert tours. Everything suddenly happened as if for
the first time: even standing alone at her grave after all
the grieving crowd had left. When—as so often, but this
time especially welcome—Gerda and Hans Erich Riebensahm celebrated my birthday with me, the first one without Irmel, the children gave us a special present. At the
instigation of Margit, our indispensable nanny, they and
some of their friends had rehearsed bewitching tableaux
vivants. One especially, a rococo minuet, brought tears to
Hans Erich's eyes. Costumes, concept, and performance
on the broad roof terrace enchanted us. I was strangely
moved by the grace of the girls in Greek garments, the
reflection of the sun sparkling in their hair ornaments,
against the background of springtime greenery ruffled by
the wind. It was a way to reach out for Irmel's jubilation
and joy: For once since the funeral I did not feel compelled
to move away from her, in the direction of instability. Nor-

mally I was troubled and pained by the contradiction between the unchanged four walls and the flock of female
relatives who had alighted and temporarily made their
nest there, without understanding. When they went so far
as to invite unwanted overnight guests, I retreated.

I did not regain full command of my abilities until I
met Ruth. The relationship had its complications, but it
was unexpected, gladdening, and enriching. Irmel and I
had too carelessly measured everyone by the same standard. Now I was confronted by differences, and to my
astonishment I saw myself compelled to recant or redis-
cover. It had been in the fragrant springtime garden that
I had first realized that the children needed a mother; I
also understood how difficult it would be to reconcile the
children's needs with the demands of their father and a
woman who was a stranger to them. Such musings were
to prove justified all too soon. It was now my fate to stagger
from one strain to another.

During a visit to Amsterdam without Irmel, the city
was windswept, with an autumn chill. Sviatoslav Richter
was staying in the hotel room above mine, and I heard
him practicing Stravinsky's *Capriccio* into the night. When
I mentioned it to Nina, his wife, somewhat later, I saw
startled faces—in part because he was just beginning to
study the work.

The following day Gerald Moore accompanied me in
Brahms' *Schöne Magelone* in the marvelous large hall of
the Concertgebouw. When the entire stage is sold out, the
auditorium has literally ideal acoustics, and the audience's quiet and concentration almost envelops the singer.
The press reactions—perhaps precisely because of the
standing ovation—were widely divergent.

Ovations can be given in very different ways; hardly

any two are alike. The most moving moment for me may have been the time in 1971, after my debut recital with Daniel Barenboim in Israel, where I was the first German soloist to appear; at the close of the concert the audience spontaneously rose to its feet and cheered me. This made all the difficult preliminary negotiations well worth the trouble.

It took me a while to understand that in the United States whistling is a form of approval. When at the end of a Hugo Wolf concert in San Francisco I heard whistles, I thought the audience was rejecting me; I did not immediately recall how often during my time as a prisoner of war and in the postwar period in Berlin I had heard Americans respond positively in this way.

By the way, during the Nazi dictatorship one hardly ever heard vocal acclaim. I have observed that loud and cheerful applause as an expression of joy gradually increases from totalitarian systems to capitalism. Recently I gave a recital based on Heine poems for the first time in the East Berlin Schauspielhaus, and I found myself on the dividing line between East and West as far as applause went as well. In the Soviet Union or other Eastern-bloc countries, vocal ovations are extremely rare; they will break out in Hungary, at most. In this Western-oriented, comparatively free enclave they sound almost as they do in Paris . . .

In Amsterdam I spied Frank Martin's and his wife's smiling faces in the audience. After the concert he offered me the leading role of Prospero in his opera of Shakespeare's *Tempest*, a complete setting of Schlegel's translation. The lean-faced composer with the ready, cheerful laugh had written the part with me in mind, but in the end I was unable to participate in the production. Shortly before the premiere at the Vienna Staatsoper, with Martin's friend Ernest Ansermet conducting, I contracted an almost fatal case of food poisoning from some fish I had eaten in Brussels. In the middle of the night a not entirely sober woman physician wrote the order admitting me to a hospital, cheerfully reassuring me, "You must not count on surviving."

Nevertheless, three months later I was well enough to resume traveling and singing. In Vienna, Eberhard Wächter courageously leaped into the breach and was a great success in the part. Later on Frank Martin came to Berlin to stage at least Prospero's three most important scenes with me and the Berlin Philharmonic. His *Gesänge aus Jedermann* and the part of Christ in *Golgotha* are among the most beautiful parts a baritone can attempt in contemporary music. They are imbued with a guileless piety.

Actually Britten and Pears, as well as the Martins, had planned on attending the next Amsterdam concert, but they did not arrive until the following day. We arranged a meeting at the American Hotel (which had briefly harbored Max Beckmann during the Nazi regime, as I had just read in the painter's published diaries). We talked about the following year's Aldeburgh Festival. Ben had established his own festival on the Suffolk coast, in part to give a world premiere of one of his own compositions every year. I was to perform the new songs and some of Schumann's melodramas (unfortunately we never did the Schumann).

Two years later the *War Requiem* was heard in Amsterdam. Sviatoslav Richter and his wife came backstage, and I invited myself to visit them at their hotel, where I also ran into Peter and Ben. During the lively conversation

Ben mentioned his intention of entrusting Slava and me with Brahms' *Magelone* romances at the Aldeburgh parish church. Though Britten was not overly fond of Brahms, he came to the rehearsals, curious to see how I would get along with the Russian giant of the piano. . . . During the concert itself Ben was the page turner.

That evening in Amsterdam saw the birth of another plan: Ben wanted to conduct a recording of Tchaikovsky's opera *Eugene Onegin* with Vishnevskaya, Peter, and me. Unfortunately the project came to nothing, perhaps because of the Russian language; I might possibly have been able to read a transliteration and understand it, but Peter could not master it.

The following autumn, after the Edinburgh Festival, I was looking forward to singing the *War Requiem* in the Benedictine Abbey in Ottobeuren (in Bavaria) on the occasion of a major German-English conference. Though I got up at six in the morning, anticipation was no match for the fog that prevented any plane from taking off from Edinburgh to London. A car took my secretary, Diether Warneck, and me to Glasgow, where we caught a direct flight to London. But we missed the connecting flight that would have taken us in time—at least in time for the dress rehearsal with Ben and Peter—to Ottobeuren. For three hours a Lufthansa blonde tried to find seats for us on scheduled flights that had long been sold out. When this exasperating attempt came to an end, I boldly decided to charter a small private plane—whose pilot, however, had first to be persuaded to leave his own wedding: no small task, as may be imagined. After two more hours we finally soared away in a grand flight in the miniplane that would, we hoped, land somewhere in Germany—as close to Ottobeuren as possible—after a nonstop flight of three and a half hours. The likable man at the controls (the pilot version of the steadfast jack-of-all-trades is the same all over the world) navigated and calculated all the way. He also had me spell the name of Memmingen, which I mentioned as a possible landing strip. After much radio discussion he persuaded NATO in Frankfurt to give us permission to land at the military airport at Memmingen. No sooner had we happily begun to set down than the radio announced that the general was holding an inspection, and we could not possibly interrupt. We could see even from the air that people were nervously running around the little landing strip. When we finally hit the runway, the military gentlemen were taken aback by the presence of civilians. The customs inspector, arriving quickly from town, seemed to find it extremely difficult to process us. Time passed. In spite of his nervousness, the pilot began to assume an expression of some complacency. Knowing that in ten minutes he would be on his way home, he smiled at me. "It's very exciting, isn't it?"

With lights flashing, the police escorted the car we had been given to Ottobeuren, though not before placing one last obstacle in our way: "Your passport has not been renewed."

Close to fainting, I managed to voice a simple "Yes, it has."

After a quick glance, the officer admitted, "Oh, excuse me. But not your Herr Warneck's passport . . ."

But there too he was out of luck, and was forced to mumble "Excuse me" once more.

By the time we saw the abbey before us in the dusk—the scene of my childhood holidays, where I first understood what a powerful instrument the organ is when to my intense delight the choirmaster played for me alone, on the oldest of the three instruments, Mozart's Fantasy in F minor—the dress rehearsal had long since ended without me. Ottobeuren, overrun by visitors and noisy, as it was, could not prevent me in my exhaustion from sleeping deeply before the concert. A brief conversation with the chamber orchestra before the performance had to make do, and Ben steered us safely through the shoals.

Deeply moved after the concluding "Let us sleep now," I heard from a distance the voice of then Federal President Lübke saying to me, "We've met in Berlin."

At a time when he intensely disliked playing the piano in public—he had undergone his first serious operation—Ben assigned me at least half a lieder recital for his festival. At the same time he hatched a plan to perform Schumann's *Scenes from Goethe's Faust*, an idea that delighted me after having waited so long. After all, this music was among the favorite works of my models Julius Stockhausen and Johannes Messchaert. Ben wrote, "The more I study the work, the more I find it beautiful and interesting. There are two or three weak passages, but Schumann himself stated that the whole thing should not be performed in one evening. I'm working on a few cuts and am looking forward to performing this great work with you." A P.S. asked, "Do you have any suggestions for our Schubert in other recitals? Have you discovered some beauties?"

Schubert with Ben! That ought to take me a long way toward understanding the greatest of lieder composers. Over and over, when Ben would interrupt himself during rehearsals at his old piano in the wonderful large studio of Red House to think out loud about tempi and techniques, I needed only to keep my ears wide open to profit from his ideas.

Schumann's *Faust* cost him a great deal of energy. But when the impressive, dedicated performance was over, the applause kept swelling and would not die down. I can still see Ben, tottering slightly during and after the performance. Tall, slightly bent forward, he stepped to the conductor's podium. The concert was held at Snape near Aldeburgh in the auditorium he had built himself and had now rebuilt a second time after a fire. Ben's slight tottering made him seem like a tall tree shaken by the wind. His "Wonderful" at the end was almost inaudible. He seemed like someone who makes a religious profession in a delirium. Blissful and exhausted, he held out the score to the public in honor of Schumann.

This concert kindled considerable interest, and many conductors performed the work soon afterward. I made use of the invitations to work my way further into the character of Faust. Back in Berlin, the Constable clouds from Suffolk stayed in my mind, with their rush to change color and possibly bring rain. I gratefully recalled a conversation with the Duchess of Kent, whom I met in Ben's splendid library at the reception after the Schumann oratorio.

Listening to Ben talk was a special event. Unlike so many conductors, he had no mannerisms at all. He was much too much of an original to seem like an actor, as is true for most of the lions of the podium. No one ever caught him playing a role. He spoke quite rapidly, but without tripping over his words; one could not tell from his speech that often several thoughts were occupying him at once. Everything he said revealed a nature dedicated to order, and he had nothing but contempt for the fascination with accident that had overcome the avant-gardists of the day. Inspiration was much too precious to him to misuse on any sort of exhibitionism. Nothing repelled him more than an effect for its own sake, no matter how repeatedly he achieved powerful effects, with whatever uncompromising means. He would suddenly make room for them in unexpected, astonishingly new sounds, only to limit them again at once, for the sake of clarity. He was opposed to musical deluges, and carried simplification to the extreme of the spare indications in his later church operas.

On the other hand, it was only logical that Ben hesitated to participate in the movement to rid composition of extramusical elements, such as the New Viennese School introduced. The inspiration for any composition, sentiment as reflection, the poem, the concrete effect of orchestration—all were called into play when he composed. The result was what today is considered nonabsolute music. The consequent judgment was often the result of a misunderstanding, and yet was perhaps acceptable to him: He still makes music. He dares to make it. He is an "après-gardist."

Britten did not consider himself above writing music that was easy to perform and that communicated directly, such as the *Cantata Misericordium* for the centennial of the Red Cross in Geneva. The other composers commissioned to write for the occasion were Frank Martin and Witold Lutoslawski; one was intent on being "modern," while the other was inappropriately playful. They could not compare with Britten. I greatly enjoyed the effortless rehearsals, in part also because Ben accommodated me with such overwhelming cordiality and generous recognition and aided Maître Ansermet, who was old and already ailing.

Ben and Peter are no longer with us. The Dioscuri are surely missed in many lives for their human decency and helpfulness, seriousness in artistic matters, and warmth of feeling. Inspired singers are rare; Peter was one of them. And he had such an extensive knowledge of literature that in his search for operatic material and for poems to serve as the basis of musical settings he repeatedly struck gold, smoothing Ben's way to creativity. He was helpful in other ways as well. As a teacher he trained voices to Ben's particular style. As an organizer he took care of numerous details, when it was a matter of engaging artists for Aldeburgh or when they had questions concerning possible transpositions or the performance of Ben's music. But his voice rose above all else; he was able to preserve it even as he grew older, and we never grew tired of admiring it. He was aided by his dramatic flair and his stage presence, which made him the ideal protagonist of the operas written by his life's companion. Sir Peter can serve as a model of British unobtrusiveness, a warm and lively host, a man ever ready to offer help.

Even by the 1950s a visit to Switzerland for West Germans meant setting foot in a bucolic land, a pristine and tidy territory. This impression is modified only by a closer look. In 1953 Dr. Othmar Schoeck surprised me with a letter from Switzerland, asking me to come to Zurich to sing his *Lebendig begraben*, based on Gottfried Keller's work. I wrote back to express my pleasure in this opportunity to discover a different, less well-known Keller. But I also warned him that some passages in the very low register would have to be transposed. Schoeck reassured me:

I thoroughly appreciate your reservations, but I do not find them so insurmountable. When such a marvelous opportunity beckons to bring the work "to life" through your performance rather than letting it be "buried," it would be a downright miscarriage of justice not to make the necessary concessions. The strength of the voice in relation to the orchestra will only be improved by the pointing (by which I mean transposing the notes to a higher register) in the few recitative passages. As a "concerned father," I place such important aspects (for me at least, as well) into your hands, which I know to be loving ones from your cordial letter, and I hope with all my heart that my ardent wish to hear you sing this work will be fulfilled."

I traveled from Freiburg to Zurich by train, quietly enjoying the passing landscape. It was surely a good thing that the day before the performance Erich Schmid, the conductor at the Tonhalle, took me firmly in hand. The song cycle *Lebendig begraben* is rhythmically and tonally composed in such a way that it is easy to stumble.

But now the master, his wife, and his daughter were waiting for me in the small house under flowering trees on Zurich's Lettenholzstrasse. At the sight of my baby face, Schoeck seemed somewhat annoyed as he welcomed me. Then he went to the piano and began to play. We worked through the whole forty minutes of the work without stopping. (Just as, in this work, the flow of the voice is rarely interrupted.) Somewhere near the middle I noticed that his clouded brow smoothed out, that his concentration on the score was displaced by delight, and that at times he averted his face to conceal his emotion. I am sure that Schoeck had not heard his cycle for decades, not since the death of his friend Felix Loeffel (portrayed with so much character by the Swiss painter Cuno Amiet), who had sung it repeatedly after its world premiere in the 1920s. After the elation and the transfiguring joy brought to the man who is buried alive—symbol of the artist suffering from creative sterility—by his impending death, Othmar Schoeck jumped up to embrace me. And now our friendship was as natural as possible.

Then there was the first performance of the cycle *Nocturno* in a version with string orchestra conducted by Paul Sacher. Not long afterward Schoeck celebrated his seventieth birthday, and a ceremonial song recital was held in his honor at the Kaisersaal in Ottobeuren in connection with the German-Swiss Congress. First the master was given the Federal Merit Cross, then it was my turn to sing a whole sequence of lieder he himself had arranged. The Swiss pianist Margrit Weber accompanied me; the grand piano was placed in such a way that she could see the guest of honor. Both of us noticed at almost the same moment that during the song "Jugendgedanken," set to a poem by Keller, Schoeck became flushed and leaned weakly on his delicate wife, Hilde. Margrit struck a few wrong notes, and I had to swallow before I could go on. But everything went off smoothly, and later the two Schoecks insisted on climbing the stairs to my rustic room to thank me and stay for a chat.

I saw Schoeck again in the midst of Margrit Weber's large family in Zurich. I could not stop scrutinizing his frightened, deeply depressed face and wondering at the accuracy of the remarks he sometimes—though rarely—interjected into the lively conversation, removing the pipe he otherwise kept clenched between his teeth. When I lived in Zollikon, outside Zurich, for a short time, he was no longer among the living.

I still feel a need to sing his songs, such as the cycle *Unter Sternen*, which I performed in 1986 to commemorate his hundredth birthday, even though every performance outside Switzerland meets with misunderstanding or arrogantly false judgments ("Helvetianism," "provincialism"). True, Schoeck is not Mozart or Schubert; he is not even Hugo Wolf, whom he admired so much. He too, like Wolf, took the concept of cycles so seriously that he created whole notebooks, each with a unified theme, and therefore susceptible to monotony, because the composer wished to remain completely in the background, allowing the poet's words alone to dominate. But his word-stressing composing style is sensibly considerate of the poem, and his harmonic impulses frequently correspond strikingly to the poetry's inner life. I find it highly gratifying that at present some of Schoeck's numerous operas are enjoying a revival on the musical stage.

No matter how harsh and dry Schoeck's tonal structures may seem, they also contain a trace of exuberance and of the ecstatic. Nevertheless, the singer must invest more in his task than will be realized in the outward performance.

When I first met Boris Blacher on the stairs leading down to the Berlin subway, I had already sung his radio opera *Die Flut*, based on a libretto by his student Heinz von Kramer. I had enjoyed the performance on the Hessische Rundfunk, conducted by Otto Matzerath. Blacher initiated the mutual exchange of opera libretti between students and teacher; thus he himself wrote the splendid scenario for Gottfried von Einem's *Dantons Tod*. When he headed the conservatory, Blacher said to me time and again, his chatty tone slightly tinged with a Russian accent, "Don't you want to teach here?"

But I was rather put off by what he generally said next: "All you have to do is look in for a minute or two now and then. Your assistant will do the rest."

He viewed teaching entirely from his perspective as a composer, and perhaps he was unable to imagine how much time singers need before they feel secure and are truly adjusted to the teacher's idiosyncrasies. Real work can begin only after a period of such absorption.

It was not only in his views that Blacher seemed delicate, modest, unemotional, and uninterested in systematics. It is true that the part of his compositional work that dealt with opera had of necessity to encompass longer musical stretches because the text so demanded. But his oratorio *The Grand Inquisitor* reveals clearly that he always aimed at the tersest solution, persuasive in short passages. Elimination, concision, and at times witty summation were Blacher's special strengths. And the "Three Psalms," written during the war, which I was the first to perform in the 1960s, were typical of these traits. The long biblical texts are over in seven minutes. Blacher seemed pleased with my rendition: He made me a gift of his holograph score.

Amiable, with a dry wit, Blacher once served as the announcer at a conservatory concert—he, the director. He stuttered mightily and basically said only what was already in the printed program. Much furrowing of the brow and an embarrassment tinged with sarcasm involuntarily created the impression of a naive person. His apparent personality was not unlike his music: There too naive and meaningless phrases run up against mathematical trickiness. Themes are abruptly introduced, only to be abandoned again just as quickly. Blacher was not given to commenting at length on his own ideas. He seemed to fit in well with the students of those years, the young women in miniskirts and the young men bearded like old men, concealing the souls of children.

His directness and openness stood him in good stead when the occasion arose. Once, when Gustav Rudolf and Ilse Sellner had given a lavish garden party, a few guests—politicians, actors, and singers—remained behind and started a discussion. One stage director pontificated at length about the advantages and disadvantages of literary opera. When he finally fell silent, Blacher could be heard to say, "That's the most errant nonsense!" Relieved laughter!

At a time when bad health was already making Blacher's life fairly unbearable and his academic activity had shifted to research, Blacher and two other music professors had a cozy meeting in Hans Erich Riebensahm's house. Ruth and I were also present. Glib and mumbling as usual, Blacher crowned the evening with the remark, "Nowadays we don't give a shit about works of art. But measurements—ah, measurements!"

Among his troubled listeners Ruth was the only good sport, expressing some appreciation for his remark; the others failed to comprehend that Blacher's irony was directed at himself. Just at that time he was studying acoustical measurements of every sort.

Lean and not very tall, Blacher moved loosely, deliberately, and with exaggerated relaxation. When he and his enchanting wife, the pianist Gerty Herzog, came to dinner at our house, he loved to discourse drily, in his Berlin German with the Russian overtone, on music, culture in general, life, and money. When he sat across from a respected ideologue, he might present a cynical indifference to cultural questions. But this facade concealed a search for strength and simplicity, for the essentials. And as Aribert Reimann told me often enough, Blacher trained his students to develop whatever was specific to themselves, to find their own style. Only someone with something to say can travel the road of a composer.

It is not my purpose here to discuss Blacher's work, but I do wish to speak briefly about the oratorio *The Grand Inquisitor*. It is based on a text derived by the conductor Leo Borchard from a chapter in Dostoevsky's *The Brothers Karamazov*. The work was completed in the small house on the Schützallee, not far from ours, into which Blacher had moved. It was during the period just after the war— in a Berlin that had not yet been divided—that Blacher's powers came into their own. His music could be heard on both the American-licensed and the Russian-sponsored radio stations, in the theaters, in the concerts of the Philharmonic, and in the opera house. Christoph von Dohnanyi conducted the second performance of the *Grand Inquisitor*—the first had taken place in 1947 in the Admiralty Palace—on Radio Free Berlin. The material has a utopian feeling, with an apocalyptic mood. Returned to earth, Christ meets with the highest representative of ecclesiastical power, the Cardinal–Grand Inquisitor, and is greeted with the words, "Thou hast come to hinder us."

Blacher solves the stylistic problem of the overwhelming reproach with striking simplicity, by leaving narration and elaboration to the chorus and assigning the role of the priest to the baritone. Of course the chief effect is

---

meant to come from the chorus, which is also given the longest passages of the hour-long composition. The Inquisitor's recitative style is close to baroque models. I invested—successfully, I believe—my vocal line (limited by Blacher to small tonal increments) with as much neutrality as possible. And lo, the effect was a perfect balance of chorus and soloist.

My strongest impression among my many experiences of Blacher's music remains *Hamlet,* arising from a 1940 symphonic poem and revised ten years later in the Deutsche Oper in cooperation with Tatiana Gsovsky into a full-length composition for ballet. Here the law of artistic economy, which all of Blacher's music observes, reaches its peak. The orchestral sound is hard, clear, elastic, and, as it were, painted in primary colors—an hour of post-Stravinsky music, but without frenzy.

Many decades earlier I had met Blacher's outstanding student, the modest and unassuming Aribert Reimann. At that time we were in Berlin preparing the premiere of Henze's opera *Elegy for Young Lovers* for Schwetzingen, and he was teaching me the part of Mittenhofer at the piano. Since then there have been countless occasions when Aribert unlocked new works—not only his own compositions—for me; his judgments helped to determine my way of listening to and assessing contemporary music. Though I was the first to perform some of his works ("Totentanz," "Zyklus," "Wolkenloses Christfest"), it is of special satisfaction to me that a small hint on my part, given repeatedly, instigated his greatest effort at opera to that time—*Lear.*

Our collaboration on this project did not take the form

outsiders like to imagine. I gave no instructions and made no suggestions. I did not discuss how the vocal tessitura was to appear, whether this or that had to be differently arranged depending on my strength, and other such details. Aribert was aware of the situation, and acted accordingly. A sensitive and gentle accompanist, he had already been entrusted by a great many beginning singers in his conservatory classes (now equivalent to my courses at the Berlin Musikhochschule), as well as by successful and experienced performers, with their first or subsequent steps. He had an unerring sense for what was latent in and possible for the voices for which he wrote. His most recent opera, *Troades*, demonstrates this skill very clearly; the musical traits of each of the leading female characters are appropriate to the best-developed capacities of that particular voice.

The stringency with which Reimann developed his art, arising on the one hand from the Second Vienna School and on the other from his spiritual mentor, Boris Blacher, has proved what a responsible artist, and how rich in inspiration, he is. He has bypassed fashion and short-lived experiments to find his way to ever more direct and moving expression, which does not ignore the impulses and burdens of the present. If, we take his concentrated, unerring working methods, as signposts for the road ahead of him, we can be sure that he will continue to refine a language that can be performed and elaborated.

I spoke earlier of the principal giant of emerging modernism, Igor Stravinsky, in connection with Busoni's *Doktor Faust*. The German premiere in Berlin of his cantata *Abraham and Isaac*, to be sung in Hebrew, was imminent.

Of course I was as unfamiliar with this language as I had been with Hungarian when I sang Kodály. It took a great deal of time to pound the part into my head; composed in a strictly post-Webern style, the cantata was rhythmically quite tricky. The master, communicating from the United States, admitted freely that he would not be able to conduct the work himself because it was too difficult for him. I confess that this was something of a relief, since the reports I had heard about Stravinsky as a conductor had not been ecstatic. I rehearsed a phonetic version of the lyrics a few times with a likable young Israeli.

Then the master himself arrived, together with his Boswell, the conductor Robert Craft. The first sight I had of him were white wool socks under galoshes as he got out of the limousine. Then he made the effort to climb the seven steps of my house in the Westend, having first counted them out loud. He gave the impression of a small, delicate pile of rubble with completely undiminished ambitions, including that of being a musical innovator. While we rehearsed, we sat around the coffee table, making little use of the piano. The master indicated his approval of my new knowledge. His only suggestion was that I place somewhat more "a-ha" in the Hebrew stresses. Craft beat time precisely and was forbearing in his criticism. But whenever the master intervened, Craft shouted impatiently, "Shut up."

On leaving, Stravinsky joked, "I love the trombone so much—that's why I now suffer from thrombosis."

And with a significant look he added, "I thank you for taking time for this work. It is very important for me and for music in general."

He did not leave without having written in my guest

book, "To my favorite singer"—no doubt a gross exaggeration.

Stravinsky had an astonishing will to live. He attended many of the Berlin Philharmonic's rehearsals of the other items on the program for the ceremonial concert, which had been arranged at the suggestion of his friend, Nicolas Nabokov (cousin of the novelist), who at that time headed the Festival Weeks. And the *Abraham* cantata, with all its changes of tempo and its uneven beat, purred along smoothly, without any kind of "accident," causing Craft to exclaim while he was still on the podium, "It's amazing, amazing, no mistake!"

Shortly before I went on stage, my heart already beating hard, I was asked to pay my respects to Federal President Lübke. He spoke of the expense, given the large number of participants, of the Britten performance in Ottobeuren. Before I arrived at his box, he had, with exquisite tact, asked the baritone Heinz Rehfuss (singing in *Renard*) why on earth I was coming as well. Of course that singer did not waste a moment in reporting this query to me, with a certain amount of glee.

Stravinsky, whom the members of the audience honored by repeated standing ovations, was beaming in high good humor. He dominated this concert, which was moving in many respects. As he embraced me, his comment on my contribution was, "You are an angel."

Whenever the mail brought me an issue of *Musica viva*, published in Munich, I admired the quality of the covers and the interesting photographs and drawings that accompanied the informative text. In the postwar period it was unique. The creator of this periodical and the founder of the concert series that went with it was Karl Amadeus Hartmann. Long before I met him, this first and most productive series of new music stuck in my mind—situated in Munich, of all places, with its rather conservative attitude toward the arts. Hartmann's own compositions were only sparingly featured in the programs.

Long before I appeared as a soloist in his series in the Herkules-Saal, Karl Amadeus had sent out feelers in my direction and spoke with me whenever the opportunity arose. After practical matters had brought us together, he confessed that he wanted to write something for me. It was to be the work that today is considered the most important in his entire oeuvre: the *Gesangsszene*, based on a fragment of Jean Giraudoux's play *Sodom and Gomorrah*.

This was late in the autumn of 1961. In February 1963, when I thought that Hartmann must be hard at work completing the composition, I was shocked by the news of his death. In our first bewilderment we had to assume that his departure also meant the end of the Musica viva concerts. But at this precise moment it was shown on how firm a foundation the series rested. Ernst Thomas and Wolfgang Fortner took over its direction, first on an interim basis and then, beginning in the summer of 1964, permanently, to continue the work along the lines Hartmann had laid out. The *Gesangsszene* was never completed; after an enormous crescendo in the orchestra, the finale has to be spoken by the singer. There is some justification for this conclusion, since Hartmann had always said that the final sentence—"It is an end of the world, the saddest of all"—would have to be recited. And yet I cannot help myself; despite the effectiveness of the sudden, naked words, I always seem to hear a powerful, fiery chorus surrounded by sharp, cutting sounds that put everything heard so far in the shade—a single inexorable swelling. I wish the composer had had time to write this ending.

Hartmann had always been fascinated by Jean Giraudoux's mixture of elegant surface and prophetic depth. He had planned an opera of *Ondine*. Hartmann's own commitment to the dramatist's words is first of all musical. Unlike other composers of his day, he does not overemote with upswings, with dramatic surges of excitement; rather, he uses the sound as a means of expression more subtle than words. The *Gesangsszene* reveals this clearly, since in spite of its link with the text, it follows its own musical development. Its symphonic character marks it as something like Hartmann's own Ninth Symphony. At the outset, long before the human voice enters, the essential message of the text has been fully stated by purely musical means. And even under the vocal line, the orchestra remains detached from the verbal meaning of the text, referring to it at most in those passages where no doubt is possible of his power of expression. In this way Giraudoux's text is raised artistically to a plane for which it had not been intended. Hartmann imbued it with the power of Old Testament images, of everything that had made him suffer; war, strife, obtuseness. It was against these that he wanted to make his listeners newly conscious of life's beauty.

Some technical burdens are imposed on the singer by the necessity of having to master lines structured both in relation to intervals and melismata, since each makes different demands on the voice. Dry declamation and bel canto follow one on the other without transition.

The world premiere in Frankfurt was conducted by Dean Dixon (now also deceased), a bright, idealistic musician, the first black conductor in postwar Germany. He immersed himself in his work.

Karl Amadeus, a man who enjoyed being with others and engaging them in conversation, could spend a long time sitting in the hotel lobby with one other person and talking about, say, painting, impulsively, committedly. He had wanted to become a painter himself, following a family tradition that included his father and a brother who were graphic artists. He also talked about the postwar days in Munich, when the city was still in ruins, when cultural life had dried up, and how he had begun in makeshift, unheated rooms to give concerts that had to be adapted to whatever musicians were available. He engaged contemporary players who, like him, had been ostracized during the Nazi period. The year its founder died, the Musica viva enterprise was in its eighteenth season, and thanks to Hartmann the capital of Bavaria had become the internationally respected stronghold of modern music. My son Mathias introduced me to the opera *Simplicius Simplizissiumus* when he staged it for a performance by the Berlin JEM (Junges Ensemble für Musik). In 1935 Hermann Scherchen had taken the scenario from the famous baroque novel and arranged it for Hartmann, who was his friend and student. The work was to show how a pure, ingenuous nature makes its way through murderous times. I recognized in it the basic traits of Hartmann's temperament: compassion, indignation, vulnerability, and anger.

We never wrote to each other. Impatient, he preferred to reach for the telephone; he listened carefully and replied excitedly. He did not talk about his own music except on the occasion when he showed me a preliminary draft for the *Gesangsszene*, and his face glowed as he demonstrated his intentions. When he discussed other composers, Hartmann could be very discreet—that is, his eyes would veil over. If his questioner persisted, he changed the subject. One primary tone ran through his personality, with all his obvious zest for life and humor—the ability to grieve, not complaining about the evils of the world but indignant and powerfully accusing, as in his symphonies. Critical opinion was quick to label him an expressionist, and therefore believed itself entitled to shove him into the après-garde. He wanted to create great music, never wavering in the face of the universal belief that it is shattered form alone that can express the new claims of freedom.

All the friends of those years have grown old. Karl Amadeus enjoys the advantage the dead have over the living: More and more clearly he has become who he was.

It was 1974 in Warsaw. The infernal destruction of the entire inner city by the Nazis could still be felt, though the Poles had brought loving pride and enormous financial resources to reconstruction. Accompanied by Sviatoslav Richter, I gave a lieder recital in the beautifully paneled auditorium of the Philharmonic. After the concert the ambassador of the Federal Republic of Germany hosted a reception. Among the guests drawn from the worlds of culture and politics was Witold Lutoslawski. I was struck at once by his strong face, somewhat reminiscent of Paul Hindemith's. We quickly found ourselves engaged in shop talk about the possibilities open to composers nowadays.

Lutoslawski had to reply with a startled no to my question whether he had written anything for the baritone voice. But my way of putting things and my tendency to seek out areas of deep spirituality must have won him over sufficiently, since soon he laid all other work aside to write a lengthy scene for me with orchestral accompaniment. It did not take him long to find a text, "Les Espaces du Sommeil" by Robert Desnos, a French poet who had died of exhaustion at the age of forty-five, imprisoned at Theresienstadt, one month after the end of the Second World War.

The fluid diction of the poetry, which like a rondo repeats the incantatory phrase, "You are," offered Lutoslawski a variety of approaches to a musical work that made experimental use of all the techniques of song and inflected speech. The vocal line is embedded in a subtly differentiated orchestral sound. The music arouses strong images, associations, and feelings in the listener, creating a communication between interpreter and audience of a kind that could not be consciously striven for, and could not have been more welcome to me.

The work monopolized Lutoslawski for a long time. He spent about three years organizing musical material that combines emotional elements with the logic of serial thinking. The world premiere on April 12, 1978, with the Berlin Philharmonic conducted by the composer, was highly successful. It reaffirmed the standing of the master, sixty-five years old at the time, as did the subsequent performance in Amsterdam and the recent recording of the work.

8

"Deren Ton mir in die Seele hallte"

From time to time the name of Johannes Messchaert played a part in my life; he was one of my ideals. My beloved teacher Hermann Weissenborn mentioned him repeatedly, contrasting him with younger singers, such as Heinrich Schlusnus. A frequent visitor to my dressing room in Düsseldorf was Franziska Martienssen-Lohmann, familiar to earlier generations as a teacher (Elisabeth Grümmer and Kurt Widmer were students of hers) and musicologist. She raved about Messchaert whenever she wanted to flatter me.

The elegant old lady heard me sing for the first time in 1948. I had just returned from imprisonment and was singing Brahms at an exchange concert of the Academy

in the auditorium of the Weimar Academy to an enthusiastic student audience. Ludwig Hoffmann was at the
piano. He shone in his solo numbers, such as Balakirev's
"Islamey," with its thundering octaves. Much later Frau
Martienssen wrote to me, "It was overwhelmingly obvious
at once that what stood before us was an incarnation of
the lied, in the devastating penetration of precisely these
songs, and precisely in those days, when we still had so
much to fear."

In her reference work *Der wissende Sänger*, to which
I contributed a short introduction, Franziska Martienssen-
Lohmann refers to Messchaert again and again. It was
also from her that I learned of a Messchaert student in
Tokyo, who had communicated the desire of the Japanese
audiences for my visit. Her description of the flourishing
musical life there, marked by reverence and respect for
Western culture, contributed substantially to my decision
to appear in Japan in 1963.

When Wolf Rosenberg published his book *Verfall
(oder Krise) der Gesangkunst*, in which he pulled me to
pieces in his prejudiced way, I was comforted in my
depression by her words:

> If you look around the world long enough,
> you will see ever more clearly that everything
> great is always pulled down into the dust by those
> with wretched little viewpoints. (You only need
> to read what his "contemporary" underlings
> wrote about Goethe.) The attacks you are exposed
> to in articles and books only increase the loyalty
> of your genuine admirers. All of them find such
> calumny incomprehensible. We must learn to un-
> derstand that these writers are looking for some-

thing in particular: to amass whatever material comes to hand that can be used to increase the publicity for a surefire best-seller; and what could be more obvious than precisely that singer who has the largest audience and whose artistry makes him the true representative of a German generation whose youth was marked by the enormous experience of the war and the "and yet . . ." possible only to humanity. Last year I heard your *Winterreise* again. It is as if in each generation this work had a unique interpreter, someone who purely and simply reflects the truth, the essence precisely of this whole generation through such works. Stockhausen's renditions must still have had some gentleness (after all, his programs included *Frauenliebe und -leben*), which was far from Messchaert's magnificent sound quality, which was almost instrumental, like a violin. Two wars came between the two. Then you came. And that remains and stands above the present day.

I encountered the name of Messchaert once more. In Vienna Maria Litschauer brought a woman to see me; though very old, she was still full of life. Her sparkling eyes fascinated me. She had been a student of Brahms for a number of years. With shaky fingers she pulled a photograph from her purse; it showed her teacher cheerfully hugging her. She was one of Brahms' late-in-life flames—of whom there were not a few—to whom he would say, "If you're upset about anything, come to see Johannes, he'll make it all better."

She had often spent lively hours with the lieder singer

Messchaert at Brahms' house, and she confirmed for me what several old people had said in Vienna: I sang in the manner of Messchaert.

Anyone who never knew Elisabeth Grümmer, and most especially never heard her phenomenal voice, cannot truly know what human and artistic integrity are. It was not until I heard Richard Strauss' *Four Last Songs* in all their metallic yet velvet tone color that I realized that these songs dealt with parting from worldly things. Elisabeth Grümmer seemed more genuine and heartwarming than others because she had disciplined herself to acquire what probably none of her colleagues had mastered to the same extent: beauty of voice paired with clarity of diction. In this she strove to emulate her colleague from the previous generation, Lotte Lehmann. And because each word came so clearly from her lips, she was able to convince her listeners with everything in her widely varied repertoire and enthrall them. She was aided in her efforts by what she had learned as an actress during her first eight years on the stage. Besides her assured presence, she had come to understand the importance of purity of vowels. Today the idea that understandable language depends not only on consonants but at least as much on the clean shaping of vowel sounds like antiquated wisdom. This is necessarily what frees and enhances the meaning of musicalized poetry. Small wonder, then, that any sort of mannerism that hindered this effect made Elisabeth Grümmer react as if she were allergic to it. Wherever she was, bell-like laughter was as common as sudden tears of disappointment.

When she and I were studying *Figaro* with Carl Ebert—I believe it was in 1952—I was startled to notice that my Countess was withdrawing to a corner of the stage, sobbing softly. I followed to ask what was troubling her. It turned out that in the fire of the verbal duel, which we were singing in German, I had overstretched the tempo of the secco recitative, (perhaps to come closer to the Italian sound) to such an extent that Elisabeth scarcely knew where she was, and could no longer enter when it was precisely her turn. But because she was so straightforward in her explanation, the damage could be easily repaired. Serious and disciplined, she endured endless rehearsals. But if she felt in the early morning of an evening performance that any aspect of her voice was not what she considered correct, she would stubbornly cancel her appearance.

On one occasion, however, she did not. The opening of the Deutsche Oper was to be filmed, and her absence would have upset all the participants' expectations of having their work documented. So she sang Donna Anna in spite of her indisposition, and today's viewers of the film should be told that in subsequent performances, which were not filmed, she produced genuine miracles of sound and intensity.

It was also her Donna Anna that won Elisabeth Grümmer the special favor of the great Wilhelm Furtwängler. She appeared in some of the performances of his *Figaro* cycle, and shortly thereafter she became Furtwängler's Agathe in a much admired but not uncontroversial Salzburg premiere of *Freischütz*. Her Agathe was a miracle of tenderness and vocal splendor. Both roles are preserved in pirated recordings, outstanding documents among her unfortunately very few recordings.

Almost to the end of her career Elisabeth Grümmer entrusted herself to the care of Franziska Martienssen-

Lohmann as a voice coach. And here Grümmer learned what it meant not only to concentrate on opera but also to study the lied for its value and effect. For eight years she sang lieder recitals—generally with Aribert Reimann at the piano—and made radio recordings. These include particularly valuable recordings of Schumann and Wolf; it is to be hoped that a record company will soon release these from the archives.

As soon as Franziska Martienssen could no longer teach her master classes in Lucerne, Elisabeth Grümmer stepped into the breach. I believe that she was able to teach with greater calm and ease in this city than in Berlin or Paris, where at the very end she tried, under chaotic conditions, to train the next generation of operatic voices.

I mentioned *The Marriage of Figaro*, in which I was privileged to sing the Count opposite her in Paris, Vienna, and London. She was a Countess who knew as no one else how to walk the thin line between a slight stupidity and charm on which this role teeters in ever new and fascinating ways. In this opera, as in *Rosenkavalier* and others, Frau Grümmer moved through all the women's roles in their various ages, presenting each persuasively in its own way. I saw her, for example, as the title character in *Rosenkavalier* conceived in very masculine terms under Ebert, and shortly thereafter as the Marschallin, given to melancholy avoidance of the inexorable course of time. In this part especially she demonstrated an extraordinary fidelity to the notes. And it is not only in this context that I should mention her life's companion, Hugo Dietz; a pianist, he helped her with unflagging meticulousness to master her material.

Elisabeth Grümmer always hesitated to deal with contemporary music. Nevertheless, at Tietjen's request, she attempted Wifried Zillig's inexpressible opera *Troilus und Cressida*, though it was not our voices that won it its unexpected success. She sang in the legendary Deutsche Oper performance of *Peter Grimes*, which represented a belated recognition of its composer, Benjamin Britten, in Berlin. She dared to attempt some lieder by Othmar Schoeck, and even Aribert Reimann's Hölderlin fragments. But what will live in the memory of those who heard her is more likely to be her Fiordiligi in Carl Ebert's exemplary staging of *Così fan tutte*, the Countess in Strauss' *Capriccio*, Bach's Passions, in which I was several times privileged to sing with her (even in Vienna, under Furtwängler's extremely subjective baton, which she followed effortlessly), or as Elisabeth in *Tannhäuser*, in which, as Wolfram, I can only confirm that I heard the despairingly resigned words "He will never return" sung with greater intensity than by any other performer of the role.

Elsa in Wagner's *Lohengrin* may be called her most perfect accomplishment. It also represented an indirect connection with Bayreuth, which on the whole engaged her far too seldom. In the Deutsche Oper, directed by Wieland Wagner, she sang an exquisite Elsa, as she did on the recording of the Vienna staging. Rudolf Kempe was our conductor. She, like me, esteemed him particularly for his integrity. It was Kempe, too, with whom she recorded Brahms' *German Requiem*. I heard her for the first time in this work in the Städtische Oper, with the unforgettable Artur Rother conducting, and was at once deeply moved. "A brief time of toil and labor"—it was for Elisabeth Grümmer also the "deep comfort" of which Jesus speaks to Sirach in the Bible verse Brahms chose for his requiem.

Elisabeth Grümmer's "ancestor" in the German repertoire, perhaps the only one, was Lotte Lehmann, to my eyes and ears—even as a very young record collector—a monument among the vocal giants of the 1920s and 1930s, alongside Lauritz Melchior, Alexander Kipnis, and Frida Leider. She was given the lion's share of vocal recordings on the old Odeon label, a few of them not very successful forays into the wrong area, others sung with exquisite beauty and clarity of diction. Her recordings also included selections from *Arabella* by Richard Strauss. Because I knew these historical recordings so well by heart and ear, it made me all the happier when, after a first performance in Munich of this opera, I received a telegram reading, "Wonderful and splendid. I only regret that I could not be your Arabella. Lotte Lehmann."

When Irmel and I were traveling through California, Lehmann invited us to visit her in her house in Santa Barbara, situated in a marvelous big garden at the seashore and stuffed full of the mementos of the career of a successful artist. We were reminded of Toscanini and Bruno Walter, of the last years of refuge in Austria for the three, before the Nazis made their stay there impossible as well. We admired her numerous watercolors, among them a set of illustrations for *Die Winterreise*, in exquisite detail. We leafed through old programs and looked at photographs of her starring roles in Berlin and Vienna.

The old lady had established herself in the sunny West of the United States as a singing teacher. She had a large number of students, among whom Grace Bumbry was the star. When I was rehearsing *Macbeth* in Salzburg with Bumbry, Lotte Lehmann sat doggedly in the auditorium. Whenever there were short intermissions and I sneaked over to her to catch some detailed criticism in the half-light, she never had anything but good to say—but she said it in a slightly accusing tone, as if I should not have asked her in the first place.

During a second California visit we were sitting out-side when I was startled by a voice almost in my ear: "Old fool," spoken in the broadest possible Berlin accent. Lotte Lehmann and her friend Frances had trained a magpie to amuse their guests. We were given one of our hostess' watercolors to take with us—a "Nightmare," in a very individual style, probably created in the nervous hours before an evening performance. Unfortunately Lotte Lehmann also hoped that I could help her distribute a spoken record, on which the singer who no longer had a voice wanted to recite the old poems from her time of singing lieder with Bruno Walter or Paul Ulanowsky.

Lotte Lehmann came movingly to terms with her past when she heard one of my Schubert recitals in London's Festival Hall: "I think back with shame to my youth, when I possessed neither your kind of penetrating understand-ing nor your superior technique. I simply 'got on' with my singing, always driven by my artistic instinct. (And of course at the beginning that was enough. . . .) Understand-ing did not come for me until the richness of the voice was already spent. I am seldom satisfied when I hear my old records. There is so much that I would do differently today! But now it is too late."

In Santa Barbara we talked about photographs of me taken during the concert; my arms and hands seemed to hang lifelessly and as if they were not part of me. But then,

after seeing me in performance in Pasadena, Lotte Lehmann wrote me, "Oh, but you spoke from your head to
your heels, which pleased me more than I can say. You
were free, you did not hold back. You were singing
through and through, and for me that was the last fulfillment, the full expression of the lied. . . ."

Two men I admired from afar, Theodor Heuss and Konrad
Adenauer (who I knew liked some of my records), remained strangers even after I met them. I was astonished
when a letter from Bonn arrived at my home in Berlin; I
was even more astounded by what followed. The invitation was for a command performance on the occasion of
Mozart's two-hundredth birthday. A dinner in Cologne's
Hotel Excelsior Ernst was the only official ceremony spon-
sored by the Federal Republic; the occasion was to take
care of the annual meeting of the national employers'
association and the Mozart anniversary in one. Anneliese
Rothenberger and I were engaged to sing a little Mozart
for the dignitaries. The attractive soprano had stood side
by side with me many times before, as Susanna in *Figaro*,
for example, and during recitals. We had developed a cordial and comradely relationship. I was all the happier
therefore to share this solemn occasion with her.

It turned out that the circumstances were to put a
damper on my pleasure. The pianist was late for the rehearsal. When he finally deigned to arrive, the first waiters
were already whirling through the hall preparing for the
dinner. In the middle of rehearsing two duets from *Figaro*
and *Don Giovanni*, the headwaiter interrupted us. "Excuse me, we must establish the order of the menu. Do
you prefer singing after the soup—that is, before the fish

course—or before dessert—that is, after the main course?"

Somewhat dumbfounded, we decided, "Before dessert," thinking in this way to give the performance a little more solemnity.

How wrong we were! When the time finally came for us to sing, all the guests had been drinking wine for some time, and the faces of the two chief personages, who were sitting directly in front of us, were already turning red. When we came to the second duet, Heuss was blissfully slumbering on the shoulder of his neighbor, who was politely making an enormous effort to keep his eyes open. After some mild applause Anneliese and I disappeared into the pantry to wait for the end of the meal, when we were supposed to shake hands with the two gentlemen. Whispering, "I'm just going to freshen up a minute in my room," Anneliese slipped out. I had a half-hour in which to watch the rushing waiters; now and then I would ask how much longer the dinner could possibly go on. "It can be a while yet," I was told, or words to that effect.

When my partner returned, every hair in place, we behaved like good children, sat on a bench, and waited. The following day I had to study a new work and rehearse it in another city. When one more hour had passed, my ire rose, and I declared, "That's enough. I'm going to bed. Good night."

Anneliese was outraged; she had no intention of missing the high point of the evening. I kissed her on the cheek and made my way to the elevator, out of the baroque kitchen atmosphere. I never learned respect for highly formal, ceremonial occasions.

* * *

The tour of *Das Lied von der Erde* was not the first time I sang with the "wonder tenor," Fritz Wunderlich, who lost his life at such a tragically early age after a fall down a flight of stairs. But on this occasion we had the opportunity to blow a "lip-horn duet" together. Before we mounted the stage of the Hanover Stadthalle, I heard Fritz humming the Hunter's Chorus from *Freischütz* in his dressing room. I immediately added the second voice, imitating a horn, and what followed was a walk through the horn literature. Finally even Keilberth, whose attention had been caught, began to listen and nearly exploded with laughter. Wunderlich had in fact been a professional horn player before he chose to sing.

In 1956 during Bach Week in Ansbach we stood side by side for the first time, performing in two secular cantatas by the cantor of the Thomas Kirche. After Werner Egk had rehearsed the introductory chorale, "Auf, schmetternde Töne," Wunderlich rose to sing. I was startled when I heard him, for his voice had a bewitching sweetness combined with the necessary amount of steel, such as had not been heard from a German tenor for a long, long time.

In the intermission I went up to Wunderlich, who was waiting quietly in a corner of the hall, and asked him where he came from and how long he had been singing. So far he had appeared in public in only a few concerts (mostly accompanied by Hubert Giesen). This situation was to change with his engagement at the Württemberg Staatsoper.

In Berlin I made certain to rave to Fritz Ganss, the record producer of Electrola, about this new phenomenon. Perhaps the remarks I repeatedly let drop shortened

the time before Wunderlich's first important recording
was made. When I sang in Wagner's *Flying Dutchman*
with Franz Konwitschny, Wunderlich sang the Steuer-
mann, his voice fresh and enormously musical. Not long
after, he sang the role of Walther von der Vogelweide in
Tannhäuser with the same conductor. But his next recording, the Evangelist in Bach's *Saint John Passion*, was
his first major one. I was impressed by the relaxation with
which the young man with a glint of mischief in his eye
let the whole process of rehearsal and retakes run off his
back. Karl Forster, the conductor (priest of the podium
and head of the Hedwigs-Chor, with which I had been
connected since its first Berlin orchestral concert), had an
easy time with him. Once I sat in on the dress rehearsal
of Werner Egk's *Verlobung von San Domingo* at the Bavarian Staatsoper, and there, in the running and cackling
atmosphere of a chicken yard, I saw Wunderlich, utterly
composed, waiting to see what else might be going to
happen.

Though this outward calm did not particularly contribute to his stage performance, it did preserve the
smooth and flawless sound of his voice. This superlative
musician quickly and surely grasped both notes and presentation, and occasionally—though rarely—he would
make a suggestion for some improvement to a colleague.
In Bamberg we recorded scenes from Albert Lortzing's
Zar und Zimmermann. He did not approve of my very
broad tempo for the czar's song. I accepted his criticism
and profited from it.

After recording scenes from Tchaikovsky's *Eugene
Onegin*, in which his singing of Lenski's aria was wonderfully effortless, we flew to Vienna for the Festwochen,

sharing the narrow oven of an Austrian Airlines plane. The following day Josef Krips, known all over the world as the Frog King because of his somewhat protruding eyes, twice ran through the entire *Lied von der Erde*, justifying his assiduousness by noting that he had never worked with me before. The sculpture of the angel playing the cello on the roof of the music society building across from my room in the Hotel Imperial came to my aid in singing in the hall in the first place; the room, hot enough to cause fainting, glittered with gold. My performance was also made possible by Krips' subdued loudness and the self-transcending orchestra of the Vienna Philharmonic (it must have been they, because I can still see Willy Boskowsky, who was concertmaster at the time, sitting before me). Wunderlich found it easier to deal with the heat and the orchestral floods of the first song. Even the commas, which in rehearsal I had pointed out were going unnoticed even though Mahler had included them in the notation of the final section of "Abschied," were brought out with special fervor. Krips could breathe in the most natural way with his singers. And so it was not to be wondered at that he agreed with an interview I gave, which he read in some record magazine, in which I was asked specifically about breathing during performing. He immediately sent me a note: "If you care about breathing when conducting, you must be a good conductor. I want to hear you as soon as possible."

Alas, there was no time left for that. Perhaps he has been spared a disappointment. . . .

Karajan had his Bernstein, Rubinstein his Horowitz, Callas her Tebaldi, Toscanini his Furtwängler. Almost everyone has his adversary, his "thorn in the flesh," his rival. I actually had more than one, but the public urged a particular one on me. When Hermann Prey began singing, about four years after my debut, his voice was so differently formed and sounded so different from mine that it never occurred to me that there would not be room for both of us in the world of music. But by the time we finally shared a stage, to Günther Rennert's great delight, in his *Figaro*, we had both accumulated so many resentments that we treated each other with reserve, not to say with the utmost caution. This situation changed soon enough; at the latest by the time of Rennert's famous Salzburg staging of *Così*, we were in total harmony.

The only thing that continued to bother me was a certain involuntary repetition in the choice of program, accompanist, and cycles of song recitals. Prey was born four years after me; I performed Schumann's Op. 35 arranged by Kerner about four years before he did, performed my first cycle of lieder recitals four years before he did, was accompanied by Karl Engel four years before he was, was made a member of the Bavarian Akademie der schönen Künste four years before he was, and so on. Well, one gets used to this sort of thing. Though when I am asked, as Prey often is, to pay homage to lighter works, I must regretfully decline. For one thing, I do not acknowledge merely good and bad performances; I care more about the artistic quality or its lack in the work in question. For another, I have never tested myself to see whether I would be able to perform purely entertaining music with the same virtuosity as Hermann Prey.

Perhaps he will stop singing four years after I do, as well.

---

* * *

Usually Julia and I do not listen at hotel-room walls. Once, however, we could not prevent ourselves. During a visit to New York we were staying right next to a large suite with a grand piano. It was occupied by Maria Callas, who for so many years was a revered ideal to both Julia and me. She was rehearsing for a recital of duets with Giuseppe di Stefano, which they intended taking on a world tour. Promptly at four o'clock in the afternoon the tenor knocked on the door to rehearse with his partner. Twice she sent him away—she was not ready. Finally, at six, the two of them began singing. Julia pressed her ear to the wall so as to be sure not to miss a note. Callas' voice was strained and no longer beautiful in every register, but we admired her way of repeating, improving, and instructing di Stefano. We will never forget the soprano's artistic power, her singular stature at the height of her career.

Nor do I harbor any posthumous resentment of this Greek-American for having once made a very disparaging remark about the German lied. Not every southerner (and not every German, for that matter) is able to understand the significance of the art song.

When Richard Kraus engaged the baritone Ernst Krukowski in the late 1950s for the Berlin opera, Hertha Klust laughed at the idea that his lightweight voice was thought adequate to sing Mandryka. Before I heard him in this part in the Bavarian Staatsoper, we had met a few times, and what I remember about these first conversations is his remarkable lack of rancor about his rivals, as well as his stunning sense of humor. Krukowski used the latter to caricature singers of the previous generation who, now toothless, express outrage at the "young people": "When I was still singing in Eckernförde in the first rank, beginners would not allow themselves such things!"

This man, who got along with everyone he worked with, knew early on that he had a fatal illness, but he tried to fight against the loss of voice that was its inevitable consequence. I was therefore all the happier that during the rehearsals for *Meistersinger*—in which I was to sing my first Sachs under the stage direction of Peter Beauvais and the difficult-to-follow baton of Eugen Jochum—a critical situation arose. The singer scheduled for Beckmesser had evidently taken on too much and wasn't able to master the part in time either musically or dramatically. Shortly before the opening it became necessary to find a replacement—and we did not have to search far. Ernst Krukowski—called Kruki by everyone—had served as understudy, and he eagerly stepped into a part he had sung countless times in the previous staging by Wieland Wagner. Relief shone from Beauvais' melancholy features; as always when he was worried, he was chewing his tie. Once the change was made, rehearsals proceeded quickly, and I can truthfully say that I enjoyed playing with Kruki, the archcomedian who was clever at using his vocal weaknesses to benefit his interpretation. In the final scene his Beckmesser, in his paralyzing powerlessness, grew into a figure of tragic stature.

From the beginning of rehearsals Peter Beauvais had shown himself to be a musical director who was good for the work. Without looking at the score, he was fully capable of prompting me, who had just learned the part, both musically and verbally. I have never met another stage director so familiar with all the roles. And if sometimes it was difficult for his slightly hoarse voice to be heard above the choral crowd and their intermission babble, in this *Meistersinger* he nevertheless managed something that nowadays can seldom be carried off without embarrassment: a concept that followed Wagner, completely, including Jan Schlubach's posterlike decorations. Wagner's precise instructions for the final scene, with its apotheosis of Sachs, contained a number of traps for the singer. During the dress rehearsal I thought of a new solution: to move quietly and modestly through the crowd until I was out of sight. Beauvais was enthusiastic: "A stroke of genius!"

And surely Sachs' gesture of modesty was a reflection of Beauvais' own nature. Though Peter attained a certain renown as a director of opera, he has never been given his due. When we worked on a new production of *Arabella* in Munich, many critics recalled the old staging, which was adapted to the style of the 1960s, and overlooked all the enchanting Viennese fin-de-siècle details Peter, who had done his homework, had added to the two final, less compelling scenes.

Peter also engaged me to play the role of the emperor in Heinrich von Kleist's *Kätchen von Heilbronn* when he staged the work for television. Owing to the biting cold during the outdoor shooting and my considerable stage fright at a quite unfamiliar line of work, with its emphasis on dramatic minutiae, the result was not satisfactory. Nevertheless, those weeks taught me something about filmmaking and the patience with which a director of such precision could work. When my fear of the dialogue and my lack of self-confidence were at their height, he would whisper to me, "Just don't let yourself get crazy."

When Beauvais died, in the midst of working on his first major movie based on his own script, the only great German director of television movies left us. To many he seemed withdrawn, since he was always thinking about some project, absorbed in plans that were often meant for the distant future. He was a quiet man; his work was also quiet. He loved internalized emotions (when it came to the supersensitive camera as well) and hated exaggeration of any kind, because he was searching for truth. Even his laughter was, as it were, internalized; it could sound strangely like gulping. He worked relentlessly until the required feeling, the expected reaction, came almost of itself. He knew how to conjure something out of thin air, to lure the appropriate thing—including color and movement—out of his co-workers. To this end he could be flirtatious as well as infinitely patient.

On one occasion, however, even two hours of interrupted rehearsals did not bring about the desired result in the third act of *Meistersinger*. In spite of all Beauvais' powers of persuasion, our Stolzing insisted on walking arm in arm with Eva, while Sachs bursts out, "Always and ever, nothing but making shoes, that is my lot." The tenor simply would not accept Peter's argument that, recognizing Sachs' jealousy and astounded by it, Stolzing must let go of Eva for a moment. He countered the director's every attempt at compromise with "I'm satisfied"—and he won.

Beauvais' working method was quite different from that of Jean-Pierre Ponnelle, who was more inclined to proceed from the external to the internal. Ponnelle was more likely to seek the echo of the music in the stage action by working from the periphery.

9

"Hingeschmiedet zum Gesang"

I t is time to remember my beloved Gerald Moore, whom a benevolent fate brought to me in 1952. As I have probably already made clear, there were more opportunities in Vienna than elsewhere to meet outstanding people (though, unfortunately, such meetings did not always lead to friendships). For a long time Walter Legge had been the head of the classical division of London's most important recording company and, as mentioned, he had founded the Philharmonia Orchestra. After a Furtwängler concert in Vienna, he invited me to meet the most famous of all accompanists, Gerald Moore, in London and to cut our first record together. It was not only that Legge's words had a magnetic effect on a beginner; they also had the weight of a command.

As we flew into London, Irmel and I enthusiastically watched the sunset over the water. At Heathrow an enchanting car stood waiting for us, Mr. Legge—who, exceptionally, had come himself—standing at its door.

The following morning, in our old-ladies' hotel, which had been recommended for its quiet, we encountered the "raw breath of reality." In spite of repeated calls to room service, breakfast did not arrive. Our English was not good enough for curses and scolding. Contrary to our usual custom, we made the pilgrimage, much too late, to the hotel lobby. When we asked where our longed-for breakfast might be, we received the chilly inquiry, "You want breakfast?" So we ordered all over again; what we were served turned out to be salty ham minus the egg.

Thus the Abbey Road Studio saw me late by a half-hour on the very first of the five recording days. But no one was annoyed with me.

To a young man who collected records these rooms were holy. I had read that Gigli, Schnabel, Gieseking, Edwin Fischer, the tenor John McCormack, and countless others had toiled here and called the place their torture chamber. These same walls and these same recording dignitaries, now of an advanced age, were in turn to capture my singing tones in the grooves, in dulcet monophonics on shellac, turning seventy-eight times a minute.

A stocky, jovial man made himself available to me for the entire time. His name was Gerald Moore, and I had noticed that name on almost every page of every available record catalogue. He seemed to accept completely whatever I lightheartedly proposed, agreed cheerfully, and put it into practice. Walter Legge, as supervisor of the recording, wanted to follow his usual habit of involving himself in shaping my understanding (of some Hugo Wolf lieder and Schubert's *Schöne Müllerin*). Estimating the situation subjectively, I thought I should stick with my own ideas, and he soon fell silent. He never forgave me. Even after his death his memoirs accused me of having been "difficult" and of not allowing friendship to develop. Nevertheless, I visited him whenever a concert brought me to London, and enthusiastically listened to records with him. And we made great plans for new programs with his wife, Elisabeth Schwarzkopf, a wonderful hostess.

It was with Elisabeth that I performed the first lieder recital in the newly built Royal Festival Hall. It was she too who shared with me the *Italienisches Liederbuch* in my debut concert in New York's Carnegie Hall. She recited a moving paean of praise when the order "Pour le mérite" was conferred on me. And she missed none of my recitals that were nearby Zurich. I believe that Elisabeth and I did our part in preserving world recognition for lieder even after 1945. And I am eternally grateful to her husband, whose lower lip could curl dangerously when he gossiped about others, for bringing me together with Gerald Moore.

Gerald's kind words kept up my courage and strengthened me. Since he remained calm and made no errors during our recordings, I loved the sessions. They put me into the state of mind I need to sing my best. Gerald and his equally witty wife, Enid, invited us to their home when they were still living in Kathleen Ferrier's former apartment, which was quiet and handsome and had a view of much greenery at the center of London.

During our first visit we saw little of the city itself. Once, however, Gerald said, "Let's go to the cinema."

And on a Saturday night, of all times, the four of us

pushed our way into one of the large downtown movie houses. Even before we got there our eyes were strained by the neon advertising signs, unfamiliar in postwar Germany, that lit up the streets. (Two days later the sporadic power cuts returned, and the neon lights went out.)

We were also surprised at the standing-room admissions to the movie, which was all that we could get at that late hour. Constantly changing location while the film was running, we were shoved along with the crowd lining the walls. For a long time we could only see either the feet or the shirt fronts of the actors on the screen. Arrived at last at the very first row, we were asked to turn around and get back on the end of the line. All the spectators were talking, smoking, or eating; the floor was covered with ashes and paper. The mystery story on the screen seemed almost irrelevant.

Gerald was hardly one to be easily disconcerted. But once I was singing the Schubert lied "Auf der Bruck" in Berlin, having just learned it, and could not for the life of me remember the beginning of the third stanza. I turned to Gerald beseechingly, but between Schubert's rhythmic trotting, I was given only a whispered snort, "I'm too busy riding."

When we were recording songs from Wolf's *Spanisches Liederbuch* at the Abbey Road Studio, we had a guest. Walter Legge was planning a recording of Schumann's *Dichterliebe* with me, with Edwin Fischer at the piano. Legge was never very considerate when it came to understanding psychological nuances; he sent the great man to watch Moore and me record, so that he could judge for himself. This was soon to prove a fatal decision, since Fischer placed himself right opposite me, up against the other side of my microphone, so that its stand was almost touching his sharp knees. Fischer stared at me unblinkingly. The first one to be disquieted was Gerald, as became evident from the wrong notes he struck. I ended the take, a decision that did not make Gerald more confident. Then I began to sing nonsense words and to babble apologies. Fischer's light, almost hypnotic eyes were still fixed on my face, the white-blond curl over his forehead stood out in the darker room. All my inhibitions grew worse whenever Fischer made such remarks as, "I understood all the words except . . ." or "But the previous lied was marvelous."

My disappointment was great when he politely said good-bye. I was sure that nothing now would come of Legge's project, which he had mentioned to me. It was some time before I succeeded in calming the justly incensed Gerald so that the recording could proceed.

Gerald helped me to endure my first large United States tour, and much more. We were welcomed to the land of liberty by a brusque customs official and a long wait before we were allowed to get into William Stein's car. In Washington Mr. Stein invested all his pride in showing us the Lincoln Memorial the very first day—but he couldn't find it. It was an hour before, discouraged and without having reached our destination, we returned to the hotel. Gerald made for the porter at once and asked where the Lincoln Memorial was. The man seemed miffed: "It's right around the corner, a three minutes' walk."

Gerald gave a wicked grin. "See Washington the Stein way."

The glittering lights of New York put on a show for

us. As we got out of the taxi with Gerald and Dr. Otto Hammer, our guide, our eyes were caught by the moon, which eclipsed the other lights.

We had known Dr. Hammer in Berlin, where as a United States cultural officer he had lived and held court in a splendid mansion in the Dahlem district. That time was long past, and now he was eking out a bare existence, living in an apartment facing a dark courtyard and working as an occasional chorus singer at the Metropolitan Opera. His pretty and lively wife, who was from Berlin and had been ceremoniously married to him in the presence of all sorts of West Berlin dignitaries, had left him long ago.

Hammer steered us to Rockefeller Center, to the Radio City Music Hall, an enormous movie theater. On the giant screen an outsize Cinderella was bending over an equally large Prince. After *Cinderella* there was a short intermission, during which the mighty Wurlitzer organ resounded from every nook and cranny. The virtuoso organist remained invisible to us all. But soon a curtain was lowered and a hundred-man orchestra, hidden until that moment, began to play—we could not believe our ears—the original prelude to *Parsifal*. What could this mean? The curtain rose on the ladies and gentlemen of the chorus, marching, in costume as nuns and priests. And that was not all: More of them, singing melodies from *Parsifal*, approached the audience at left and right on side stages. Someone whispered to us, "The Easter show."

The music soon switched from *Parsifal* to sugary tunes, more and more nuns and angels (identified for us as the ballet) holding palm fronds marched forward, accompanied by flabby choral singing and thick orchestral sounds. The side stages, decorated with huge haloes, soon filled up. A stalking dancer, miming a priest, used a long stick to light an "eternal flame" that glowed red. A "Hallelujah" sung at breakneck speed brought that part of the show to a close.

Hardly had our eyes recovered from all the glitter than a menacingly large Easter bunny, complete with eggs and chicks, filled the stage. The stage floor then rose to reveal a trained-dog act. Poodles in sparkling collars jumped to the tune of the orchestra that a moment ago had been playing *Parsifal*. The nuns, angels, and priests had become worldly bathing beauties, singing suggestively. Abruptly the orchestra rose, moving backward when it had reached half-stage height to make room for the chorus, which, draped in flowers, was pushing an enormous flower cart. Then the orchestra soared all the way to the top. The hundred instrumentalists, thirty yards up in the air, cheerfully played on. But there was more rushing down below: On a new moving stage the Rockefeller Girls were rising. Tap shoes moved at the ends of about two hundred legs of exactly the same length; behind them the flower chorus, above them the orchestra sang and played on. Since we were sitting close to the stage, we had to stare into each girl's bored or sad face; some of them must have been well past forty and looked miserable. One of the "ladies," who kept to the background, was limping. I am sure her shoes, which she had to put on three times a day perhaps for months on end, were pinching her.

When the staged springtime, with its at least four hundred participants, came to an end, hardly any hand moved to applaud. And in no time the movie, with the pretty plastic Cinderella in wide-angled sound, filled the screen again. Gerald and I had the same thought: Tomorrow a single singer and a single pianist were supposed to present Schubert lieder, without a stage show, relying on their inner resources.

Town Hall, where I made my debut, was more than sold out. The stage seats and all standing room were gone, and those waiting in line for tickets were turned away. During the concerts the expectant seething restlessness could be tamed only gradually. It was followed by breathless silence, ending in profound emotion. Many people pushed their way into my dressing room; I particularly noticed the wonderfully serious and enthusiastic blacks among them.

Ann Colbert took my American fate into her capable hands immediately after my first agent, the unfortunate Mr. Stein, declared bankruptcy. It was through her that we met John Coveney. The head of EMI's U.S. division, Angel Records, he became a guardian angel and ever-helpful New York "companion." After every concert, whether a lieder recital or with orchestra, he fervently gave himself over to the enjoyment of Ann's chicken soup, sitting at her large, round table late into the night and digging deep into his trove of memories. They dealt mostly with singers. He had been a friend of Maria Callas, he regularly kept in touch with Lotte Lehmann, occasionally he wrote little essays about various old friends for the Metropolitan Opera's magazine. It was Coveney who gave the eulogy at Lehmann's funeral in Santa Barbara.

Whenever we met, he would begin by telling us with great pleasure all the latest inside gossip of the Metropolitan, especially the negative kind. We never arrived in a new hotel room (generally to be changed for another) without finding flowers from John. And before the trip to the airport, when we were headed back to Europe, either a sizable package of records or some other gift stood beside our luggage. John also gave Julia suggestions for possible purchases. He was tall, lean, and long-legged, with slightly curly salt-and-pepper hair. Always impeccably dressed, with a carnation in his buttonhole and smelling discreetly of cologne, he would accompany Julia to the shops, explaining to her in his broad, slow, clear American English what she could safely buy and what it would be better to pass up.

His obsession with singers was such that he never missed an important opera premiere in the United States. But he did not travel to Bayreuth or Salzburg. In 1937 he had tried to visit the Salzburg Festival, but the air already smelled too sharply of National Socialism for his taste; he made no further attempts. However, he had saved all the brochures from that first time, and kept being surprised at how cheap travel had been in those days. If I was awarded a Grammy—the American prize for recordings— he would be the first to tell me the news. Time and again he held up to me the model of Lehmann, who had given fifty recitals in the sixteen postwar years of her career; I was the only one who could dare to match her, he said. But I could not bring myself to become such an expansive presence—beyond the cycles already mentioned—on the New York stage. Coveney was able to manage only a single recording session with me in New York: baroque arias with Jean-Pierre Rampal, the great French flutist, and his accompanist, Robert Veyron-Lacroix.

I could never get much out of "big-city excitements," such as bar-hopping and dancing, for their own sake. Nevertheless, John, a benevolent spirit able to conjure up tickets even to permanently sold-out hits, invited the Moores and us to a performance of *Cabaret.* Our pleasure was great, especially at the landlady played by Lotte

Lenya-Weill. Why European productions of the musical never quite achieved the quality of the original Broadway production is something of a mystery to me. After all, provocative dancing, working up to verbal climaxes, showing off pretty voices—performers can do that there as well as here. But this production—long before the film by the way—demonstrated once again that native elasticity and lasciviousness, and the swing of the music, are, for inexplicable reasons, inimitable.

It was also with Gerald that we flew back to Europe, but not until we had had literally to stand up to the then customary ritual of departure with the tax officials. Even the most celebrated had to make their pilgrimage to this authority to document their income. The amount of tax assessed depended on the personality and mood of the official. We were assigned to an agreeable man who let us go without paying a cent, while Gerald lost a lot of money to his cynical Cerberus—a loss he swore about on the entire flight back.

We returned to the United States many times. Each time our beloved Carnegie Hall represented the high point of the tour, in both the quality of the audience and in the fear of failure.

Only twice did I see Gerald alone on the stage. In Toronto my recital was scheduled for two o'clock in the afternoon, at that time the usual hour for the women's clubs, where by definition no men were allowed to be in attendance. The friend with whom we were staying stopped her car at a department store. When she saw our bewilderment, she told us simply to go in and find the elevator. We were to take it to the seventh floor, where we would have no trouble finding the concert. And so, forge ahead into the noontime crowd to celebrate the

Dichterliebe somewhere. At the indicated floor the loud-speaker announced, "Children's wear." We got off any-way. A silent man in livery was waiting and led us to a greenroom whose door opened onto the stage. And what a surprise: a pretty auditorium with about eight hundred seats and good acoustics. Before we started on the Schu-bert, Gerald went on the stage alone. I was about to follow him, but he gestured to me to remain behind. His fabulous touch coaxed the British national anthem from the piano; clearly he had practiced it often and had long since be-come used to performing it.

The second time I saw Gerald alone on stage he was playing a version of Schubert's lied "An die Musik," which he had chosen as his theme years ago for his series on the BBC. He played it at the conclusion of his farewell concert in the Royal Festival Hall before almost five thou-sand listeners who had come to say good-bye to their be-loved Gerald Moore. Elisabeth Schwarzkopf, Victoria de Los Angeles, and I accompanied him in song that night. Countless tears flowed. After the standing ovation, Gerald asked the listeners to resume their seats, and he took leave of them with his signature tune.

On one occasion Gerald literally shed tears of laugh-ter. I was supposed to illustrate a little lecture he was giving with musical examples. It was to take place in the SFB television studio, at that time still located in Berlin's NAAFI House on Theodor Heuss Square. There was an inhumanly long lighting rehearsal. December winds were blowing outside, but the studio was glowing with heat. Added to these discomforts was a noticeable nervousness on the part of the technicians, who were not thoroughly trained. At last, when I was to make my entrance before the rolling cameras down a little wooden staircase, one of the steps broke. With a crash I fell headlong. I was not hurt, however, and tried to look amused. Gerald howled with laughter; he had already begun lecturing and had to stop. Unfortunately he was the only one in the room who was laughing. The technicians had to set up everything one more time. Their expressions were bitter.

In 1962, when Gerald and we were staying at the Ritz in Paris, the city was caught up in the Salan trial, with its consequences in Algeria and on United States policies in Europe. In their nationalist intoxication the crowds sang the "Marseillaise" when the commutation of the general's sentence to life imprisonment became known. A noisy crowd of supporters of French Algeria were demonstrating outside the Palace of Justice. It was late when, coming from Munich, we arrived at the hotel, which looked out on the Place Vendôme; the desk clerk anxiously checked a list to see whether we had made our reservations long enough ago, suspicious-looking as we were. (Since then we have been forced to adopt a considerably more cautious attitude toward matters of security.) The hotel, which we were trying out for the first time, tormented us with drilling noises, spike heels on uncarpeted floors above our heads, marital strife and joys behind the thin connecting door, and general door-banging through paper-thin walls—all thrown into the bargain as a matter of course in Paris. Irmel, saddened by my expression of suffering, was growing more nervous by the hour, and Gerald, whom we had once again invited to supper in our room because the restaurant downstairs repelled us with its fish smells, drafts, and noise, now took his revenge on Irmel over a small difference of opinion they had had in Munich: He made fun endlessly of the "quickness" with which she prepared everything. Howling winds outside, scudding clouds, and sporadic showers mixed with hail reflected our mood. The exuberance we had just experienced, as so often before, had to be paid for with the "blues." But after a day in which hotel noise and weather had made us almost unable to struggle on, the Schubert recital in the totally reliable Salle Pleyel had magical restorative powers, and the enthusiasm of the audience, which was bubbling like champagne, knew no bounds.

Iceland was the only place Gerald did not like. He was bothered by the sulphurous steam that rose from the ground everywhere. The people ate too much chocolate too frequently for his taste, making them fall into sweet slumber during the concerts. The only thing that escaped his criticism was the soup served in the hotel.

Gerald was an enthusiastic walker. But in Berlin, which I too loved for the endless footpaths in its three forest preserves, it was difficult to show him the beauties of nature. Every day everywhere the Occupation Powers' military maneuvers had soldiers popping up from every bush or standing guard at every turn. I will never forget Gerald's dumbfounded expression. We Berliners have always been happy that we are being protected, but of course a visitor was disturbed by the maneuvers.

In the meantime the sinister Wall was erected, over the belated protests of the vacillating Western powers. It put an end to the "display window" that was West Berlin. We were compelled to adopt a solidarity of the status quo. In July 1962 the fleeing Peter Fechter bled to death as the police watched. Suddenly the population grew emotional. An absurd situation arose: The Wall had to be protected by the Western police. Nevertheless, in December 1963 the historic moment came when the agreement was concluded concerning border-crossing permits. People went to visit their family and friends on the other side. They happily endured long waits in the early dawn hours. And life went on within the 120-kilometer wall, resigned but in—unasked-for—safety.

Gerald had never seen crows in such masses as can be observed over West Berlin. He was speechless with astonishment as they arrived in a thick cloud to settle on the trees where they slept, screaming and cawing and hacking at each other. Then suddenly, as if on command, silence fell.

"I wish I could fall asleep like that," Gerald said, impressed.

The movies continued to fascinate us. When we treated ourselves to *Ben Hur*, a by no means worthless epic, we came to see the touching simplicity of Gerald's feelings; though we had long suspected this side of him existed, he had never shown it so nakedly before. The depth of his emotion was almost infectious.

It was with Gerald that I brought out one of the first— probably the very first—long-playing albums. In Berlin Electrola recorded Hugo Wolf's Möricke lieder. Fritz Ganss, that gnarled Hessian, was at the time the head of the company. Though he was a champion of music, and there was nothing he did not know about human nature, he always stayed behind the scenes. Earlier he had been chief dramaturge at East Berlin's Komische Oper, and had persuaded me to visit Walter Felsenstein, its manager, in his office.

Felsenstein, casting a commanding glance at me, called out, "Come and work with us. We're the only ones that will let you train yourself adequately for *Don Giovanni*."

I beat a hasty retreat. I had just been hired by Tietjen.

Ganss was now concerned to keep a handful of singers—names he himself had launched—loyal to the Electrola label and to give them appropriate material to record.
I had recorded a great many performances with him in
the Zehlendorf Protestant parish house. Horst Lindner, its
chief technician, and Christfried Bickenbach, the production head, were outstanding in their jobs. Here too I met
Rudolf Schock, still in his "serious" phase of singing opera
and concerts. I had already been absolutely captivated by
this tenor when I heard him sing Ottavio in *Don Giovanni*
at the Admiralspalast.

Erika Köth had just been discovered in Munich;
Schock and I were smitten by her Musetta in selections
from *Bohème*. From the old Lindenoper days the soprano
Erna Berger, whose beautiful voice never let her down,
blessed as she was with a timbre like that of a child, sang
Mimi and then Madame Butterfly. Hermann Prey, and
later Fritz Wunderlich, also became part of the group, both
recruited by Fritz Ganss.

About ten years after the first taping of Hugo Wolf
lieder, Deutsche Grammophon asked me to record all the
songs for male voice by Franz Schubert. This huge undertaking brought Gerald and me together again inter-
mittently, each session for a considerable time, in the
former movie studios in Tempelhof.

"Coming to" after any prolonged period of concentrating on producing correct and relaxed sounds, it would
be a mistake to go looking for company. Even an otherwise
sociable person will feel strangely isolated at such a time.
The student movement, which was just awakening then,
may have contributed to the feeling—for no matter in what
tone its echo came to our ears, it caused deep depression,
there being no way of knowing where its apparent arbi-

trariness would lead. And everyone over forty, whether he wanted to or not, began to look inward, asking himself where he might have contributed to the mistakes that had led to it.

The disconcerted observer felt the lack of any constructive element in the pronouncements of the young people. At best they strove for remote, unrealizable ideals—insofar as their revolutionary jibberish could be deciphered at all. Today we realize more clearly than we did at the time that their critical drops of water hollowed out more than one stone of dead convention. They helped to change some things, making it more possible to end the Vietnam war. They took some effective steps in opposing stagnation in the universities. They did not let themselves be intimidated by the need for internal calm in the fortress that was Berlin. And, most especially, they left us with the realization that not everything needs to be resolved by resorting to police violence. Reality and the policies decided upon by governments must not diverge too widely. To do nothing but hope, overlooking deeply rooted discontent, can only lead us astray.

Today every young person should be encouraged once again to take action against apathy. Whatever was said at the time, however, about "revolution" only added fuel to the flames of unfocused discontent.

The Schubert recording sessions always led us away from these and other confusions, back to essentials. In spite of the abstruseness of the lyrics, this lifework, produced in only fifteen productive years, is a continuing joy, a story with no ending for the lieder singer. I felt immediately at home, even in the songs that were new to me. Over and over I admired the scope of Schubert's expression and his artistic sensibility. Whether he worked in an

Italian or a pre-Wagnerian style or in Bach's, form and style were always congruent. Sometimes, before returning to Schubert, I found my voice thin and overextended; in Schubert it quickly regained its full sound.

Occasionally, as the working sessions went on, Gerald tended to become somewhat dry and unimaginative. At such times I arranged our rehearsals to permit greater liberties of interpretation, and discussed all the details ahead of time. I always came back to Karl Jasper's healthy adage: "The guiding principle of your actions must be whatever you have recognized as right, even if it leads to lonely, unconventional decisions."

Suddenly I had to give up the Schubert recording for a while. I had been on my feet through all the sessions so far, and I had begun to suffer vertigo and slight nausea. The fussy company physician did not know what to say, not even about the fact that in the course of the day my blood pressure dropped much too quickly. A week passed before it finally occurred to me to put on my reading glasses. It was the obvious solution to my problem, though we were slow in finding it.

In the end we listened to all the tapes in one final session that took nine hours. During the last two I felt feverish. The entire team—including the producer Rainer Brock and the technician Hans Schweigmann—who had grown close in the three years of recording, also complained of aching joints and the onset of the flu. So I took to my bed and stared at the thermometer, which registered 39 degrees Centigrade. When my racing heart did not slow down, I called my guardian angel, Dr. Rudolf Zimmermann, in Starnberg. He had always known what to do, and this time was no exception. An injection restored me to normal within an hour. I was almost always filled with

joy, even euphoria, when I returned to Munich from Zimmermann's clinic in Starnberg. Because he invariably did
the right thing, singers from all over the continent beat a
path to his door.

As the Schubert recordings were completed, the troubling student unrest also came to an end. All that remained
was long hair, which to Gerald seemed to exemplify a lack
of imagination and conformity. Soon the longhairs began
to take over the television screen. The cultural magazines,
lacking any real insight, began to flirt with the principles
of emptiness, ugliness, and sterility. Inaction became important, any form of concentration was rejected. The mod-
erates welcomed conformity on an international level. A
modern plague spread, more virulent than any previous
temptations.

That Gerald continued to accompany me in the recording studio for some time after his official retirement,
which he did for no one else, makes me happy to this day.

Gerald was also a popular lecturer and a witty com-
mentator on himself in several books. In his overly modest, utterly unassuming *The Unashamed Accompanist*, he
exposed the often inadequate skills of the professional
accompanist. As a result he acquired the status of a legend;
I had followed his career from the time I was a child, when
I had seen the name of Gerald Moore richly represented
in all the record catalogues, long before I ever met him.
After the war, when the first record encyclopedias were
issued, Moore appeared on almost every page of these
walks down memory lane.

On various occasions Gerald has praised me orally
and in writing. As a final word, I can only attempt to give
back to him some of all that he has given me. The rhythm
that he particularly praised in me was one of his own

principal virtues. He walked hand in hand with his partner, whose mainstay of meter and breath was never sacrificed. He never lost himself in details but always followed to the end the larger line initiated by the composer. His perfect legato playing contributed to this effect, as did his many nuances of attack, which never became independent to the detriment of the work.

When I think of the many pianists with whom I have shared a stage, I realize that there are a few preconditions I wish to mention briefly. Of course the quality of an accompanist largely depends on the singer. If the pianist knows what he wants and can give good reasons for his choice, he may take the initiative without qualms. Unfortunately many a lieder accompanist relies on receiving the lyrics and their meaning predigested by his partner, unless he has played the works before. This attitude generally goes hand in hand with a certain inability to subordinate sufficiently the colors of the piano part to the voice. I am reminded of the otherwise reliable Leo Taubman in the United States; occasionally he did not understand what it was he had to reproduce until after the second performance. This situation can also hold true for pure instrumentalists, as happened with Fritz Neumeyer, who understood a great deal about his cello and the piano and the literature for them but had only a peripheral understanding of the lied. So what we are dealing with is the necessary independence of the "accompanist," who is to be a partner in the duet and a nonserving slave.

Nor can playing for lieder serve as a refuge for those pianists who could not make it technically on their own. No matter how reverently I think of Michael Raucheisen, with his years of experience on the concert stage and his resourcefulness at finding unknown or rarely performed lieder, I shudder at the thought of his instrumental carelessness when we recorded Beethoven's folksongs, not to mention his frenzy to finish a postlude as quickly as possible so as not to distract attention from the vocalist.

Accompanying is not merely a matter of pianistic technique; pianists may be skilled in playing the larger genres, such as sonatas, but these are different from lieder. Accompanists must also be sensitive to detail, which in classical solo works tends only too frequently to be ignored. That is to say, it takes time to learn even a simple piece composed of plain chords, such as Schumann's "Lotosblume." Some piano students in my lieder class who are familiar only with the solo literature leave me with the impression that it is precisely this that makes difficulties for them. But beyond this point, they do not sense how important breathing is even in these short forms. All too frequently breathing is thought to be superfluous; though the sonata player seldom encounters it so unmistakably, it is obviously in the very nature of song and is inherent in the composition. The way from the lied to chamber music should be the right road for many. Some people cling to the erroneous belief that power resides exclusively in the spacious instrumental works and not in the delicate lieder form. The facts, and many small piano pieces, argue otherwise.

Many "standard" accompanists provide now one, now another singer with routine piano playing. Such jumping around has damaged the reputation of the keyboard player. For even in the best circumstances he can only pretend that he can quickly adjust to each singer. In fact it is an impossibility. Loving change as I do, I have no

objection to bringing inspiration and renewal to the interpretation through a new partner. But such a shift takes
time, just as even great tennis players need time in which
to adjust to their opponents' peculiarities. Working together on the stage and in the recording studio in many
ways resembles a ball game between two equals. In my
opinion it affects the listener when singer and pianist are
well adjusted to each other. The lieder interpreter is constantly being faced with new challenges, new situations.
Without the use of gestures to underline his intention, he
must re-create the psychological process of which the
poem represents a segment. Unlike the opera singer, he
cannot describe a figure through appearance, behavior,
and character development. Only through his own position, glance, or degree of tension—generally unconscious—may he visually express the piece he is singing.
On such occasions the pianist must not disturb the image,
for instance with his habitual facial expressions. And yet
neither should the correct attitude be confused with indifference. Thus the otherwise admirable pianist Paul
Ulanowsky, an almost ideal traveling companion, remained remote in performance to such a degree that when
I appeared with him in the United States, in spite of its
transparency, his playing was felt only as gray, as no
longer capable of interaction. Only when the pianist is
centered within himself, thus free to express himself, to
share in experiencing the mood of the work, is he prepared to enter unreservedly into the dialogue with the
singer. His physical involvement must reflect his playing,
based on the particular lied. This is where the tonal values
of performance are gained.

* * *

The only time I participated in the Casals Festival in Prades in the hot south of France, Gerald also accompanied me, in spite of a long-standing quarrel with Pablo Casals. The grand old man lived in the white former gatehouse of a little castle glimpsed in the huge park behind cast-iron gates through the trees. We climbed the narrow wooden stairs to his living quarters and found him in an easy chair, smoking his inevitable pipe. He greeted us with a tired gesture that hinted at the many unwanted visitors he had to deal with daily. A notably large number of women and girls from all over the globe went in and out—nieces, aunts, students, and gate-crashing Festival fans. Some kept house for him, others—the prettier ones, as far as I could see—spent the whole year as disciples in Prades. The master rewarded even the slightest help with an embrace and kisses on both cheeks—surely going beyond Spanish good manners. We did not stay long, since the first concert was to take place that night.

Brahms' *Vier ernste Gesänge* were performed with piano accompaniment in the extremely handsome thirteenth-century church. A magnificent and somewhat intimidating early-baroque altar of a sweeping splendor dominated the scene. The sound also seemed to me uniquely dry.

Irmel, the cellist, had to remain in the audience, which, much to her sorrow, prevented her from watching Casals warm up, as I was able to do. Lacking other space, he sat in the sacristy in the midst of all the other soloists. While violin, viola, and clarinet doodled scales, he steadfastly played one Bach suite after another, as if he were the only person in the world.

He listened to my Brahms songs sitting in the open doorway. His attempt, after I finished, to kiss me on both cheeks miscarried because of the difference in our height. The clarinet quintet and string sextet were faultlessly performed, but the second cello left the church in a rage, rejecting all praise with an impatient wave of her hand. None of the listeners who pushed their way backstage paid her any attention.

On the final day of our stay we met her. Madeleine Folley lived in the United States. A student of Casals, she and other Americans had been organizing the Festival for years. She had corresponded with us as well, without the smallest compensation from Festival funds. She had admitted that the Prades cult had made her a little bitter, that her inner strength was being consumed and her playing compromised. Organizational work was considered completely unimportant. Furthermore, all of Casals' many relatives, who helped organize the Festival, made every action twice as complicated through the very specifically miserly intent of keeping from the participating artists even the slightest remuneration. (We too had difficulty being reimbursed even for part of our travel expenses.) In Prades they did not like to pay honoraria.

Casals had powerful hands with stubby fingers which, in spite of his eighty years, were always placed precisely on the strings. He was always humming. You could feel that he rarely planned finger placements or bowing motions ahead of time (in sharp contrast to, say, Enrico Mainardi). It was as if at the moment of playing he was composing the work anew. His articulation could still be unbelievably powerful and passionate, never languishing or ardent, as is easy for the cello, but always lean and authentic in expression. Occasional glissandi or portamenti revealed some weakness—the only indication of his age. Most of the time he was able to avoid them.

The following evening, again in the church, I sang the *Winterreise*. With the help of an electrician willing to dim the lighting, I tried to soften the effect of the oppressive baroque altar behind me—without success. The electrical power failed, however, at the beginning of "Lindenbaum." Total darkness engulfed the room. But without being in the least hampered, Gerald played on, not even hesitating at the difficult transition to the final stanza. I therefore was finally able to enjoy this lied fully concentrated on the music. At the last chord the floodlights unfortunately sprang back into service.

By the way, I was startled each time when at the end of every single song the master's bass voice could be heard from the first row saying, "Lovely!" He "whispered" the word to the Pure Elisabeth from Brussels, who was sitting next to him.

For a long time Pablo Casals was a unique example of instrumental "perfection" because of his novel technique and his unusual concept of the rubato. There followed a time when cellists seemed to gather together only to perform something approximately matching the Spaniard's playing in technique and inspiration. Technical skills developed rapidly, perfection followed upon perfection, and a virtuosity now seemed possible for which the time was apparently ripe. One talent above all others captivated listeners with its spontaneity and the will to reveal the music's inner life: Jacqueline du Pré.

Some are taken from us long before they stop breathing. When I met Daniel and Jackie Barenboim—only just married in Israel during the Six-Day War—in Rome, both of these superbly talented musicians glowed with fire and inspiration. It was not difficult to realize that Jacqueline was an outstanding interpreter. I heard the two of them play Beethoven sonatas before an undeserving audience—the listeners did not pay much attention—in the auditorium of the Accademia Santa Cecilia. One truly enthusiastic listener, whose total absorption was evident even from his back, was Carlo Maria Giulini, who sat many rows in front of me. I was aware that the now dreamy, now tempestuous woman on the stage was demonstrating an artistry without limits. She moved easily and quickly, throwing back her long blond hair, and when the music seemed to call for a sforzando, she struck the strings with the bow. She indulged in generous variations in tempo, but they were always subordinated to the meaning of the work and therefore sounded entirely natural.

The following day, during lunch on the open terrace, she explained that she did not intend to become one of those "traveling musicians" who must perform day in, day out. She wanted to spend a lot of time with Dany, be there for him, and simply enjoy being alive. Whenever I saw the two of them again, I was made happy by the harmony between them—in their character, their working discipline, their strong will and ability to concentrate. Temperament and wit melded all these into an exquisite relationship.

Jackie did not find an instrument that truly satisfied her until shortly before she had to stop playing. She always complained how little color the cello basically allowed, and she expressed envy for the human voice, in which the word alone can conjure up so many more shadings of expression. When she at last found a cello in Philadelphia that met her needs, the range of colors in her repertoire also seemed to increase.

Around this time I was in New York; we were staying at the same hotel, and that same week. as a "dress rehearsal" for upcoming concerts, Jackie and Dany played for me the César Franck Sonata in the arrangement for cello. I could not hold back my tears at the absolute harmony the two achieved. Later, in Paris, I recorded Hugo Wolf with Dany; Jackie, her face bright red, turned the pages, which spurred me on all the more.

This woman, who was all motion, contracted multiple sclerosis, the paralyzing disease that has not yet been understood and is difficult to diagnose. We were recording the Mozart Requiem in a London church when Dany seemed to become fully aware of the tragedy that had struck him. He called an orchestra intermission earlier than planned. I felt my deepest bond with him, beyond all our artistic solidarity, when, after sending the orchestra away, he fell sobbing into my arms.

Daniel Barenboim gave every sign of being a many-faceted musical genius. And if today it were still the custom to compose with Mozart's naturalness, he would hold a place at the top of this discipline as well. When his father, a highly respected piano teacher—first in South America, then in Israel—brought nine-year-old Dany to see me in my dressing room in Vienna, I could not have anticipated the good fortune that I would later experience in our friendly collaborations. A Schubert recital in the Royal Festival Hall and some Mahler cycles with the Philharmonia Orchestra gave me an opportunity to admire his versatility. And there followed work upon work, each newly brought to life by his conducting or playing. A phenomenal memory helped him to hold almost the full canon of the piano literature in his head—and his fingers. Relying on his expansive nature, I made ample use of this facility when, all too rarely, we could share a few leisure hours. He immediately fulfilled all one could wish for in a performance.

Most of the time, however, Dany is zealously at work on three problems at once. It was always a special pleasure for him to play Hugo Wolf's Mörike lieder. At our first rehearsal of a program composed of them in New York, to be performed in Carnegie Hall, the following happened: In the midst of the thundering octaves on the galloping "Feuerreiter," which he was playing at sight, he jumped up: "Excuse me, one moment please."

He ran to the desk where he had spread out the score of Furtwängler's huge piano concerto, which he was about to perform with Zubin Mehta in Los Angeles. Humming softly, he stared at the notes for a few seconds, then darted back to the piano and resumed playing. While the Wolf was absorbing him—not the easiest score in the world— an entirely different work was running simultaneously through his head.

I learned to admire Barenboim as an opera director as well. He provided my Count in *Figaro* and Amonasro in *Aida* with the most beautiful possible support and the most subtle accompaniment. He claimed that he did not understand Robert Schumann's very special rubato, that he approached it incorrectly. And yet he played it so much more beautifully than all the others, precisely because he was very given to a romantic range in the tradition of Wilhelm Furtwängler. Nor can I think of any more idiomatic interpreter of Edward Elgar's symphonies. The memory of a rehearsal of the Second with the Berlin Philharmonic stays with me because in the course of the rehearsal a bored orchestra, predisposed against the work, became, by the intermission, a happily debating and entranced musical team.

I felt supported and relieved when Dany accompanied me on the stage of the Mann Auditorium in Tel Aviv. I was giving the first concerts there by a German artist, singing in German to boot. It is impossible to "make amends" for what happened in the Nazi period, but I hoped to create a narrow opening to that spirit of German culture that has nothing in common with the Nazis.

The long negotiations with Wolfgang Lewy and Mr. Cohen of the Israel Philharmonic Orchestra paid off, and the moment was well chosen. With a trembling heart I stepped in front of an audience of every age group and from every country in the world, all waiting expectantly. The reactions in the various seating locations and from the young people sitting on the steps in a dense crowd varied widely, running the gamut from nostalgia to fascination. But approbation was universal and could not have been more cordial. Dany played for me in a mixed Schubert program, consisting mostly of little-known lieder and few favorites; a Beethoven program; an orchestral concert with works by Mahler; and finally Schubert's *Winterreise*.

Klaus Geitel, who went to Israel with us, wrote in *Die Welt* that the current generation of Israelis had no feeling for Mahler, any more than did the orchestra. Such a statement did not really apply to Israel, where Mahler's music had been regularly and intensively promoted. It is true, however, that since that time Bernstein, Kletzki, and Mehta have brought about an enormous increase in the share of the repertoire devoted to Mahler.

I was deeply impressed by the land of milk and honey,

and not only by the holy sites in Jerusalem, where the various religions live in close proximity and yet maintain their independence. Though the Israelis have had a hard economic struggle, they have created an island of fertility and culture, which contrasts only too sharply at the nation's borders with the surrounding desert, causing envy.

The factotum of the Israel Philharmonic Orchestra, Joseph, often drove us through the country, explaining knowledgeably and turning away all thanks with "You are mostly welcome." What we saw did not really correspond to what we had come to expect from reading about it. In the midst of all the beauties of land and sea, of crowded cities, fields, and shores, lives a people that has newly discovered itself, newly shaped itself into a group that can defend itself, young, beautiful, and working for the future. No one looking in from the outside and troubled by its bellicose outward appearance should ignore the fact that Israel's highest aim is to live in peace with its neighbors, to trade and traffic with them. . . . And I will always be grateful to Dany for the opportunity I had to step on this soil with him as my companion.

It was while I was at the conservatory—that is, during the war—that the pianist Wilhelm Kempff introduced me to three of Mozart's piano concertos. He played them in the Beethoven-Saal with a chamber orchestra conducted by Fritz Stein, who at the time was head of my music school. There is no way to describe the emotion that overcomes me when I first hear an important work by Mozart. I was sitting on the stage behind the orchestra; a sense of ecstasy filled me as these treasures reached my ear for the first time. I was especially fascinated with the soulful and at the same time unearthly way Kempff rendered the D-minor Concerto, both dramatic and precise. In some indeterminate way his conducting matched his appearance: blond hair, looking wind-blown, above a strong nose, a tall, slender body . . . That evening I came close to taking him for a heavenly messenger. The Brahms B-major Concerto, conducted by Eugen Jochum, strengthened the impression.

I did not see Kempff again until after the war. A favorite of the gods, he settled in a castle not far from Bayreuth with his wife and daughters. The master had been aware of my festival debut, and now he took pleasure in entertaining Wolfram and his flirtatious wife at his home.

In 1964 I had a somewhat odd idea. I wanted to make a complete recording of lieder composed by famous interpreters. The idea had suggested itself when, during the performances of *Doktor Faust* by Busoni, someone sent me four of his songs set to Goethe lyrics. At the same time Kempff sent me a small bundle of his own piano songs. Thereupon he accepted my invitation to accompany me himself in some songs on texts by Conrad Ferdinand Meyer. The remaining songs—among them some by Fritz Busch with viola (played by Rudolf Nel), Bruno Walter, and Enrico Mainardi—were accompanied by Jörg Demus.

Kempff entered the studio with the deliberate dignity of the master, as if to rid himself of the particular excitement of his own works. Testing the two grand pianos put out for the occasion, he produced an astonishingly firm, even thunderous tone, only to turn to his own creations with that much more enjoyment of the details. The recording of the songs, all of which remained well within the limits of conventionality, went off without a hitch.

While we were still in the studio, Kempff told many

stories about the operas, oratorios, and chamber works he had written long ago. His mood, already sunny, heightened to a kind of ecstasy. No surprise, then, that in the inscription in his beautiful handwriting on my copies he called May 18, 1964, "one of the most blessed days." He came along home with me; he was in the mood for a declaration of thanksgiving, and so he played to a tiny audience, listening excitedly, until late into the night. My mother, who during her youth in Potsdam must have been in love with the boy wonder at the organ, sat as close to the piano as she could, her cheeks bright red, and did not hesitate to make more and more requests. And Kempff outdid himself as he broke into a wealth of improvised Schubert sonatas, Liszt sonnets, Schumann cycles, and Debussy preludes. He seemed to like the long music room crammed with books and scores, as well as the children (who had been allowed to stay up), because they stayed so still and quiet. I noticed how much more surely and accurately he dealt with the music he was interpreting. There was no sign of the detailed key work, the fingering in the middle voice, that had tended to make me uneasy on earlier occasions.

At our last meeting in Tokyo, Kempff was able to take only short steps as he moved to the piano. He had a special fondness for Japan and had made the effort because there he enjoyed unlimited adoration and—as he did all over the world—a huge audience. I was amazed to hear his trembling hands managing the tricky parts of Schumann's *Kreisleriana*. His second concert was all Beethoven. In the intermission I went up to him and looked into a frightened face: "The Waldstein Sonata is next! I can't play that any more. Don't listen. . . ."

Now the old man, seriously ill, is in his beloved Pos-

itano, where he had experienced recuperation and the joy
of teaching. There he waits for the last curtain call.

I have already mentioned that I took special pleasure in
adjusting to Sviatoslav Richter's ideas. This Russian—
intense, even lionlike on the stage—had a mother who
lived in southern Germany. He therefore had closer con-
tacts with the West than did other Soviet artists. Since the
French have given him a festival "of his own" in Touraine,
he can be heard more frequently in France. He cherishes
that country if only because there the "young men shout
so wonderfully"—a circumstance that I also like because
this acoustic reinforcement also helps me to shine.

When, after prolonged "horse trading" with the Soviet
authorities, we finally were allowed to give a recital together in the Soviet Union, I came to know Richter as an
extremely vulnerable, sensitive man. Both he and his wife,
Nina Dorliac—formerly a famous singer—found it more
difficult than others to endure life's injustice. He had acquired two adjacent apartments in an ordinary high rise
and had knocked out the walls between them, giving the
place a certain comfortable expansiveness. In his home
Richter regularly organized small exhibitions of paintings
and drawings. I happened to be there for one of them,
which included portraits of himself and of close friends
and family members, among them especially valuable
drawings by I.J. Repin and Oskar Kokoschka. I met the
widow of Shostakovich and the violinist Gidon Kremer.
Kremer and I stood at the huge windows with their wonderful view of Moscow and talked about the unfortunate
effects of isolation on Soviet musical life at the time.

The next time I went to Richter's home for a rehearsal,

he and I stood looking at the same panorama. I asked him about the histories of some of the houses I saw. He answered sadly, "All that's been studied so little."

The abrupt change from despair to action and back again, those specifically Russian traits, marked him as well. I shared a car with the Richters to go to the concert hall. When we came in sight of the expectant crowd of people without tickets blocking the street and the traffic, he drew back anxiously. Because the magnificent conservatory auditorium was undergoing renovation, we had to move our recital to a hall built in the Stalin period, with very poor acoustics. But Slava was not in the least disconcerted; as always, his playing was impeccable. Literally as always: I have never yet caught him in a wrong note, and hardly ever in an omitted one. His playing is marked by an impeccable, straightforward, as it were, beauty, which succeeds most strikingly in balancing the levels of volume. And he manages to do this with acoustics of the special difficulty presented by the huge medieval barn in Tours, with its sandy floor that nips any resonance in the bud.

Slava's joy in successful concerts is totally unbridled; his disappointment when they are less successful has tragic overtones. He was therefore deeply wounded that the conventional audience in Leningrad felt our Wolf recital to be too difficult and "modern."

The concerts themselves were by no means the most significant aspect of my visit to Russia. To wander alone across Red Square and observe the "pilgrims" from all over the world as anxiously, reverently, or curiously they gawked at the changing of the guard at Lenin's Tomb, the occasional black limousines with politicians arriving or departing, or the groups of picturesquely garbed tourists from the interior—these sights offered scope enough for astonishment. To sit in the Bolshoi Theater, looking down from one of the boxes at the countrified audience who did not know what to feel about the *Stone Guest* by Alexander Dargomyshsky, noting the anxious timidity of the cultural officers who shared my box; to see the bored routine of the conductor, Mark Ermler, who surely was not at all eager to lead the hundredth performance for an ever-changing but always untutored audience; to listen to the voice of Vladimir Atlantov, who was doing the tenor role of Don Juan, surrounded by the utmost mediocrity and old-fashioned "modernism" from the 1950s—these were, of course, eclipsed by visits to museums, especially to the Hermitage in Leningrad, where the lecturer in art history, over my protests, closed the Rembrandts to the Sunday public so that I could indulge my enjoyment of art undisturbed. But I could not stand before the magnificence of the *Prodigal Son* and *Danae* with an entirely easy conscience. And the yellow palace facades and the different-shaped bridges of Leningrad enchanted me, although the streets were always crowded and busy. Everything I saw made up for the icy drafts in the "luxury hotel," for the dark brown soup in the bathtub that hardly seemed suited to washing, for the lone potato on a plate that was given the name of supper. . . .

Working with major soloists fulfills its high purpose only when, a partner in the enterprise, I feel open to suggestion and correction. This was true particularly in Israel when I was to conduct Alfred Brendel in one of his standards, Mozart's Piano Concerto in C-major, K. 503. Julia and I learned of his arrival late at night at the Israel Philharmonic's guest house only after we had long since gone to bed. We had not, however, been able to fall asleep, partly because of my excitement at the coming event, partly because of the storm rattling the windowpanes. Our chief nourishment during the unusual Israeli cold wave was delicious soup in a huge thermos bottle, kept filled by Mr. and Mrs. Redlich, who did a splendid job as house parents. No sooner had we arrived than we were shown the huge kitchen, and we were encouraged, should we be overcome by an attack of hunger, even during the night, to help ourselves. That first night Julia did feel drawn to the monster refrigerator that housed yoghurt and all kinds of drinks. To her surprise, she found a tall man bent over into the open refrigerator. He straightened up and turned around, sleepy, rumpled, and blinking through his glasses. It was Alfred Brendel. After each had explained, quite unnecessarily, "I was just looking for a snack," they introduced themselves.

When we got up the next morning, we could hear that Brendel was already busy practicing. Excited and a little abashed at such fortitude, I knocked on his door to receive my first instructions from him; he was cordial but firm in his ideas. During the rehearsal (we had only one) all went well; I was relieved to find that there were no grounds for my fears that I might encounter difficulties in working with someone so given to sharp definitions of sound. Though onstage at the keyboard he seems fanatic or dreamy, he can laugh like few others. In the intermission, after the rehearsal of Schumann's Third, he gave his opinion: "What you make of this music—it's astonishing. . . ."

In the final movement of the Mozart piano concerto there was a moment when the harmony between us was not fully present at the outset. In the third of the concerts he suddenly played as I had expected, not without making the notes f–d sound louder than the rest.

At lunch Brendel revealed himself to be a collector of inadvertent blunders and howlers in newspapers; he conjured a large number of such clippings from his wallet.

We went straight to the United States from Israel. There we met Brendel and his beautiful Reni (at the time they were engaged to be married) again when he played a matinee performance at Carnegie Hall. I remember particularly the *Kreisleriana*, which was analytical to an unprecedented degree and yet pulsing with passion. An all-Beethoven program (part of his cycle spread out over the winter) with the Berlin Philharmonic also earned my complete admiration. He played as masterfully as ever, but afterward, when I opened the door to his dressing room, he waved me away: He was running a high temperature.

Not everyone was so considerate. Often I would be warmly embraced by people with colds; after one such encounter in Chicago I came down with an extremely serious case of the flu the following day. Adrift in a foreign country, I subjected myself to acupuncture treatment by a solemn Chinese who, with the assistance of a gigantic, athletic black, made smoky sacrifices—as mysterious as they were malodorous—on my parlor table; alas, they were fruitless.

After Brendel and I performed the *Winterreise* at Carnegie Hall, we "cemented" our friendship by visiting a small exhibit of surrealist art on Fifth Avenue. This excursion was wholly to Alfred's taste. He had a soft spot for bizarre, outrageous things, and he showed us some of them he had collected in the top floor of his house in London's Hampstead. The dominant curio on the shelf was an exquisite statuette; a three-legged animal shaped like a grand piano, with the head of Alfred Brendel.

We enjoyed the pleasure of quiet cameraderie and an unobtrusive recording team throughout a series of television tapings with the stage director Klaus Lindemann. The only problem that arose was that on the day set aside for a rehearsal a number of distant microphones were tuned in to the technical apparatus, and people may even have taped the event, which was not what either Alfred or I intended. It is true that the result, which Lindemann proudly played for us, was so full of revelations and interest that we gladly approved it for presentation.

I thank Alfred for thinking of me as a professional musician, so that we could tell each other freely what was on our minds, which led to productive exchanges. And I believe that the concerts and recordings we shared reflected them. In London so many dignitaries and such a glitter of gowns attended our performance at the Opera that the event resembled a state reception. The large hall was as silent as if a spell had been cast over it; we seemed to be playing just for ourselves. After "Leiermann" many listeners audibly drew in their breath, as if to keep themselves from sobbing, before the applause broke out.

We have still not realized our plan of spending a vacation together somewhere at the shore, not stirring unless we feel like it. But we must hold onto our daydream; it deserves it.

10

"Habe gelernt und geschrieben"

Gerd

German singers may sound somewhat strange in Italian opera, no matter how polished their pronunciation. I was therefore all the more eager at my first visit to the fairy-tale city of Naples (before a mixed audience containing both nursing mothers and adolescent children) to be persuasive. This was in 1955; I was engaged to sing with the Scarlatti orchestra under Franco Caracciolo Mahler.

When we got out of the car in front of the San Carlo theater, Hans Werner Henze and Ingeborg Bachmann came to meet us, happily holding hands. They had just moved into a house in the hills above the city and seemed like a blissful brother and sister. The fruit of this encounter, the first time Henze had heard me sing, was his *Nea-politanische Lieder* the following year, based on poems in the local dialect. Welcoming this attempt at a new melodics, I gave the songs their world premiere with Otto Matzerath and the Hesse Radio Symphony Orchestra. Hans Werner was more than pleased with the result.

I had no hesitation in using my influence with Frau Schiller and Deutsche Grammophon, and soon the company had agreed to record the *Neapolitanische Lieder*. The recording session was held in the Siemens mansion in the Lankwitz section of Berlin, which has since been the site of many of my lieder recordings. The founder of the firm had had the handsomely proportioned auditorium built and decorated in gold and white in order to indulge his hobby—conducting an orchestra hired for the purpose. To set up and dismantle the electrical equipment in that hall is relatively easy, and though the acoustics sound extremely sharp, especially in the microphone, they are therefore all the clearer and more vivid. During the recording Hans Werner sat silent and shy to one side, hardly daring to intervene in the orchestra's proceedings, though he did not seem to agree with every detail. This was the first of Henze's works to come out on records. Richard Kraus, whom I have mentioned before, was the conductor.

Years later, during the rehearsals for the Berlin world premiere of *Elegy for Young Lovers*, directed and designed by Henze, Ingeborg Bachmann came to our house. She seemed insecure, and she no longer appeared thrilled when Henze arrived. She had lost him and with him, she thought, the whole world. She impressed me as someone who makes life difficult for herself. As if visually to emphasize this attitude, her hair was excessively bleached. I was rather startled by her covertly amorous glances between moments of glassy distractedness. She raved to our small group about—Klaus Kinski. Almost in the same breath she began to discuss the pros and cons of literary opera, exemplified by *Don Giovanni* and *Lulu*. She knew what she was talking about: She had worked for a long time on the libretto for Henze's *Prince of Homburg* and painfully arrived at the conclusion that strict literalness could only do harm. Inevitably the conversation turned to the relationship between music and language. Ingeborg Bachmann's view was that today language was no longer capable of meeting the intellectual demands made by music, with all its accumulated technical skills of simultaneity. That was why for the first time in the modern period the two arts had reason to take divergent paths.

But the question immediately followed: Must singing come to an end altogether? With all the firmness of which her shy, soft voice was capable she said, "On this planet, where the clouds always roll in again because emotions are sent packing and many thoughts no longer find support, people over and over become newly aware what it means—the human voice. . . ."

At that, I forgot what had seemed to me a discrepancy that appeared to hold her back inwardly and outwardly. Her eyes no longer seemed cold to me, no longer contradicted her shy, sensitive being as her beautiful figure opposed her ugly hairdo.

I learned from television about the uncertain political stream into which Ingeborg Bachmann subsequently fell. But even though every adult is free to commit himself to whatever cause he chooses, I nevertheless felt that she did not really mean it with all her heart. She sounded as if she were not speaking genuinely, as if it was an automatic commitment to anyone who was "against the system." I'm sure the trauma of living through the Nazi period as a child played some part in her actions. Ingeborg Bachmann was the instrument of her own destruction; she searched for death until she found it in Rome, in agony.

I prefer Ingeborg Bachmann's poetry to her prose; I am in awe of her literary skill; no one since has been her equal. Her lines comprise a flight forward that describes the poet's entire life.

Ingeborg Bachmann encountered Paul Celan, the other great German-speaking poet of that day, when, shortly after the war, he left the East to live in Vienna. His poems caused a sensation that in retrospect is hard to understand. But after all, even for me they meant a first encounter with all that had been declared as no longer possible in the cage of the National Socialist years. I did not begin to explore the aesthetics of Celan's lines until Aribert Reimann composed his first lieder cycle to Celan's poems. The songs made a vivid but ambivalent impression. As people left the auditorium, some muttered scornfully, "We created the dark into emptiness. . . ."

In Paris, where Celan went in 1948, there were few opportunities for the poet to prove himself. Claire Goll indignantly prattled to me about the effrontery with which Celan had plagiarized her poems and those of her late husband, Ivan Goll. I did not believe a word of it, if for no other reason than that Claire had just dedicated a poem to me—especially written for me—whose weakness made the opposite seem more likely. The eighty-year-old woman, who was wearing a flaming red wig, asked at the last moment for "a little bench, over to the side" for my lieder recital. Celan was not the first poet whose life she

had made difficult, in one way or another, and I am sure
that her husband was not exempt either. Perhaps she was
taking her revenge for the many injustices she had suffered in her life.

I have often sung Celan, and always with conviction.
Only once was I privileged to shake hands with the shy,
withdrawn poet. After a Wolf recital in Paris that included
Mörike's "Weylas Gesang," a short man with glowing eyes
pushed his way into the room. Apparently in some kind
of shock, he pushed Francis Poulenc and his friend Pierre
Bernac, who were talking to me, to one side, to blurt out,
"But that's an inconceivable poem, the one about the land
of Orplid, I've never heard anything like it, you can't describe it, and it's deathless, 'Weyla's Song.' "

That was all he wanted to say. No sooner did he finish
speaking than he made his bashful way back through the
throng. When Paul Celan drowned himself in the spring
of 1970, had he relinquished all hope of seeing the land
of Orplid? The chief cause of his death was exile.

In 1965 Heinz Friedrich coaxed me outside my familiar
world of scores and notes. In Ruth's elegant parlor the
polymathic publisher suggested that I compile a book containing the most frequently sung texts to German songs
with piano accompaniment, and write an introduction to
it. This conversation led to a continuing exchange that
was not affected even by long periods of being out of touch.
And the fact that we quarreled over a number of musical
questions only increased the intensity of our dialogue. The
lengthy correspondence between us is really very interesting, extending so far over two decades. (I always answer personal letters myself, and by return post.) I feel it

a very serious loss that the wonderful custom of letter writing is withering away, displaced by telephone and Telex.

Heinz Friedrich's sure and single-handed restructuring of the Deutsche Taschenbuch Verlag from nothing to one of the most respected paperback publishing houses in the world is evident almost entirely between the lines. His natural tendency to scholarship, to introspection, and to friendship conflicts with the need as a publisher to create something substantial, to organize chaos into form. His office building in Chiemgau is typical of him. Originally a farmhouse, it was brought there from some distance, to win new respectability as the home of Friedrich's enormous library (perhaps the largest private library in Germany) and his various collections. It was a Herculean effort, but he needed to secure the proper environment for quiet writing and thinking. (Gottfried Kraus did the same in Austria.)

Heinz has mastered the art of friendship, as no one else has, never forgetting about the other and yet practicing restraint. He is as critical of the cultural situation, of forced or frivolous progress, as he is life-affirming and optimistic at heart. People with his general outlook probably tend to unite powerful contradictions within themselves. In Heinz Friedrich's case I note the unfortunate effects of the dispersal of Munich's intelligentsia in a section of the city that for all practical purposes stretches from Fürstenfeldbruck to Prien and where, because of the distances, people see each other so rarely that it takes a great deal of effort to keep any friendship alive.

A pleasant relationship, with agreement on many vital issues, also came about with Maria Friedrich, the indefatigable head and intellectual center of the company's juvenile books. In 1985 Heinz Friedrich's kindness to me culminated in a wonderful event. Having by then been elevated to the presidency of the Bavarian Academy of Arts, he loaned me the sacred rooms in the Munich Residence for a retrospective exhibition of my paintings and a splendid banquet in honor of my birthday. With Julia's energetic help, the event included a reunion with friends in an informal, loving atmosphere that enfolded me and moved me, far more so than in Berlin, which was much more Spartan in the equivalent instance.

Both ceremonies were accompanied by exhibitions of my paintings. In Berlin, Dr. Ulrich Eckhardt opened the doors of the Festspiel-Galerie on Budapester Strasse. So many members of the press and public attended the opening that one could not look at the pictures in peace. My friend and colleague Elmar Budde, who taught at the same academy as I did and with whom I was doing a new edition of Schubert in the Peters publishing program, initiated the viewers into my paintings by pointing tellingly to the structurally dominant role of the brushstroke, the line in my work.

In Munich, Werner Spies spoke at the opening. The longtime assistant to and friend of Max Ernst, he had an intimate understanding of Picasso's art and was also internationally esteemed for his skill at mounting major exhibitions throughout the world. His judgment of me was surely too favorable, the result of a friendship that has grown out of many yearly meetings in Paris, where he lives.

Given the wealth of possibility for artistic expression today, the standard of quality is, on the one hand, very complex, on the other, enormously simple. I mean that when the intensity an artist puts into his work communicates itself to the viewer, it must surely have something to do with quality. I have had many conversations about the meaning of art with other painters—sometimes when we have worked together—such as Ursula Fischer-Fabian, the wife of my friend Siegfried whose estate adjoins mine. We live in a time in which people no longer know how to look at art and in which verbal communication is deteriorating and actually becoming increasingly insubstantial. But the sensual power of art grows more important. In spite of the flood from the media that inundates us all, art holds its own to this day. The age of reproduction has not yet managed to defuse the originality of the work of art. There is in us a deep and undeniable need to see art as a confrontation and provocation, as well as a confirmation that cannot be imitated or replaced by any other reality. I believe that the ability of painting to answer this need is more complete and comprehensive than is generally understood or taught.

The study of drawing, color, and composition that has engaged me since my childhood has enriched my life with vital stimuli. My special love has always been for the French artists of the nineteenth century, but the impulse to paint seriously myself came from the late works of Paul Klee. The fact that there are some people courageous enough to let me exhibit now and then has taught me how exciting it can be to hang pictures properly, how unimportant it is when dogs in the manger scornfully pontificate about the "painting singer," how much joy there is in reading a review that shows understanding.

* * *

It was easy to see that the handbook of song lyrics Heinz Friedrich had planned answered a real need among listeners and readers. The situation was quite otherwise for the next demanding enterprise, inaugurated two years later. The idea came from a well-born lady from Wiesbaden. Susanne Brockhaus, a direct descendant of the talented Leipzig branch of Richard Wagner's family, headed the famous publishing house. Even before I met her personally I had written a foreword to Jörg Demus' *Vom Abenteuer der Interpretation* for her. Her appreciation was expressed in words borrowed from *Meistersinger*, "A word from Sachs, that means so much."

But now she invited me to go somewhat more deeply into the songs of Franz Schubert; I had just devoted myself to them for the collected edition, and had accumulated a great deal of research in the process. The result was a work that not only enjoyed a respectable success but, most especially, gave me infinite pleasure. That is, apart from one terrible mishap: We were staying at the Savoy Hotel in London, usually a satisfactory domicile, conducive to work. But one day I innocently left my lengthy manuscript, which I always carried with me on my travels along with a portable typewriter, lying on the desk. More fatally, the stack of pages, which normally I guarded like a precious treasure, was sitting on top of a pile of newspapers I had finished reading. With no evil intent, the maid threw the whole stack of newspapers and manuscript into the trash. And with merciless speed the trash made its way down to the basement, to the paper shredder. I returned scarcely an hour and a half later, to discover my manuscript gone. The whole hotel staff searching in a panic could not bring it back to me. "Too late," was the death sentence.

After a period of physical debility and sleepless nights

broken by every sort of nightmare, I was just working my way back to ordinary well-being when I received a letter from Susanne Brockhaus expressing her hope that I was young enough to start all over. She would not admit how old I already was by 1969—" 'born 1925' seems totally unbelievable to me," and she had been about to have a "misprint" corrected in the encyclopedia. Of course Frau Brockhaus hoped that, in spite of many other obligations, it would not be long before my book would take shape again.

A year and a half's work in the paper shredder—I cannot think of anything comforting to say. Perhaps I am filled with enormous admiration for the way you immediately and unhesitatingly went back to work. I find that altogether splendid. Were I given to quoting, I would have to begin with Goethe—"Allen Gewalten" (die Maid) "zum Trotz sich erhalten" and "die Arme der Götter herbeirufen," but you were there before me! And I should have to quote Schopenhauer, your fellow author on our list: ". . . for only the conviction of the truth and importance of our thoughts gives rise to the enthusiasm that is necessary for the tireless endurance everywhere to care for the clearest, most handsome, and most powerful expression." What do you think of my wise philosopher, who is generally scorned as a pessimist?

I started over, using the few sketches and excerpts that had survived. Soon, in April 1970, Frau Brockhaus wrote me, "I must tell you that I am setting to work with the greatest pleasure, for I find the beginning beautiful and promising."

I met with the aristocratic but unaffected lady at the Schlosshotel Kronberg and enjoyed her cordial candor. We were surrounded by a royal library of large old tomes and warmed by a huge fireplace. She persuaded me that my plan of including the original line drawings from Schubert's texts might not meet today's demand for half-tone reproductions, since they might strike the reader as old-fashioned. So we agreed on reproductions of old copies of the illustrations. Later, when I sent numerous revisions to the publisher, I received a written confession:

> You have touched on passages about which I myself was not easy. You have gently turned and worded wherever I failed. Since the days of William the Great [she meant Furtwängler], who also ennobled my suggestions with shadings of his own, I have not seen anything like it. How marvelous—I thank you so much.

When the great work was coming to an end, in 1971, Susanne Brockhaus and I drew a breath of relief, since I was about to embark on a series of major vocal obligations. While on a visit to the Leberberg in Wiesbaden, I had occasion to admire Wagner's Dresden library (since donated to the foundation in Bayreuth). The book of his that carried the greatest number of marginal notations was—the Bible.

Although correspondence about the Schubert book, with suggestions for illustrations, corrections on galleys, and the like, had died down long ago, Susanne Brockhaus became concerned with Kristina's ill health. She suggested that Kristina come and stay with her for a longish period of time, under the care of a single physician. In the meantime, however, Kristina moved to New York, which turned out to be necessary as well as useful, since there was a suitable physician in that city.

In 1974 the *Frankfurter Allgemeine Zeitung* printed prepublication sections from my next book, *Wagner und Nietzsche*. It had involved my switching over to the Deutsche Verlags-Anstalt; and Frau Brockhaus, with the generosity I had already come to know, wrote:

> There has been a flood of literature on Wagner for more than a century. Little of it good and much of it mediocre or not good. What makes your book stand out for me are the noblesse and fairness with which you have portrayed the characters. Precisely in the case of material so laden with emotion, this is enormously difficult and perhaps for that reason rare.

This letter was a source of strength when the first diatribes appeared. I could also recall the fact that after all, Frau Brockhaus was a decendant of Richard Wagner's. (I did meet with approval from various sides, such as the Nietzsche-Gesellschaft Sils-Maria, the pianist Richter-Haaser, and Manès Sperber.)

Between enthusiatic echoes from a song recital I gave near where she lived, I then learned of an accident, a fire, and finally a pulmonary embolism that heralded her end and made me fear for a friendship that I had cultivated far too little. I could still manage to contribute some recollections to a book about Enrico Mainardi, and there was a plan for a biography of George Szell in which I would have had a share. I was about to perform my first Sachs in Berlin, and Frau Brockhaus was determined to attend. But her doctor, "cold and heartless," canceled her plans. My final news of her concerned the Japanese edition of the Schubert book, which had just been published and in which she took special pride. (Translations into English, French, Italian, and Hungarian followed. My other books have also been translated into various languages.) I could have wished for more frequent meetings and longer dialogues with this grande dame of the publishing world.

When I had just turned forty, I received a letter from Felix Berner. He was the guiding spirit behind the Deutsche Verlags-Anstalt in Stuttgart. At that time, before I ever thought of my Schubert book, Berner asked me to write my memoirs. I was reluctant, however, to write them in the form he was thinking of, not yet—actually, never. Thus he was the first to approach me with the suggestion that I work on a book that would be entirely my own.

Berner waited patiently until the time was ripe for a different book. Susanne Brockhaus graciously allowed the changeover to DVA necessitated by the new plan, since she knew only too well that the work neither fitted easily into her music series nor could be absorbed into the general Brockhaus list that was more directed to reference materials. The idea of examining those unequal friends, Wagner and Nietzsche, had intrigued me since at the age of seventeen I had read the strange utterances on this subject by Nietzsche's sister Elisabeth Förster-Nietzsche. Four years before the Nietzsche book was published, I asked Berner if he was interested, and he was. Without fettering me contractually, the eloquent but reserved Swabian came to Berlin to discuss the project with me. By the time Berner remembered me on my fiftieth birthday, all the work and minor problems of this book were behind me. Two brief quotations from a Wagner dictionary, concerning Hermann Levi, had accidentally been printed without a source reference. Berner supported me nobly, allowing for late insertions into the proofs, and pacified the publisher of the "plagiarized" author as well as the author himself. In July 1974 the moment came when I received the very first copy of *Wagner und Nietzsche*. Berner's cover letter read:

> It is a special pleasure to be allowed to send you herewith literally the first copy of our book. I have this moment received it from the bindery. Should it be too fresh and therefore warp a little, I beg you to overlook this. I am sure that the book will make its way. Prepublication in the "Frankfurter Allgemeine Zeitung" [arranged through the advocacy of Joachim Fest] is a very positive sign and will do its part to find still more readers for the book.

Given the subject, disparagement and snide remarks had to be expected. Nor did we have to wait long, though they could not prevent a substantially enlarged paperback edition from being published by dtv. Felix Berner must also be given credit for having brought me together with Frau Ulla Küster for editorial advice and help; since that time she has overseen the translations of a work about me and of other books of mine (such as the one on Robert Schumann, and *Töne sprechen, Worte klingen*). My continuing ties with her, the daughter of one of the most respected book retailers in the history of bookselling, are of inexpressible value to me.

Felix Berner, a publisher of the old, personal school and a collaborator with a great feeling for others, eager to work with and know them, worried about the structure of an uncompleted book, gave advice, and repeatedly—concerning the Schumann book—reminded me to write for readers with only an average interest in music, who would not always be as conversant with the biographical and historical background as my manuscript assumed. Berner summed up the result as follows: "I think that we have nothing to be ashamed of. I even believe that it has turned out to be the *very best* of our music books to date."

This was our last joint book. I am deeply grieved that I cannot offer him these memoirs and ask for his opinion.

When we had acquired our "beautiful slope" near the Starnberger See, a friendly gentleman in the neighborhood wrote to me, the beginning of a closer acquaintance. His hyphenated name was not unlike mine, so that the post office sometimes had difficulty making the right deliveries. His name is Sebastian Fischer-Fabian. His wife is Ursula, the painter, but at the time she did not call herself that, since she had—for the sake of her sons and her home—laid her brushes aside. The man of the house not only wrote in a variety of forms, which secured him a permanent place on German best-seller lists over many years with his historical writings; what was more important, and had greater consequences for me, was his consummate skill in bringing people together and encouraging stimulating conversation. Whether the speaker is the writer Herbert Reinecker, the actor Axel von

Ambesser, or the program director of the ARD, Dietrich Schwarzkopf, always—and intensified by the women present—the topics touched on catch fire, furnishing material for weeks of reflection. The shy Heinz Rühmann and his wife were very much part of the circle, as was Rolf Pauls, the former first German ambassador to Israel. More than once I felt that I had gone back more than a hundred years, to a time when conversation and the ability to listen were taken for granted. Fischer-Fabian, a former journalist, had learned to ask questions in a way that encouraged the other to respond freely. Unfortunately I am not sufficiently familiar with his interviews with actors, reflecting his passion for the theater. But I was grateful that an hour-long television interview with him went off as simply and light-heartedly as possible.

Dealings with people to whom music meant far less than it did to Julia and me seemed complicated at first, for no one is willing to put aside completely his deepest interests. But as it turned out, Siegfried, the nephew of the one-time head of the Berlin Philharmonic, Ernst Fischer, is prepared even in this field to ask questions that compel me, more than him, to reflection.

At every opportunity Ursula and Siegfried escaped the "suicidal climate" of the Alpine foothills by going south, a form of travel not equally available to those of us who travel constantly. Instead we would listen to their stories and look at Uschi's sketches, which were resonant with the local atmosphere.

In my opinion, those books of her husband that illuminate history and provide information have over the years become more concise and convincing. When I was in Montreal I had occasion to marvel at the universal distribution of Fischer-Fabian's cheerful, reflective, and humorous publications. On the bookshelves of the hotel lobby I was happy to be greeted by his volume *Das goldene Bett*—even though it had been placed on a bottom shelf.

Most painters have no idea how good it is for their work when they do not spend months living in isolation. I therefore never regretted any occasion when I succeeded in luring Uschi into my basement studio with its direct access to the garden. In the past ten years her work has developed from the exclusively black-and-white line, the dot, the plane, into the canvases of an imaginative colorist. There is nothing more wonderful than a long silence during work, when two artists are hatching their separate works, only now and then uttering a sigh or muttering a technical remark. The cry for help, "Oh, look . . . ," can distract the other from his own daydreams and release him back into work.

When not long ago Uschi had her first one-woman show, I was asked to say a few words. My notes contained everything I needed. But I was thrown into difficulty by the man who introduced me placing me on a staircase landing without any light whatever. One should not have to speak of complicated technical matters in front of prominent listeners unless one is used to professorial lecturing. All my stammering, however, could not rob Uschi of her well-deserved success. Whenever we have to make rational decisions, Uschi's benign imagination always furnishes us with good advice. From me she can learn—at least in painting—a bit of spontaneity, can receive a little encouragement to "destroy" earlier methods and styles. What is friendship? Taking and giving, simply, with an open heart.

Postlude

No matter how tempestuous and unexpected they may have been, I think more light-heartedly and happily about the last decades of my life than about the time that went before. When I try, as I write, to recall the years since Irmel's death, they appear to me as an astonishingly brief period, all their dismaying fullness notwithstanding—like a single school year, perhaps, or the time it takes to learn one's first opera. In other words, I have more memories of the twenty-one-year-old than of the forty-five-year-old.

Since that time there have always been new threats to inner security, to the vital spine. Too many things have happened, both frightening and encouraging.

It began with the anguishing need to go on living and

working when my inner existence had been seriously jeopardized. I could not quite keep up with Ruth Leuwerik's literary knowledge nor her cultivated elegance, and yet—to the surprise of both—she brought me back to myself. That our intimacy faded was probably caused by the fact that both of us are naturally independent types.

Nor could my life with beautiful young Kristina from New York be permanent. All efforts to free her from a dependency failed: Its roots in her childhood could not be laid bare.

It was not until ten years after Irmel's death that I met Julia. I could give her my understanding and my utmost admiration, and she returned my feelings. I have told the story of how we met, how we found our way to each other. Today Julia shares all my fears and joys.

Index

INDEX